Foreigners in their Own Land

A Mexican American Studies Reader

First Edition

Edited by Erika R. Rendon-Ramos, Ph.D.
University of Texas Rio Grande Valley

publisher colophon

cognella
SAN DIEGO

Bassim Hamadeh, CEO and Publisher
John Remington, Managing Executive Editor
Gem Rabanera, Senior Project Editor
Rachel Kahn, Production Editor
Asfa Arshi, Graphic Design Associate
Kylie Bartolome, Licensing Associate
Natalie Piccotti, Director of Marketing
Kassie Graves, Senior Vice President, Editorial
Jamie Giganti, Director of Academic Publishing

Cover image copyright © 2012 iStockphoto LP/Monica Rodriguez.

Printed in the United States of America.

cognella® | ACADEMIC PUBLISHING
3970 Sorrento Valley Blvd., Ste. 500, San Diego, CA 92121

Contents

Introduction

FOREIGNERS IN THEIR OWN LAND IS a textbook that challenges the typical master narrative method of storytelling. A master narrative is told, by and large, from one point of view—most often, that of the "victors" or, in the case of the United States, the Anglo perspective. This book champions the voices and stories of Mexican Americans and is written for individuals interested in learning about the Mexican American experience in the United States. It is, more specifically, geared toward students who have little or no knowledge of Mexican American Studies (MAS) and are looking to explore a range of themes to introduce them to the subject.

The purpose of the textbook is to raise awareness about an often-marginalized minority group and demonstrate how the Mexican American story can be interwoven with a traditional, American master narrative. It provides a thematic overview of issues that have shaped the Mexican American experience in the United States while simultaneously covering centuries of history. Readers will gain an understanding of the diversity of the Hispanic culture and of how Mexicans are one small part of the Hispanic story.

The concepts introduced in this book can be applied to multiple facets of our personal and professional lives. I want to encourage readers to be open-minded and accepting of diversity in all its forms—including ways of thinking, learning, and applying their skills. This is in addition to recognizing the cultural diversity that exists in the United States with the multitude of minority hyphenated identities. The readings are written by scholars from a range of disciplines—history, political science, sociology, criminology, and anthropology, to name a few. This exposes students to different methodologies, styles of writing, and viewpoints. The textbook is a valuable resource because it is written from several angles rather than one dominant perspective. It gives students the freedom to challenge their points of view alongside those introduced in the book.

The book is organized into six chapters—I and III include one reading each, while II, IV, V, and VI contain two readings. Each chapter covers a different theme: US-Spanish Heritage and Exploration; Mexican Women in the 19th Century; Mexican Lynching; Immigration: the Bracero Program; Education; and Borderlands and 21st-Century Mexican Americans. Every chapter begins with a brief introduction to the topic and scholar(s), is followed by the main reading, and concludes with discussion questions. These questions have been developed as both a check for understanding and to encourage the reader to reflect on the reading's connection to their personal lives and contemporary representations of Mexican Americans.

Foreigners in Their Own Land highlights the Mexican American experience in the United States. Some textbooks have undervalued the importance of including the stories of minority groups in favor of a master—and Anglo—narrative. Their histories add layers, depth, and richness to our understanding of American life and culture. Their stories inform debates and current movements; historical context is everything. My hope is that this book is the first of many that students read to learn about historically marginalized people.

Chapter 1

US–Spanish Heritage and Exploration

Editor's Introduction

Chapter 1 is devoted to US–Spanish heritage prior to the Mexican–American War of 1846. The history of Mexican Americans in the United States often "begins" after the Mexican–American War, when the United States acquired half of Mexico's territory and roughly 80,000 Mexican citizens. However, Mexicans lived in what is now the United States for centuries prior to the war. Spanish presence in the Americas dates back to the late 15th and early 16th century. This chapter focuses on the 18th century and the development of a racial hierarchy that continues to impact race relations in Latin America today.

Social identity and race in Spanish America is important because it provides the foundational knowledge necessary to understand how and why these issues remain relevant. While it is important to understand how race and racism affect minority groups, it is equally important to understand how racism is internalized within minority groups. Mexicans have been discriminated against by Anglo-Americans, but Mexicans also have an internalized racism against their own ethnic group. For example, on the one hand, it is often a compliment to be called or considered *güera* or *güerita*, blonde or fair-haired and fair-skinned. On the other hand, being called *indio*, or a person of indigenous background and typically darker-skinned, is often an insult. It is easy to dismiss these comments without delving deeper into why these beliefs are engrained in Mexican culture. Learning about the *sistema de castas*, or caste system, provides a glimpse into the history of racial classification that informs the present.

Scholarship on Mexicans in the US Southwest and South has emphasized their existence post-1848 when the Treaty of Guadalupe was signed, granting the United States over half of Mexico's territory. However, there is much to know about the political, social, and cultural environment of Mexicans, and Hispanics in general, prior to the Mexican–American War. Reading 1.1, "Social Identity on the Hispanic Texas Frontier," by historian Gerald E. Poyo, begins to fill this void by highlighting the complex relationship between race and class on the Hispanic Texas frontier. Poyo analyzes "why the Mexican indigenous elites in the Southwest appropriated a Spanish identity for their own advantage after 1848" through two case studies: San Antonio de Béxar and Nacogdoches. He reveals how, despite US racism penetrating Texas, Tejanos "reinvented the social definitions from their own tradition of social identity in the eighteenth century" and did not fall into a clear-cut black versus white dichotomy.

This reading was chosen because it illustrates the complexity of the *sistema de castas*. The *sistema de castas* was a Spanish colonial social system in the Americas that created a racial hierarchy to reflect the *mestizaje* (racial mixing) that was widespread in New Spain. At the top of the hierarchy were *peninsulares* (peninsular-born Spaniards), followed by *criollos* (American-born Spaniards), and finally, Indians and Africans. The mixing of these four groups resulted in the *castas* that composed the middle racial groups. There were 16 total *casta* designations. While one might assume that such an extensive racial hierarchy would cause a rigid distinction between peoples, the reality is that the system was quite fluid. Poyo's reading illustrates how race and class materialized differently throughout the Spanish empire. The system was malleable and one's position in the hierarchy was influenced by a number of factors, including physical appearance, local politics, social standing, and geography.

Poyo's reading allows one to evaluate the diversity of Spanish America. Spanish America was vast and expansive and it varied greatly based on one's location—specifically one's distance from the "center," Mexico City. Understanding the complex nature of race, class, and geography in Spanish America sets the foundation for understanding not only tensions and disputes that arose based on one's connection, or lack thereof, to the capital, but also race relations as they might play out in the future.

Social Identity on the Hispanic Texas Frontier

Gerald E. Poyo

Introduction

Historians of the United States-Mexico border long ago began to construct the historical narratives of the regions from Texas to California under Spain and later Mexico, but only in the last twenty-five years has socioeconomic and cultural research on this region and time period begun to illuminate the important themes that conceptually integrate the early years to the post-1848 experience of the United States.[1]

United States historiography has generally acknowledged the Spanish and Mexican borderlands historical tradition, but not sufficiently to warrant more than an introductory overview when offering an historical overview of those regions. This is why, for example, we still hear Steven F. Austin referred to as the "Father of Texas."[2] Even the revisionist Chicano interpretations of the 1960s and 1970s, written by Mexican American scholars trained in United States history, viewed the pre-1848 periods as irrelevant for Chicano history.[3] Though this idea continues to be advanced by some Latino historians, for the most part the relevance and importance of the earlier period is now recognized.[4] A solid historiography that demonstrates the continuities across the centuries and sovereignties now exists.[5]

In order to appreciate the processes of integration and change that nineteenth century Hispanic Borderlands communities underwent as they became part of the United States, the societies they came from in the previous century and earlier must be understood. Mexican residents of the Southwest became Mexican Americans. They moved from traditional Hispanic societies into Euro-American dominated societies, giving rise to complex relationships, not only between Hispanics and Anglos, but within Hispanic communities themselves. Much has been written about the nature of relationships between Mexicans and Euro-Americans after 1848, but the processes Hispanic communities themselves underwent in the new political, socioeconomic, and cultural environment are just now being addressed.[6]

In the case of Texas, historians point out that many of the relatively economically well-off leaders of the newly annexed communities tended to make political and economic alliances with Euro-Americans, often by marrying off their daughters to Anglo immigrants, while the *pobres*

Gerald E. Poyo, "Social Identity on the Hispanic Texas Frontier," *Recovering the U.S. Hispanic Literary Heritage,* Vol. III, ed. María Herrera-Sobek and Virginia Sánchez-Korrol, pp. 384–401. Copyright © 1998 by Arte Público Press. Reprinted with permission.

faced oppression and became a permanent underclass to meet the labor needs of an expanding capitalist frontier.[7] This stratification and indeed definitive splitting of *mexicano* society under United States rule prompted some of the Hispanic landed elites, and others who perceived a need to distance themselves from a Mexican identity, to characterize themselves as Spanish. While the precise process by which this Spanish identity emerged and consolidated in mid-nineteenth century Texas has not been studied, the emergence of a Spanish ethnicity among certain segments of the Hispanic inhabitants of New Mexico is well documented. During 1821–1846, the Hispanic residents of New Mexico generally referred to themselves as Mexicans, but once the region came under United States control *nuevomexicanos* began to refer to themselves as Spanish-Americans. According to Richard L. Nostrand, "In New Mexico, the use of "Mexican" declined while that of "Spanish-American" gained momentum. By the 1920s "Spanish-American" was widely entrenched. By the twenties, moreover, "Spanish-American" or simply "Spanish" had come to be much more than a euphemism for avoiding "Mexican"; it was now a genuine ethnic identity with overtones that were cultural and racial."[8] In the Southwest many members of the Hispanic communities claimed a direct lineage from Spain, and denied any substantive identification with Mexico and Mexican immigrants who arrived in the late nineteenth and twentieth centuries.[9]

While the need by the indigenous Hispanic elites in the Southwest to separate themselves from a Mexican identity was clearly calculated to defend themselves against Euro-American racism and discrimination, it is also true that the concepts chosen by these elites did not emerge from a vacuum or solely from definitions imposed by the arriving Euro-Americans who tended to call the rich "Spanish," and everyone else "Mexican." Spanish/Mexican communities brought with them into the United States already established social attitudes and structures that underwent alterations and transformations as they confronted Euro-American society. To understand why the Mexican indigenous elites in the Southwest appropriated a Spanish identity for their own advantage after 1848, the origins of this identity in the centuries prior to United States occupation must be studied. This paper explores the Texas case.

During the eighteenth century residents of the Spanish American province of Texas developed a regional identity that manifested itself in a variety of ways. The area's relative isolation, and its ranching, agricultural, and commercial economy created a fiercely independent population that jealously defended their autonomous way of life. Scholars have highlighted local politics in defense of autonomy, commercial ties to the east, and a ranching culture as aspects of an emergent Tejano identity during the course of the century.[10] One aspect of Tejano identity that has not received ample analysis relates to social identity.

In 1912, José María Rodríguez, a descendent of San Antonio de Béxar's early settlers wrote in his memoirs that La Villita, a barrio on the east side of the San Antonio river, "was settled by some of the soldiers that came with the Mexican army and those who had intermarried with Indians, and were not supposed to be the very best of people." "In fact," Rodríguez continued, "there was a great distinction between the east and west side of the river." "The west side of the river was supposed to be the residence of the first families here ... the Canary Islanders ... [who] took great pride in preventing any intermarriage with mixed races and when one did mix he lost his caste with the rest."[11]

Rodríguez no doubt acquired this uncomplicated understanding of Béxar's late eighteenth century system of social stratification through oral tradition, and it was consistent with the best traditions of the long-standing myth of Hispanic segregation and purity on Mexico's northern frontier provinces. Though racial exclusivity or purity simply did not exist in San Antonio or in any other colonial era communities on the northern frontiers of New Spain, Rodríguez's remembrance does conform with the fact that a Canary Islander or Spanish identity was an important aspect of social organization in the late eighteenth century. While the arrival of Euro-Americans to Béxar in the early nineteenth century clearly changed, deepened and hardened ethnic and racial cleavages within Mexican and Mexican American communities, remnants of the social identity forged during the eighteenth century persisted in the minds of the descendants during the next century. Social stratification existed but how did it evolve and how was it defined?

New Spain's *Sistema de Castas*

Attitudes about social status in late eighteenth century Borderlands communities, as throughout Spain's American empire, derived from the assumptions inherent in the so-called *sistema de castas*, or caste system. The colonial Spanish American social system included a racially inspired hierarchy of status which placed peninsular and American-born Spaniards (*peninsulares* and *criollos*, respectively) at the top and Indians and Africans at the bottom of the social structure. Mixtures of these groups, known as *castas*, fell in-between, each possessing their particular political, economic, and legal place within society.[12]

In attempting to understand New Spain's social system, historians have inquired into the relationship of racial hierarchy inherent in the system to occupational position and social status in general. Some have argued that a person's racial background played a crucial role in defining occupational possibilities and social status. Others suggest that by the middle eighteenth century race had disappeared as the primary determinant of a person's occupational position or social status.[13] Whatever the case, race, class, and social status were intricately intertwined in a complicated hierarchy not easy to sort out that categorized people in census documents according to their *calidad*, "quality," or worth. The difficulty of interpreting the meaning of *calidad* is pointed out by Rodney D. Anderson, for example, when he notes in a study of race and social stratification in Guadalajara that, contrary to expectations, the census of 1821 contained a large number of *españoles* who held low status occupations. In explaining why so many people with Spanish designations held low status jobs, Anderson suggests that "it just might be possible that the low-status Spaniards"... closely resembled Indians and castas because they *were* Indians and castas, generously provided the label of "español" by politically sensitive census takers using more flexible criteria than in the past."[14] This is a crucial observation because it suggests that while the *sistema de castas*, with its clearcut *español*, *criollo*, *casta*, *indio* and *negro* designations, created the fundamental frame-of-reference for categorizing people socially in the census throughout the empire, in reality, the practical workings of the system was subject to highly complex manipulations of the census according to the political, economic, and social crosscurrents of particular communities. Anderson's observation is useful for our analysis of the Texas frontier.

The categories of *calidad* recorded in census documents theoretically attempted to conform to the ideal system of racial hierarchy required by law, but in fact, a person's *calidad* designation also included other considerations such as wealth, military rank, or other characteristics that might lend individual prestige. Spanish censuses often did not register an individual's race at all, but rather his "quality" or status in the community beyond race. The problem with making generalizations about what *calidad* meant in eighteenth century New Spain, of course, was that its definition varied from community to community. In some places *calidad* might relate closely to race while in other locations economic position or some other indicator of status might be more important than racial background. Thus any analysis of social status in a particular colonial Latin American historical setting confronts the fundamental problem of discerning something about the history of how the local community defined *español*, *mestizo*, or any other designation, which takes us back to Anderson's observation about Guadalajara in 1821. If, in fact, the low status *españoles* Anderson alludes to were actually Indians or *mestizos* it seems evident that in Guadalajara the meaning and usage of categories of *calidad* had moved away from a racial definition. In the case of Texas, the exact meaning of a category of *calidad* and its implications for local social relations may only be understood and evaluated through research into the specific dynamics [of] the province's individual communities.[15]

Bexar's Demographic Development

An analysis of San Antonio de Béxar's census of 1793 seems to confirm José María Rodríguez's remembrance that his ancestors were Spanish. The census reveals that 63 percent of Béxar's household heads were *españoles*, while only 24 percent were *castas* and another 13 percent were *indios*. But at the same time, Rodríguez's historical memory does not incorporate Anderson's insight that what you see in the census documents may not be what was. In fact, the historical literature suggests that social development in eighteenth century Texas was indeed fluid and flexible. Alicia Tjarks observed some years ago that "as a consequence of the mixture of race and classes, Texan society [of the late eighteenth century] experienced an increasing upward mobility." "It is remarkable," she continued, "that, along with the continuing concept of a caste society, differences due to skin color and other related circumstances were reduced to such a point that a society definitely heterogeneous, both in its origin and its composition, emerged in Texas." The socioeconomic dynamics in the late eighteenth century, she concluded, "encouraged a strong social and ethnic mobility, tending toward a free and heterogeneous society."[16]

Tjark's article supported the generally held assumption that racial distinctions on the frontier were less sharp than in more settled areas, but the article is less successful in providing an understanding of the interplay between *calidad* and social status in Spanish Texas. Texas frontier communities were socially fluid but how did this fluidity also contribute to the emergence of a Spanish or Canary Islander social identity that endured in oral tradition for over a century?

We may begin by looking at Béxar's demographic development during the century. In 1718 Indians and soldier-settlers from communities in northern New Spain such as Saltillo, Monclova, and Monterrey founded the mission and presidio communities that eventually became San Antonio de Béxar.[17] Béxar's military rosters did not include information on racial background, but frequent testimonials by missionaries and Spanish officials indicates that most residents were *castas*. Fray Antonio de Olivares of Mission San Antonio de Valero complained that almost half of Alarcón's recruits were "mulattoes, lobos, coyotes, and mestizos." He expressed prevailing *criollo* attitudes toward people of color when he noted that the inhabitants were "people of the lowest order, whose customs are worse than those of the Indians."[18] Of the fifty-four families living in the presidio in 1726, most were of mixed racial backgrounds according to the military commander. Demographic growth during most of the century came as a result of immigration. Béxar received a one-time influx of 56 Canary Islander immigrants in 1731 and a larger number of immigrants (reflected in the censuses of 1790s) of mixed-blood heritage who arrived from Los Adaes [close to Natchitoches, La.] and New Spain especially during 1760s–1780s.[19] By the late 1770s, Fray Agustín Morfi estimated that the town, presidio, and missions that composed the community of Béxar included 514 families. Of the 2,060 persons, "324 are Spanish or as they commonly say 'de razón,' 268 Indians, 16 mestizos, and 151 'de color quebrado.' According to Morfi, over half the residents of the settlement were identified as non-Spanish.[20]

For the most part people who travelled to Texas came from the lowest rungs of northern New Spain's economic strata and, as the testimonials and data suggest, they were heavily of mixed-blood social backgrounds.[21] At the same time, as we have seen, by the 1790s most residents in Béxar appeared as *españoles* in the official census returns. The *calidad* designation of *español* was clearly preferred, but, given the demographic history of the region, it cannot be understood as an accurate racial indicator. What then did *español* mean? Clues to this may be gleaned by tracing Béxar's social development.

Defining *Español* in Bexar

To begin with, it is helpful to recognize that the founders of Béxar recognized the importance of being español in colonial New Spain. Recruited primarily in Coahuila and Nuevo León where they participated in the *sistema de castas*, the soldier-settlers who resided in the presidio associated status with being *español*. As leaders of this new and isolated community, the prominent *vecinos* (residents) took the opportunity to define social categories, which they did to their own benefit.

Despite their mixed-blood heritage, almost from the beginning the most prominent military settlers in Béxar, with the cooperation of the friars, recorded themselves as Spanish in offical marriage, baptismal, and death records.[22] They became the community's *españoles* and, very often, the children of these Spaniards by Indian wives also received an *español* designation. Already during the 1720s the emergent community conformed to the prejudices inherent in a *caste system* that gave preferences to people of Spanish or white backgrounds. Despite the fact that few in the community were actually ethnically Spanish, even on this isolated frontier inhabitants understood that to be declared Spanish in official documents carried a certain distinction. The most prominent residents took on the Spanish designation and established the rules for gaining access to it.

While a concern with being known as Spanish already existed among Béxar's early settlers in the 1720s, this concern seems to have become even more exaggerated with the arrival in 1731 of a contingent of Spanish immigrants from the Canary Islands. They established the formal villa or town of San Fernando next to the presidio and missions along the river. These *isleño* immigrants did not occupy high socioeconomic rank in their place of origin, but on immigrating to their new home the Crown empowered them economically, socially, and politically. On arriving to Béxar, they received titles as *hidalgos* and obtained the best lands in the area. They also gained exclusive control of the *cabildo*, or city council, which they used to try to maintain a monopoly over farm lands and water rights in the region. They emerged as the region's recognized, though bitterly contested, elites and, as a result, the importance of being known as an *español* grew even more dramatically.[23]

The value of having an *isleño* or Spanish identity is evident in many documents of the era. Those with the appropriate genealogical credentials often prefaced their requests for land grants with allusions to their Canary Islands origins or parentage, hoping that their cousins on the city council would reward this distinction with the best grants. Others without such backgrounds often had to be content with smaller, less strategically located lands without water rights. When the mixed-blood Mexican soldier-settlers complained to authorities in Mexico City about their displacement and obtained decrees ordering distribution of farm lands and water to them, the cabildo ignored the directive for most of the century. The cabildo provided the Canary Islanders with the political authority to maintain their advantages and status to redefine social relations in Béxar.

While the Canary Islanders attempted to maintain an exclusive position within the community, their small number resulted in frequent interactions with the Mexican families of the presidio community. Intermarriage and economic cooperation led to an overall integration that blurred distinctions between the two groups. By the end of the century, the children and grandchildren of these two groups composed the local elite and it is evident that they established the standard for being Spanish in the local version of the caste system. Since the offspring of the two groups were in the majority of mixed-heritage, presumably representing many shades of color, actual race receded as an important determinant for attaining the Spanish designation in Béxar's census and other documents. In fact, since most people were actually mestizos or some other race mixture, Spanish simply became the term used for most people in Béxar, including 63 percent of the town's household heads in 1793.

The Workings of *Calidad* and Status in Bexar

Clearly, by the end of the eighteenth century Bexar's system of social stratification in principle adhered to the caste system which by its very nature discriminated against non-whites. Indeed, residents of Béxar aspired to be *españoles* because it was a prerequisite for obtaining respectability, and for being a member of the elite. *Españoles* held most of the land, were eligible for the honorific title of *don*, and held political office. The 1793 census reveals that a strong relationship existed between *calidad* and occupation. Take, for example, the relationship between being *español* and being a *labrador*, or an individual with access to land. In Béxar, only 23 percent of household heads were *labradores*, a rather restricted percentage. Of these *labradores*, 73 percent were Spanish. This relationship suggests that residents of Béxar perceived advantages in being recognized as *españoles*.

Nevertheless, despite the ideal of stratification in the *sistema de castas*, fluid local practice allowed the great majority of the town's inhabitants to define themselves, or be defined, as *españoles*. Béxar's society incorporated the ideological framework of the caste system but circumvented its exclusionary aspects in local practice by allowing "worthy" people of any racial background "to pass" as Spaniards. In effect, the designation of *calidad* in Béxar's census records and other documents did not reflect an individual's race but rather the level of acceptance or status in the town. People born in the town or individuals who gained a certain recognition had a greater possibility of being *español* than a person without status, who remained a *casta* or Indian in official documents for a longer time, particularly if his skin was dark. This is reflected in the census documents when comparing *calidad* and nativity. It is also reflected in the case histories of individuals.

The relationship in the 1793 census between *calidad* and nativity suggests that immigrants to Béxar could not expect to be recognized as *español* immediately. In 1793, 74 percent of the native born enjoyed the designation *español*, but only 49 percent of immigrants achieved this desired status. The dynamics of *calidad* designations in Béxar seem to have made distinctions between long-time community residents who descended from the *primeros pobladores* (founding settlers), and new arrivals.

It seems, then, that a desire to be recognized as Spanish existed and that, in general, native born people had a birth right to that status while immigrants usually achieved it by proving their "worth" to the community. But how did this passing of people into *español* status actually happen? While this is extremely difficult to know for sure, one interpretation may be that their status changed as they achieved reputation. Land acquisition provided one avenue. By the time of the 1793 census lands around Béxar were at a premium. The threat of Indian raids meant that only lands within the vicinity of the presidio could be effectively used, limiting the lands available for official distribution by the Governor and Cabildo. People competed for land and distribution criteria had to be established. The statistics suggest that land was technically only for people who fit the local definition of Spanish, but the reality of the local practice, which allowed for "passing," provided opportunities for *castas* to recieve land. They merely became Spanish, it seems, once they acquired land based on their individual merit and reputation in the community.

But the process was even more complex than just land acquisition. Two individual case examples illustrate more effectively how newcomers in Béxar managed to establish themselves as respected Spanish residents of the community. In the 1770s, José Manuel Berbán arrived to live in Béxar from the east Texas community of Los Adaes. A former member of the Adaes presidio, Berbán and his neighbors relocated to Béxar in compliance with the governor's orders to abandon the village. Béxar's first census taken in 1779 described Berbán as a *mulatto* (of black and white heritage) of 38 years who worked as a *campista* or farm/ranch hand. Between that time and 1792, Berbán married Teresa de Armas, daughter of a prominent Canary Islander family. In the 1792 census he appeared as a *mestizo* (of indian and white heritage). In 1796 Berbán gained election as a member of Béxar's city council and five years later he became the cabildo's city legal officer. He also gained sufficient position in the community to file a complaint against an important citizen, Santiago Seguín, for assault. In Béxar's 1803 census, our subject is registered as Don Manuel Berbán, *español*, *labrador*.

During his thirty years or so in Béxar, Berbán had risen from obscurity to prominence and respectability. Bérban, however, was not unique.[24]

Also consider the case of Pedro Huízar, a *mulatto* from Aguascalientes, who probably arrived in Béxar in the 1770s. The census of 1779 lists his occupation as sculptor, and he worked at Mission San José. He and his wife, Trinidad Enriques, a *coyota* (of Indian and black heritage), had several children beginning in 1779. During the early 1780s, Huízar purchased several lots of land in the town from prominent Bexareños, suggesting a financially rewarding employment at San José. Huízar also became a surveyor. In 1791 he conducted a survey in La Bahía to determine the feasibility of digging an irrigation system and in 1794 he became the official surveyor for the mission lands secularized the previous year. Huízar then became the alcalde of the former mission community of San José. In the census of 1793, Huízar appeared as an *español*, thus like Berbán he too gained sufficient prominence and respectability to achieve the most desired ethnic status in Béxar.[25]

While most Bexareños achieved classification as *españoles*, that designation did not necessarily translate into elite status. Apparently, once a family became part of the community, members retained the designation of *español* even if they did not distinguish themselves economically. The 1793 census includes many cases of *españoles* who were servants and day laboreres. They did not lose their status as *españoles* simply because they failed to reach elite status, and, presumably, they retained Spanish identity for themselves and their children even if they married people darker than themselves providing they enjoyed a good name and reputation.

The data seems to suggest that race played a role in defining social categories for non-whites just entering the community, but race could be disposed of as a concern once a settler proved his individual "worth" (or *calidad*) to the broader community. Strategic marriages, acquisition of land, personal friendships, or leadership capabilities all operated to establish a person's worth and reputation. Immigrants had to gain the community's respect before becoming an accepted "Spanish" member of Béxar's society.[26] In general, Béxar's *españoles* were those who achieved full-blown acceptance as legitimate members of the community, regardless of economic or racial background. But their identity as *españoles* also depended on the existence of a group not accepted as full members of the community.

As revealed earlier, according to José María Rodríguez's historical memory, the established Spanish/Canary Islanders of Béxar's society lived in the town, San Fernando, on the west bank of the San Antonio River, while the non-established (and thus non-Spanish) group lived east of the San Antonio River on lands of the former Mission San Antonio de Valero. Once again nativity played an important role in defining status and belonging in Béxar. In 1792, local authorities finally implemented an order, originally issued in 1779, to secularize Mission Valero. The next year Texas Governor Manuel Muñoz distributed irrigable farmlands to fourteen mission Indian families, forty-two heads of household from the abandoned east Texas presidio of Los Adaes, and fourteen others.[27] Valero also became the home for hundreds of soliders and their families who arrived from Mexico during the next decade and a half. Few Indians remained in the mission at the time of secularization, but those that did maintained an Indian or at least a *casta* identity. The immigrants from the presidio of Los Adaes received the largest number of land grants. Forced by the Crown to leave Los Adaes for Béxar in 1772, after Louisiana became Spanish, many of these refugees rented lands from the missionaries, worked as day laborers and tenant farmers, or served in Bexareño households.[28] Only after twenty years, with the secularization of Valero did they succeed in obtaining lands. By the time of the census of 1804, seventeen of the thirty-three household heads (51%) of the pueblo de Valero were designated *españoles*, while the rest were *mestizos, coyotes*, and *indios*.[29] Seeminly, the residents of the pueblo slowly attained *español* designations, but a new development redefined the barrio de Valero once again. In 1803, La Segunda Companía Volante de San Carlos de Parras arrived in Texas and took up residence at Valero mission and its environs. While some soldiers lived in the mission itself, many lived with their families along the river south of the mission complex in a neighborhood that became known as La Villita.[30] By 1810, the 69 soldiers from the Parras del Alamo Company, were joined by 50 soldiers from the Punta de Lampazos garrison, and 508 militiamen from Nuevo León and Nuevo Santander.[31] It is likely that many of these also took up residence in La Villita. While the military roster of the Parras Company of 1807 does not include the *calidad* of the soldiers, the list does reveal that most of their wives were *castas*. This demographic history explain's Rodríguez's description of the residents of the Alamo as not among "the very best people."

The Case of Nacogdoches

Béxar's complex social process reflected an adaptation of the *sistema de castas* to local conditions, but it is also useful to compare Béxar's experience with another community in the province to demonstrate the uniqueness of these processes of local identity formation. In the east Texas community of Nacogdoches different conditions resulted in different attitudes about social status despite a similar demographic history.

In 1720 the Marqués de Aguayo, newly appointed governor of Coahuila and Texas, departed Monclova with some five hundred soldiers for east Texas. He established a presidio garrisoned by twenty-five men.[32] During the next fifty years the community of Los Adaes emerged. Initially the presidio provided the primary means of economic livelihood, but in time residents farmed, raised cattle, and traded with the nearby French garrison of Nachitoches. Many of the twenty-five Mexican soldier-settlers from Coahuila, which later grew to sixty-one, brought wives and families with them and their community grew to some 500 by mid-century. Like in Béxar, most were of mixed racial heritage. Among the members of the presidio in 1731, twenty-nine were classified as *españoles* (probably American-born Spaniards), while the remaining thirty-two were *mestizos* (Spanish-Indian mix), *mulattos* (Spanish-black), *lobos* (Indian-black mix), *coyotes* (Indian-mulatto mix), and *indios* (Indian).[33] In 1770, a frontier reorganization resulted in Los Adaes' abandonment and most of its residents subsequently founded Nacogdoches. The continuity in population from the first settlement to the second is clearly revealed in the family names found in the census data of the 1790s.[34]

It is evident that Nacogoches's demographic experience was not dramatically different from that of Béxar. Each was founded by a contingent of people of color and in general reflected a population of mixed background, but by the end of the century the census reveals that a significant divergence in social identity had emerged. As we have seen Béxar's household heads were 63 percent Spanish in 1793, but an analysis of Nacogdoches' census reveals that only 28 percent of household heads were *españoles*. Forty-seven percent were *castas*, 12 percent were *indios*, and 13 percent were of some other designation.[35] The differences in the number of *españoles* in the two communities is striking and cannot seem to be explained through divergent demographic experiences.

Nacogdoches' social system operated so differently, in fact, that the underlying assumptions used in the Béxar census do not apply in interpreting the Nacogdoches census of 1793. The analysis of the 1793 Nacogdoches census data departs from the assumption that *calidad* in the Nacogdoches case is probably more realistic indicator of the community's racial composition than was the case for Béxar. For a number of reasons people in Nacogdoches were not as concerned as people in Béxar with attaining the status-laden designation of *español*.

An interesting difference in the census statistics relates to the relationship between *calidad* and nativity. Nacogdoches reveals an opposite pattern from Béxar. In the east Texas community, 77.5 percent of residents born in Nacogdoches/Adaes were *castas*, mostly *mestizos*, while only 55.3 percent of immigrants to Nacogdoches from the Spanish empire were *castas*. In addition, at Nacogdoches a considerable number of European and American French contributed to diluting the traditional caste designations. While immigrants to Béxar were mostly defined as *castas*, and natives were mostly *españoles*, in Nacogdoches *españoles* were immigrants in higher proportion. This suggests that the isolated residents of east Texas simply cared little for New Spain's social attitudes and accepted whatever designation they were given. On the other hand, new arrivals in Nacogdoches were more conscious of the *sistema de castas* and considered an *español* designation important.

Similarly, the relationship between *calidad* and occupation in Nacogdoches reveals a different pattern from Béxar. In Nacogdoches, 47 percent of household heads were *labradores*, and, of these, only 33.3 percent were Spanish. In Béxar a smaller percentage of residents were *labradores* and they were to a greater extent Spanish. Clearly, in Nacogdoches a much weaker relationship existed between *labrador* status and Spanish *calidad* than in Béxar. To some extent this probably reflected the fact that land was simply more plentiful in the Nacogdoches areas due to the generally cordial relations with the Indians. Since pressures on land were not great, no system of stratification evolved to define its distribution. In fact, it seems that since land was readily available few residents in the area bothered to acquire official title.

Another difference to consider relates to what must have been dramatically different attitudes about race as a result of the divergent relations each community maintained with their surrounding Indian populations. While the census indicates that the actual number of Indians who were heads of households living within Béxar and Nacogdoches were about the same, we might speculate that the attitudes about them were different. While settlers in central Texas had to contend with the warlike Apaches and Comanches and did not often mix with them socially, Adaesanos coexisted with the more settled and sedentary Caddoes of east Texas for a half century or more.[36] Adaes' general population characteristics differed from Béxar only in that perhaps the Native American influence was more recent and culturally alive. From the perspective of *mestizo* Bexareños who called themselves Spanish (most already culturally removed from Indian ways) the residents of Nacogdoches were viewed as highly influenced by Indian culture. The psychological, political, and socioeconomic need to reject Indian and mixed-blood designations of *calidad* among people in Nacogdoches was simply not as intense as in Béxar.[37]

Furthermore, in Nacogdoches no institutional basis for stratification existed as in Béxar. The local elite in Nacodoches did not have at its disposal a cabildo that it could use to manipulate class relations. This is reflected in the weak relationship that existed in Nacogdoches between the Spanish designation and the occupation of *labrador*. While a local Spanish elite did exist, whose leader Antonio Gil Y'Barbo was himself evidently a *mulatto* or *mestizo*, this elite did not enjoy the benefit of a cabildo through which to link certain social standards to acquisition of resources as was obviously the case in Béxar.[38]

If this analysis is correct, when Manuel Berbán lived in Los Adaes he probably did not have to worry excessively about becoming *español* to advance his economic interest and obtain community respectability. Nacogdoches's political and social dynamics made for a society relatively lacking in distinctions, consistent with generally accepted notions of frontier communities. The case of Nacogdoches highlights Béxar's more stratified society. For reasons peculiar to San Antonio's political, social, and economic development, prominent early settlers fervently sought Spanish status in order to more effectively manipulate the social system to their advantage. The flexibilities inherent in the system resulted in a significant majority claiming Spanish ethnic designations, which, in turn, contributed to creating a local identity based on that ethnic designation.

When José María Rodríguez wrote about his eighteenth-century ancestors in Béxar, he revealed their clear sense of social identity apart from the Mexican soldiers who had settled in La Villita in the early nineteenth century. But when they spoke of being Spanish or Canary Islanders, they did not refer specifically to nationality or race, but rather to a definition born of the old *sistema de castas* and transformed by local reality, culture and custom. Perhaps the residents of Béxar did attempt to maintain themselves separate from the soldiers in La Villita, but this stemmed not exclusively from racial motivations. Their desire for separateness was a more generalized need to defend their community definitions of social status and identity from immigrants unfamiliar with local traditions. To be Spanish meant to be an accepted member of Béxar's community to which all could aspire in one way or another but only after meeting certain conditions. People of light complexion would be accepted more easily than people of darker skin tones, but people of color could also be *españoles* by being born in Béxar, establishing a good "reputation," or attaining some level of economic or political "respectability." In Nacogdoches, on the other hand, social identity operated in a different way. To be known as Spanish was not so necessary. Despite similar demographic profiles each community created its own standards of social status and thus community identity.

Conclusion

Shortly after the arrival of the Parras military company in Béxar, the community entered a period of considerable crisis as insurgents in Mexico led by Father Miguel Hidalgo y Costilla initiated the Mexican war of independence against Spain. Texas became embroiled in the insurgencies and on two occasions during 1811–1813 Tejanos in Béxar displaced Spanish authority. Nevertheless, Spain reasserted its power in Mexico and San Antonio, and independence came peacefully in 1821. Béxar's residents became Mexican citizens of the State of Coahuila y Texas. In an 1832 petition of the *ayuntamiento* of Béxar to the state legislature in Saltillo, the local councilmen made clear their allegiance to a Mexican identity at the same time that they complained of the inadequate attention the Mexican republic gave their region. "Being persuaded, your honors, of the importance and need of this manifesto, you will surely appreciate the language of sincerity and frankness with which this body has explained its cause. In so doing, it represents the emotions that inspire its inhabitants. It does so openly, without remote thought of calling into question the sweet and valued glory of being Mexican."[39] In Nacogdoches, the Mexican population also expressed its firm allegiance to Mexico in the face of Euro-American immigration into their region.

Nevertheless, in 1836 political confrontations between Euro American settlers and Mexican authorities resulted in an insurrection that led to Texas independence from Spain and incorporation into the United States in 1846.[40] This was followed by the United States war against Mexico which resulted in the conquering by the United States of the entire Southwest. Texas' Mexican inhabitants became Mexican Americans who had to contend with entirely new circumstances and a new national identity. San Antonio's Mexican residents attempted to conform to the imposed system while those in Nacodoches actually rebelled against the new order.[41] Regardless of these distinct survival strategies, in both regions Mexicans found themselves confronted with the threat of political, economic, and social subjugation.[42]

As Euro-Americans flooded into Texas after 1836, the Spanish or Canary Islander social identity took on a new importance for Mexican residents in both San Antonio and Nacogdoches. Mexican independence from Spain had brought to an end the official designations of calidad in the census as the new nation set out to implement republican ideals. An *español* or Canary Islander identity had diminished as the region became more integrated into the Mexican nation, but the racist social attitudes toward Indians, Blacks, and Mexicans brought to Texas by Euro-Americans produced incentives for Tejanos to revive a Spanish identity as a way of separating themselves from their brethren to the south.[43] As United States racism penetrated Texas, Tejanos reinvented the social definitions from their own tradition of social identity in the eighteenth century. José María Rodríguez's reassertion of his own Spanish or Canary Islander heritage, and emphasizing its distinction from the Mexican identity "across the river," was consistent with a need to maintain a social identity acceptable within the borders of the nation to which he belonged. While the centrality of race had diminished as a feature of Tejano social identity during the eighteenth century, racial concerns clearly regained force and hardened with Texas' incorporation into the United Sates. Indeed, even into the late twentieth century, many Mexican American descendants of eighteenth century settlers in San Antonio and Nacogdoches continue to identify with their Spanish—not Mexican—heritage.

Notes

1   For a discussion of this idea see Gerald E. Poyo and Gilberto M. Hinojosa, "Spanish Texas and Borderlands Historiography in Transition: Implications for United States History," *Journal of American History* 75 (September 1988), pp. 393–416.

2   Stephen F. Austin's designation as the "father of Texas," has been universally utilized in Texas history texts since their inception.

3   The classic expression of this view is Juan Gómez-Quiñones, "Toward a Perspective on Chicano History," *Aztlán*, 2 (Fall 1971).

4   A more recent restatement, arguing from an economic rather than sociocultural point of view, is Gilbert González and Raul Fernández, "Chicano History: Transcending Cultural Modes," *Pacific Historical Review*, 63:4 (November 1994), 469–497.

5   For examples of studies that deal with the Spanish/Mexican communities across time, cultures, and sovereignties see John Chávez, *The Lost Land: The Chicano Image of the Southwest* (Albuquerque: University of New Mexico Press, 1984); Juan Gómez-Quiñones, *Roots of Chicano Politics 1600–1984* (Albuquerque: University of New Mexico Press, 1990); Thomas Hall, *Social Change in the Southwest, 1350–1880* (Lawrence: University Press of Kansas, 1989); Gilberto M. Hinojosa, *Laredo: Borderlands Town in Transition* (College Station: Texas A & M University Press, 1983); Antonio Ríos-Bustamante, "Los Angeles, Pueblo and Region, 1781–1850: Continuity and Adaptation on the North Mexican Periphery" (Ph.D. diss., University of California, 1985); Ramón Gutiérrez, *When Jesus Came, the Corn Mothers Went Away: Marriage, Sexuality, and Power in New Mexico, 1500–1846* (Stanford: Stanford University Press, 1991); Douglas Monroy, *Thrown Among Strangers: The Making of Mexican Culture in Frontier California* (Berkeley: University of California Press, 1990).

6   See Arnoldo de León, *They Called them Greasers: Attitudes Toward Mexicans in Texas, 1821–1900* (Austin: University of Texas Press, 1983) and *The Tejano Community, 1836–1900* (Albuquerque: University of New Mexico Press, 1982); Timothy A. Matovina, *Tejano Religion and Ethnicity in San Antonio, 1821–1860* (Austin: University of Texas Press, 1995); Gerald E. Poyo, *Tejano Journey,1770–1850* (Austin: University of Texas Press, 1986).

7   For a sophisticated study of the nature of relations between Euro-Americans and Mexicans in Texas, and the implications of these relations for Mexican American social structures see David M. Montejano, *Anglos and Mexicans in the Making of Texas* (Austin: University of Texas Press, 1986).

8   Richard L. Nostrand, *The Hispano Homeland* (Norman: University of Oklahoma Press, 1992), p. 16. See also Nancie L. González, *The Spanish-Americans of New Mexico: A Heritage of Pride* (Albuquerque: University of New Mexico Press, 1967).

9   For an excellent overview discussion of this issue see the final chapter of David J. Weber, *Spain's Northern Frontier in North America* (New Haven: Yale University Press, 1992), pp. 335–360.

10 See Gerald E. Poyo and Gilberto M. Hinojosa, *Eighteenth Century Origins of the Tejano Community of San Antonio* (Austin: University of Texas Press for the University of Texas Institute of Texan Cultures at San Antonio, 1991).

11 José María Rodríguez, *Rodríguez Memoirs of Early Texas* (San Antonio: Passing Show Printing, 1913; reprint, San Antonio: Standard, 1961).

12 For a useful introduction to social relations in colonial Latin America see Magnus Morner, *Race Mixture in the History of Latin America* (Boston 1967).

13   For an overview of this literature see Benjamin Keen, "Main Currents in United States Writings on Colonial Spanish America, 1884–1984," *Hispanic American Historical Review*, 65:4 (November 1985) and John E. Kicza, "The Social and Ethnic Historiography of Colonial Latin America: The Last Twenty Years," *William & Mary Quarterly* 45 (July 1988), 468–470.

14   Rodney D. Anderson, "Race and Social Stratification: A Comparison of working-Class Spaniards, Indians, and Castas in Guadalajara, Mexico in 1821." *Hispanic American Historical Review* 68:2 (May 1988), 339–240.

15   For an interesting discussion of the *sistema de castas*, including visual depictions created by eighteenth century artists, see María Concepción García Sáiz, comp. *La Castas Mexicanas: Un género pictórico americano* (Italia: Olivetti, 1989).

16   Alicia Tjarks, "Comparative Analysis of Texas, 1777–1793," *Southwestern Historical Quarterly* 77, no.3 (January 1974).

17   For information on the Alarcón expedition see Fritz Leo Hoffman, ed. and trans. *Diary of the Alarcón Expedition into Texas, 1718–1719, by Francisco de Céliz* Los Angeles: Quivira Society, 1935 and "The Mezquía Diary of the Alarcón Expedition into Texas, 1718," *Southwestern Historical Quarterly* 41, no. 4 (April 1938). For the most thorough discussion of San Antonio's demographic development during the eighteenth century see Jesús F. de la Teja, *San Antonio de Béxar: A Community on New Spain's Northern Frontier* (Albuquerque: University of New Mexico Press, 1995).

18   Quoted in Jesús F. de la Teja, "Forgotten Founders: The Military Settlers of Eighteenth Century San Antonio de Béxar," in Gerald E. Poyo and Gilberto M. Hinojosa, *Tejano Origins in Eighteenth Century San Antonio de Béxar* (Austin: University of Texas for The Institute of Texan Cultures at San Antonio, 1991), 33.

19   See Gerald E. Poyo, "Immigrants and Integration in Late Eighteenth Century Béxar," in Gerald E. Poyo and Gilberto M. Hinojosa, eds. *Tejano Origins in Eighteenth Century San Antonio*, 85–104.

20   Fray Juan Agustín Morfi, *History of Texas, 1673–1779*, trans. and annotated by Carlos Eduardo Castañeda (Albuquerque: The Quivira Society, 1935; Arno Press Reprint, 1967), 99.

21   See de la Teja, *San Antonio de Béxar*, 17–29.

22   See baptismal, marriage and death records of mission San Antonio de Valero. Photocopies available at University of Texas Institute of Texan Cultures, San Antonio.

23   See Gerald E. Poyo, "The Canary Islands Immigrants of San Antonio: From Ethnic Exclusivity to Community in Eighteenth-Century Béxar," in Gerald E. Poyo and Gilberto M. Hinojosa, *Tejano Origins in Eighteenth Century San Antonio* (Austin: University of Texas Press for The University of Texas Institute of Texan Cultures at San Antonio, 1991).

24   For information on Berbán see "Estracto General de la tropa de dicho [San Antonio de Béxar] Presidio y Vezindario de la Villa de San Fernando en que se Comprende el Padron de sus Familias, Armamentos, y Bienes Raizes que cada uno tiene. 1, 2 y 3 del mes de Julio de 1779," Archivo

General de Indias (AGI), Audiencia de Guadalajara (AG), legajo 283; "Padron de las almas que ay en esta villa de San Fernando de Austria (*sic*). Año de 1793," Bexar Archives Microfilm (BAM), reel 2; "Padron de las familias que hay en esta Villa de San Fernando, y Presidio de Béxar ... Año de 1803," BAM; and Frederick C. Chabot *With the Makers of San Antonio* (San Antonio: Artes Gráficas, 1937).

25 For information on Huízar see "Padron de las almas ... Año de 1793," household entry no. 325; Land sales Pedro Huízar, Béxar County Archives, Land Grant Series (LGS)-322 (1783); LGS-323 (1784); LGS-278 (1784). Carlos E. Castañeda, *Our Catholic Heritage in Texas, 1519–1936*, 7 vols. (Austin: Von Boeckmann-Jones, 1936–1958) v. 5, pp. 40, 42, 51–58, 177, 197.

26 Poyo, "Immigrants and Integration."

27 See "Distribution of Land of Mission San Antonio de Valero, January 11, 1793," Bexar County Archives, Mission Records.

28 See Herbert Eugene Bolton, "The Spanish Abandonment and Re-Occupation of East Texas, 1773–1779," *Quarterly of the Texas State Historical Association*, 9:2 (October 1905) and "Expediente promovido por los vecinos del extinguido presidio de los Adaes para que se les conceda algun establecimiento donde pueden subsistir con sus familias," AGI, AG, legajo 103. Copy of transcript in Barker Texas History Center.

29 "Census Report of the Town of San Antonio Valero, December 31, 1804," BA, in Carmela Leal, comp. *Residents of Texas, 1782–1836* 3 vols (San Antonio: University of Texas Institute of Texan Cultures, 1984), 3: 378–380.

30 Randell G. Tarín, "The Second Flying Company of San Carlos de Parra," *The New Handbook of Texas* 6 vols. (Austin: The Texas State Historical Association, 1996), V: 960–961.

31 Statistics found in Jesus F. de la Teja, "Rebellion on the Frontier," p. 17, in Gerald E. Poyo, ed. *Tejano Journey, 1770–1850* (Austin: University of Texas Press, 1996).

32 On the Aguayo expedition see Charles Wilson Hackett, "The Marquis de San Miguel de Aguayo and His Recovery of Texas from the French, 1719–1723," *Southwestern Historical Quarterly*, 49, no.2 (October 1945); Peter P. Forrestal, "Peña's Diary of the Aguayo Expedition," *Preliminary Studies of the Texas Catholic Historical Association* 2, no.7 (January 1935).

33 "Lista, y relacion jurada ... de los ofiziales, y soladados de este presidio de Nuestra Señora del Pilar de los Adais, 27 de Maio de 1731," Archivo General de la Nacion (AGN), Provincias Internas, vol. 163.

34 Castañeda, *Our Catholic Heritage*, v.4, pp. 273–302.

35 "Census of the Town of Nacogdoches. 1793," *BA*, in Leal, *Residents of Texas*, v.1.

36 For information on the Caddo tribes and their ongoing relationships with the Spanish and French see Timothy K. Perttula, *"The Caddo Nation": Archaeological and Ethnohistoric Perspectives* (Austin: University of Texas Press, 1992); Timothy K. Perttula, ed. "Commemorating the Columbian Quincentenary," *Bulletin of the Texas Archeological Society*, v. 63 (1992), special issue; H.F. Gregory,

ed. *The Southern Caddo: An Anthology* (New York: Garland Publishing Co., 1986); F. Todd Smith, "The Red River Caddos: A Historical Overview to 1835," *Bulletin of the Texas Archeological Survey*, v. 65 (1994), 115–127. For information on the combative Spanish-Indian relations in the San Antonio area see Elizabeth A. H. John, *Storms Brewed in Other Men's Worlds: The Confrontation of Indians, Spanish, French in the Southwest, 1540–1795* (College Station: Texas A & M University Press, 1975).

37 Castañeda, *Our Catholic Heritage*, v.4, pp. 273–302.

38 Herbert Eugene Bolton, *Texas in the Middle of the Eighteenth Century* (Austin: University of Texas at Austin, 1970), 388–389.

39 David J. Weber, ed. *Troubles in Texas. 1832: A Tejano Viewpoint from San Antonio with a Translation and Facsimile* (Dallas: Southern Methodist University, 1983), 29.

40 See Paul Lack, *The Texas Revolutionary Experience: A Political and Social History, 1835–1836* (College Station: Texas A&M University Press, 1992)

41 See Gerald E. Poyo, ed. *Tejano Journey, 1770–1850* (Austin: University of Texas Press, 1996)

42 See David Montejano, *Anglos and Mexicans in the Making of Texas, 1836–1986,* (Austin: University of Texas Press, 1986)

43 On Euro-American racism in Texas in the nineteenth century see Arnoldo De León, *They Called Them Greasers* (Austin: University of Texas Press, 1983) and James Ernest Crisp, "Anglo-Texan Attitudes toward the Mexican, 1821–1845." Ph.D. dissertation, Yale University, 1976. For a profile of nineteenth century Tejanos after Texas independence from Mexico see Arnoldo de León, *The Tejano Community, 1836–1900* (Albuquerque: University of New Mexico Press, 1982).

DISCUSSION QUESTIONS

1. Why was there a decline of the term "Mexican" and a rise of the term "Spanish" in the 1920s?

2. Why did people seek to separate themselves from a Mexican identity?

3. What role did *calidad* play in census documents? How did this impact the racial hierarchy?

4. How does the Béxar example demonstrate the fluidity and complexity of the *casta* system?

5. How could people establish their "worth" or *calidad* in the community?

6. How did Tejanos reinvent social definitions of their identity in the 18th century?

Chapter 2

Mexican Women in the 19th Century

Editor's Introduction

As the title suggests, chapter 2 focuses on women in 19th-century Mexico, specifically in northern Mexico or the present-day United States. There are two readings in this chapter—both of which highlight the role that women played during wartime. Women have been a marginalized group throughout history, often treated as bystanders instead of active agents. Contemporary historians have worked to undo this trend by researching the female experience and interweaving it into a broader historical context. The authors of the following readings, Jean A. Stuntz and John M. Belohlavek, begin to fill this void with their analysis of *Tejanas* during the Texas Revolution and *soldaderas* in the Mexican–American War.

These readings are grouped together because they demonstrate the various ways that women were involved in, and affected by, two 19th-century wars, the Texas Revolution and the Mexican–American War. The first reading, "*Tejanas*: Hispanic Women on the Losing Side of the Texas Revolution," by historian Jean A. Stuntz, discusses the daily life of women prior to the Texas Revolution (1835–36) and how they were impacted by Texas Independence and the increasing Anglo-American presence that followed. The second reading, "*Soldaderas*: Mexican Women and the Battlefield," by John M. Belohlavek, focuses on the Mexican–American War (1846–48) and the *soldaderas* who traveled with the Mexican Army to provide critical aid to its soldiers. While one reading emphasizes the impact of war on Tejana daily life, the other emphasizes the impact of the war on women who lived and worked in military camps.

Stuntz's reading examines how Tejanas were impacted during and after the Texas Revolution. Stuntz describes the daily life of Tejanas—their priorities, routines, and so on—and explains why the Texas Revolution had a devastating effect on the Hispanic women of Texas. Unlike readings that emphasize influential men of the Texas Revolution, Stuntz focuses on the short-term and long-term impacts of the war on women. She does not spend a lot of time delving into the military aspects of the war and instead highlights the challenges that arose for Tejanas as their homeland became increasingly overrun by immigrating Anglo-Americans. This reading is helpful in understanding how Tejana's lives were transformed by changing policies that were a direct result of the Texas Revolution. Stuntz's primary point is that even though historical texts have focused on how men were affected by the revolution, women suffered catastrophic losses as well. They lost their land, their rights, and "had to struggle just to hold on to the remnants of their culture." She wants readers to understand that these women who have been marginalized throughout history are an important part of Texas history, and particularly, Mexican American history.

Belohlavek's reading sheds light on the Mexican women who were actively involved in the war effort in some capacity. Additionally, it analyzes how stories of women on the battlefield became legendary in both the United States and Mexico. Belohlavek has published extensively on the 19th-century Southwest and South and the Confederacy, and his most recent research is on the role of Mexican women in the Mexican–American War and their support or opposition to the war. This new research fills a gap in current scholarship that privileges the experiences of men in the war. "*Soldaderas*" illustrates the significance of women's presence on the battlefield and in the soldiers' camps. Belohlavek argues that soldaderas were an essential element of every Mexican Army unit, performing critical roles and suffering along with their men. He states that Americans have too often marginalized their role or portrayed them as servants or slaves, which fails to encompass the impact they had on the army.

Together these readings work to illustrate the ways that 19th-century Mexican women were influenced by wartime and the various tasks they performed for wartime efforts. It removes them from the margins and places their experiences at the forefront, providing the reader with a more well-rounded understanding of two significant events in Mexican American history.

Tejanas

Hispanic Women on the Losing Side of the Texas Revolution

Jean A. Stuntz

I N 1821, WHEN MEXICO RECEIVED ITS independence from Spain, the Hispanic population in Texas had been decimated by the fighting. The three population centers, San Fernando de Béxar (San Antonio), La Bahía (Goliad), and Nacogdoches, had only a few thousand people total. Indian groups dominated the rest of Texas. By 1824, when Stephen F. Austin began bringing in Anglo colonists legally, life for Tejanos and Tejanas, the Hispanic men and women of Texas, had not improved. If anything, life was more unsettled because of the rapidly changing politics in Mexico City.[1]

During the 1820s and early 1830s, most Tejanas raised children, took care of their husbands, and participated in the social and religious rituals of Spanish Texas. They lived in *villas* (small towns) which had grown up around the missions and *presidios* (forts) created over a century earlier. The missions had by then all been secularized and either served as parish churches or had, like the *presidios*, been converted to non-religious uses. This traditional urban lifestyle preserved much of the Spanish heritage including social mores, festivals, and their legal system.[2]

Every day Tejanas got up before the rest of the family to make tortillas for breakfast. This involved kneeling on the ground while grinding dried corn between two stones to make the flour, then forming and cooking the tortillas. After feeding her family, she would get on with the day's chores. This might involve doing laundry by the river, making or mending clothes, tending to sick children or neighbors, or any of the thousands of things pre-industrial women all over the world do. It also might involve activities unique to Spanish-heritage women, such as supervising irrigation of their fields from the *acequias* (irrigation ditches), working in the shops they or their family owned, or taking their spinning to the *plaza* (town square) where they could talk with other women as they worked.

Historians are fortunate that literate people traveled through Texas during this time and left accounts of their travels. In 1828 General Manuel Mier y Terán traveled through Texas on an inspection tour for the Mexican government. His draftsman, José María Sánchez, described the ruins of missions in San Antonio as being populated by poor farmers almost totally at the mercy of hostile Indians. The botanist for the expedition, Jean-Louis Berlandier, also described the town in unflattering terms. The streets were narrow and twisted, the houses were mostly

Jean A. Stuntz, "Tejanas: Hispanic Women on the Losing Side of the Texas Revolution," *Women and the Texas Revolution*, ed. Mary L. Scheer, pp. 47–63. Copyright © 2012 by University of North Texas Press. Reprinted with permission.

thatched-roof huts (*jacales*), the people indolent and carefree. He wrote that the women dressed more like women of Louisiana than of Mexico City and that the population in general had adopted too many customs of its French and Anglo neighbors.[3]

Once Terán's expedition made it to the next largest town, Nacogdoches, the scene had changed considerably. For one thing, this town situated next to French and later American territory was quite cosmopolitan. The Spanish influence had dissipated, along with the inhabitants, according to Terán. The place was lawless because law-breakers could simply cross the border into another country, and this went in both directions. Terán thought that the Americans were much more industrious in both farming and business than were the Mexicans, and he deplored this, though he stated that Americans also worked much harder at their vices.[4]

Terán visited the tiny town of La Bahía del Espiritú Santo last. The town was poor in every sense of the word. Only about 300 people lived there and they had little food and no luxuries. Only the missionaries kept the town going, for the presidio was run by inept and corrupt officers.[5]

An American visiting San Antonio at about the same time as the Terán expedition, J. C. Clopper, found many contradictions. He praised the lush fields and huge cottonwood trees, but despaired of the architecture and the ruins of previous *presidios*, such as the Alamo. He described the houses as wigwams, with walls woven of small mesquite trees daubed with mud, and with most families having very few possessions. However, he found the young ladies very attractive.[6]

The young ladies found him attractive, too, as his father had opened a successful business in town. One mother even invited him to court her daughter. He accompanied the senoritas to the *fandangos*, or street celebrations involving dancing. These dances were strictly chaperoned to protect the young women's virtues. His detailed descriptions of the women of San Antonio betray his own upbringing as well as theirs. He spoke of their sparkling eyes and bright skin, their long black hair and rich festival clothing. He seemed somewhat chagrined that their ordinary clothing was less than glamorous.[7]

Clopper also described the making of tortillas by the women, from soaking the kernels in lye to the grinding process, done between two stones while kneeling, to the cooking on hot sheets of iron laid over the fire. He said that the women usually sang merry tunes as they worked. He marveled that the tortillas were used in lieu of utensils for eating the rest of the meal, but this was necessary as so few people owned forks. Meals and other household activities took place while sitting on skins on the ground, as chairs were rare.[8]

A young American blacksmith, Noah Smithwick, traveled through Mexican Texas from 1827 through 1836 and recounted his journeys in his memoirs. His description of a woman making tortillas matches Clopper's. Smithwick heard the sounds of singing and what he thought was dancing, but which turned out to be a woman making tortillas. He explained the process as being almost mechanical, as the woman ground the corn into a paste in the *metate* (the flat grinding stones), rolled it into a ball then flattened it with a series of pats, finally tossing it onto the hot sheet of iron to cook, all the while singing as she did so.[9]

When he stayed in San Antonio, Smithwick saw women spinning and weaving in a manner he thought most old-fashioned and inefficient. The women of San Antonio did not use spinning wheels as Americans did. Instead, they tied the end of a long roll of wool to a wooden peg, then set the peg to spinning in a bowl, using the gravity and twirling motion to turn the wool into thread. Smith-wick thought this manner of spinning took much longer than did the American way. He also criticized their manner of weaving as being inefficient. Instead of using thread for both the warp and the woof, they used it only to string the loom, then wove rolls of wool under and over the threads with their fingers. He did admit that the blankets thus produced were both beautiful and warm.[10]

It seems that neither Mexican nor American visitors to Texas in the late 1820s were impressed with the inhabitants. However, each had to concede that the women worked all day, even if they then partied well into the night. Tejanas spent many hours each day preparing tortillas and other food and in making the clothing and other textiles for their families. Visitors would not have seen the other duties of the women, such as raising children, cleaning the house, or taking care of their gardens, as all of this was done in private. The life of the Tejana before the Texas Revolution revolved around her family. This would not change much either during or after the conflict.

A few Anglo men did make the acquaintance of Tejanas and some married into the Hispanic community. Jim Bowie may be the most famous/infamous Anglo to do this. He married Ursula de Veramendi, member of a rich

IMAGE 2.1.1 Tejana type, from *Views of Mexico: Album pintoresco de la Republica Mexicana*. Courtesy DeGolyer Library, Southern Methodist University, Dallas, Texas, Ag2000.1297.

and prominent family, in 1831, after officially becoming a Mexican citizen the year before. Bowie often found himself in trouble with the law and his land speculations infuriated President and General Antonio López de Santa Anna. When that general arrived in San Antonio on February 23, 1836, he deliberately took up residence in Bowie's home.[11]

When the tensions began, most Hispanics wanted to stay out of it, seeing the Anglos as the troublemakers. However, when in 1835 Santa Anna overthrew the Constitution of 1824, many in the Tejano communities declared themselves against the tyrant and for liberty (though not for independence, yet). As Tejano men left their homes to join the Consultations, Conventions, and battles, women were left to fend for themselves. They had to do all the work they usually did, plus what the men would have done. No matter how much they supported the principles of liberty, some must have grumbled at all the extra work.[12]

General Martín Perfecto de Cos came to San Antonio with 500 soldiers to secure the area after the first rumblings of resistance. He announced that he would punish the troublemakers at Anahuac and threatened to run all Anglos out of Texas. Those Anglos who had been pushing for war saw this as the last straw. Texan rebels seized Goliad and refused to allow Mexican soldiers to remove the cannon at Gonzales. It was in this struggle that the first shots of the revolution were fired. The banner painted with the words "Come and Take It" over a cannon became the first symbol of armed resistance to the Mexican authorities even though no shots were actually fired. The Mexican troops retreated to San Antonio empty-handed. The rebel forces proclaimed victory and moved to San Antonio to take it, as well.[13]

The Texan mob arrived at the outskirts of San Antonio in October 1835. The battle of Concepción, fought near the mission Nuestra Señora de la Purísima Concepción de Acuña Mission, was a great victory for the Texans led by Jim Bowie. The Texans then set up a siege of San Antonio, which resulted in the Grass Fight, so called because when the Texans spotted a mule train with large sacks approaching the city they attacked, thinking it was a payroll caravan. Instead, all they found was grass, which the San Antonio natives had gathered to feed their livestock. Infuriated, the Texans burned the grass, only belatedly realizing that they should have used it to feed their own horses.[14]

Finally, on December 5, 1835, as many of the men were cold and hungry and ready to return home for the winter, some of the Texas volunteers decided to attack the city. Ben Milam led about 300 men into San Antonio where they fought house-to-house and hand-to-hand, forcing the Mexican soldiers to retreat from the city into the Alamo on the outskirts of town. There General Cos surrendered and promised to move his troops south of the Rio Grande, never to return to Texas. The Texans moved into the city, either paying for or commandeering quarters and supplies. They also set about fortifying the Alamo to withstand the attack they were sure would come. Santa Anna had already threatened to kill every person who had resisted his authority and had issued arrest warrants specifically for Jim Bowie for his part on the Monclova Speculations. The threat of Santa Anna's army and his reputation for violence drove large portions of the Texas population into hiding in the countryside and sent Anglos rushing east toward the Sabine River and US protection.[15]

The fighting itself, which lasted less than a year, affected Tejanas directly and indirectly. Most of the battles took place in or near the Hispanic towns, so Tejanas had to share their food, their belongings, and sometimes even their houses with soldiers. Once the anti-Santa Anna forces took control of San Antonio in December 1835, Tejanas in town sold food and other goods to the Texian army under the control of Colonel James C. Neill. The army also employed the men living in San Antonio. After Lieutenant Colonel William Barret Travis took command of the forces inside the Alamo, he also issued scrip for cattle purchased from Felipe Xaimes. The Texas government eventually paid these debts.[16]

In February 1836 the people living in San Antonio and those barricading themselves inside the Alamo heard that General Santa Anna and his army were approaching. Many of the Hispanic women and children fled into the countryside to escape his wrath though some stayed in town to convince him of their loyalty. Others joined the forces inside the Alamo.[17]

In the town of Goliad, which had grown up by the mission La Bahía, Tejanas also experienced the fighting first-hand. Captain Manuel Sabriego commanded the *presidio* there and had married a local Hispanic woman. He loyally supported Santa Anna and even raised a company of local men, mostly *vaqueros* (cowboys), to fight off the rebels. On October 10, 1835, Texian commander George M. Collingsworth captured Sabriego and took command of the *presidio*. Philip Dimmitt took charge because he was married to a local Tejana, but he was not especially suited to command. He forced the local townspeople to perform heavy labor without pay, causing many of the families to flee to the countryside and join the forces loyal to Santa Anna. General José Urrea took advantage of these loyalties to defeat Colonel James W. Fannin, Jr. and his garrison at Goliad, which ended in another massacre of surrendered Texian troops on March 27, 1836. "Remember Goliad!" was as much a rallying cry as "Remember the Alamo!" The fighting ended on April 21, 1836, with the battle of San Jacinto.[18]

After the fighting was over, Hispanics in Texas faced tremendous problems. As more and more Anglos came into the Republic, Hispanics lost status, power, and land. Some lost their lives to Anglo race-based violence. Most of the whites moving in came from the U.S. South and brought their prejudices against people of color with them. Those from Georgia especially had just forced an Indian removal and saw that as a good thing. These new whites saw all Hispanics as lesser because of their skin color and as traitors because they were of Mexican heritage. Even those who had fought with the Texians found themselves branded as disloyal and therefore subject to prejudice and violence.[19]

An example of this prejudice was Juan Seguin. Born in San Antonio to a prominent family, he became *Alcalde* (mayor) in 1833. He supported the movement against Santa Anna and was among the defenders of the Alamo. He survived because he had been sent with a message to the government before the battle. He fought with a troop of Tejanos at the battle of San Jacinto, as much a hero as any man there. He became a senator in the Republic of Texas legislature where he tried in vain to get pensions for the widows and orphans of the Tejanos killed at the Alamo. He also tried unsuccessfully to get the Texas laws translated into Spanish so the Tejanos could defend themselves in court against the Anglos. Eventually, Seguin got tired of fighting the prejudice and joined the Mexican army, though he eventually returned to Texas.[20]

Many of the wealthier Hispanic families dealt with the Anglo invasion by marrying their daughters to promising Anglos, many of whom then became city and state officials because of their wife's money. Both sides benefitted. The Tejanas could protect their families with their Anglo prestige and the men got easy access to land and power. This arrangement only lasted a few years, though, until the influx of so many Anglos and the loss of so much Hispanic land made such marriages less desirable.[21]

Religion was another cause for prejudice against Hispanics. Protestant Anglos held deep-seated hatred of Catholics and all the Tejanos were Catholic. Catholic rituals and festivals continued to take place in the Spanish towns like San Antonio and Tejanas continued to take part in the parades and celebrations. The procession of Our Lady of Guadalupe included the image adorned with flowers, women carrying crosses and banners, and girls dressed in white carrying candles in the parade. Men played music and fired their guns while everyone sang hymns. Protestants saw these parades as idolatry and proof of the ignorance and superstition of the Hispanics.[22]

For most Tejanas daily life did not change much as a direct result of the Texas Revolution, although in the long-term their lives and prospects changed for the worse. They still ground corn to make tortillas, spun thread and wove cloth, took care of their family, and participated in community events. The difference was that they now did all this in occupied territory. After the revolution, immigration from the southern part of the United States increased. These people brought with them the racial attitude that allowed people of color to be treated as less than human and any land they held to be taken from them. So even though most Tejanas did not have much direct experience during the fighting, and their lives did not change immediately, the long-term results of the Texas Revolution on the lives of Tejanas were immense.[23]

The mostly Anglo Republic of Texas legislature moved quickly to change the legal system from the Spanish to the English common law system they were more familiar with. This change took away a lot of rights from Tejanas, as the Spanish system held women to be almost equal to men. Under English common law, married women had no rights at all. Their very existence merged into that of their husbands. Under English law, a married woman could not make a contract, could not own property, could not write a will, could not sue or be sued, could not even fight for the custody of her own children because she did not have a legal identity separate from that of her husband.[24]

This was very different from the Spanish system where married women could do all of these things. Hispanic women in Texas were used to being able to transact business, sue someone for transgressions, and own and manage their own property. Legal cases preserved in the Bexár Archives give ample evidence that women in Spanish Texas knew their rights and exercised them as needed. For example in 1745, Tomasa de la Garza, a married woman, petitioned the *cabildo* (local government) for a piece of land for her family to live on. She and her husband had eight children who lived with them; one of her daughters was a widow. The government officials granted title to her, not her husband.[25]

IMAGE 2.1.2 Tejana in Baile costume, from *Views of Mexico: Album pintoresco de la Republica Mexicana.* Courtesy DeGolyer Library, Southern Methodist University, Dallas, Texas, vaultfolio-2 F1213.L45.

Under Spanish law, women could sue and be sued in their own names, even if they were married, though usually the husband would represent the wife. In 1770, don Francisco Caravajal brought suit on behalf of his wife, doña María, to gain title to land that had belonged to her grandfather. A city official had illegally given part of this land to brothers Andrés and Francisco Hernández and Andrés had sold part of his share to his niece, dona Josepha Hernández, while Francisco sold part of his share to the son of the original owner, Joseph Caravajal, dona María's father who should have inherited it to begin with. Dona Josepha Hernández, the defendant, claimed that the land was indeed hers, but the authorities ruled in favor of Dona María. Even though the husband had brought the suit, the land belonged to the wife.[26]

Spanish married women could also write wills disposing of their own property. Unlike English common law, married women under Spanish law retained their legal identity and ownership of any property brought into the marriage. María Melián wrote a will on December 3, 1740, which is a good example of Spanish inheritance laws. María had gained property in each of her two marriages and by settling in Texas. (The Spanish government lured settlers to Texas by giving them land and other property.) She devised each type of property according to the Spanish law. Property brought into a marriage or received as a gift or inheritance after the marriage was separate property, while anything earned during the marriage was community property. María had one cow that she brought into her second marriage, so this cow was her separate property. It had given birth to four calves, which were then community property. Husbands and wives each owned half of this community property. María gave two of these cows—her half of the community property—to her children. She had also received five cows for settling in San Antonio. These were her separate property and she gave all of them to her children. She divided the rest of her own property equally between her sons and daughter.[27]

These cases showed that Tejanas held considerable rights before the Texas Revolution. They could own property in their own name, which is often considered the foundation of citizenship. They could sue if they felt their rights had been infringed upon. They could write wills to dispose of their property as they wished. These rights all disappeared when English common law became the law of Texas. Fortunately, Texas legislators brought back some aspects of the Spanish system when they wrote the statehood constitution in 1845. Though the motivation to re-enact community property laws was to keep Texas lands out of the hands of creditors in the United States, women could still benefit. That was, if they had lawyers. Most people knew nothing about the Spanish community property law and it was only in cases of divorce, intestate succession, and other property battles that these laws were ever used. By that time, though, most Tejanas had been deprived of all land by violence or fraud, and did not have enough money to hire lawyers.[28]

As more and more Anglos came into the Republic and occupied more and more of the territory, Hispanics lost more and more. They lost their land to greedy, unscrupulous H, and violent Anglos. They lost the ability to control their own lives and to guide their children's future. Even in places like San Antonio, which had been mostly Hispanic, Anglos took over and made the town their own. In the process, Tejanas lost their land, lost their rights, and had to struggle just to hold on to the remnants of their culture. In short, the Texas Revolution had a devastating effect on the Hispanic women of Texas.

Selected Bibliography

Acosta, Teresa Palomo, and Ruthe Winegarten. *Las Tejanas: 300 Years of History*. Austin: University of Texas Press, 2003.

Cantrell, Gregg. *Stephen F. Austin: Empresario of Texas*. New Haven: Yale University Press, 1999.

Campbell, Randolph B. *Gone to Texas: A History of the Lone Star State*. New York: Oxford University Press, 2003.

Chipman, Donald E., and Harriet Denise Joseph, *Spanish Texas, 1519–1821*. Rev. ed. Austin: University of Texas Press, 2010.

De la Teja, Jesús F., ed. *Tejano Leadership in Mexican and Revolutionary Texas*. College Station: Texas A&M University Press, 2010.

Dysart, Jane. "Mexican Women in San Antonio, 1830–1860: The Assimilation Process," *Western Historical Quarterly* 7, no. 4 (Oct. 1976): 365–375.

Jackson, Jack, ed. *Texas by Terán: The Diary Kept by Manuel de Mier y Terán on His 1828 Inspection of Texas*. Translated by John Wheat. Austin: University of Texas Press, 2000.

McKnight, Joseph W. "Spanish Law for the Protection of the Surviving Spouse," *Anuario de Historia del Derecho Espanol*, tomo 57 (1987): 373–395.

Montejano, David. *Anglos and Mexicans in the Making of Texas, 1836–1986*. Austin: University of Texas Press, 1987.

Poyo, Gerald E., ed. *Tejano Journey, 1770–1850*. Austin: University of Texas Press, 1996.

Salmon, Marylynn. *Women and the Law of Property in Early America*. Chapel Hill: University of North Carolina Press, 1986.

Smithwick, Noah. *The Evolution of a State or Recollections of Old Texas Days*. Compiled by Nanna Smithwick Donaldson, Barker Texas History Center Series #5, 4th printing. Austin: University of Texas Press, 1994.

Stuntz, Jean A. *Hers, His, and Theirs: Community Property Law in Spain and Early Texas*. Lubbock: Texas Tech University Press, 2005.

Notes

1   For more information on the Spanish era of Texas, read Donald E. Chipman and Harriet Denise Joseph, *Spanish Texas, 1519–1821*, rev. ed. (Austin: University of Texas Press, 2010). For more information on the extent of Indian control of Texas, read Pekka Hämäläinen, *The Comanche Empire* (New Haven: Yale University Press, 2009). For an understanding of Mexican politics during the late 1820s and early 1830s, read Gregg Cantrell, *Stephen F. Austin: Empresario of Texas* (New Haven: Yale University Press, 1999), 104–131, 202–296. To get an understanding of the experiences of Spanish and Hispanic women throughout Texas history, see *Las Tejanas: 300 years of History* (Austin: University of Texas Press, 2003) by Teresa Palomo Acosta and Ruthe Winegarten.

2   Randolph B. Campbell, *Gone to Texas: A History of the Lone Star State* (New York: Oxford University Press, 2003), 97.

3   Jack Jackson, ed., *Texas by Terán: The Diary kept by Manuel de Mier y Terán on His 1828 Inspection of Texas*, trans. John Wheat (Austin: University of Texas Press, 2000), 15–17.

4   Ibid., 79–81.

5   Ibid., 151–53.

6   Ibid., 21–23, 26.

7   Ibid., 23.

8   Ibid., 25–26.

9   Noah Smithwick, *The Evolution of a State or Recollections of Old Texas Days*, comp. Nanna Smithwick Donaldson, Barker Texas History Center Series #5, 4th printing (Austin: University of Texas Press, 1994), 9–10.

10   Ibid., 34.

11   William R. Williamson, "Bowie, James," *Handbook of Texas Online* (http://www.tshaonline.org/handbook/online/articles/fbo45), accessed April 18, 2011. Published by the Texas State Historical Association.

12   Campbell, *Gone to Texas*, 116–131; Cantrell, *Stephen F. Austin*, 247–328.

13   Campbell, *Gone to Texas*, 116–122, 128–131.

14   Ibid., 128–136; Alwyn Barr, "Grass Fight," *Handbook of Texas Online* (http://www.tshaonline.org/handbook/online/articles/qfg01), accessed April 17, 2011. Published by the Texas State Historical Association.

15   Campbell, *Gone to Texas*, 138–141. See the chapter in this book on the Runaway Scrape for more on this topic.

16   Stephen L. Hardin, "Efficient in the Cause," in *Tejano Journey, 1770–1850*, ed. Gerald E. Poyo (Austin: University of Texas Press, 1996), 56.

17   Ibid., "Efficient," 63. The stories of the women in the Alamo are told in another chapter of this book.

18   Ibid., "Efficient," 62–64.

19   For more information on the Tejano experience, see Timothy M. Matovina, "Between Two Worlds" in *Tejano Journey*, 73–87 and David Montejano, *Anglos and Mexicans in the Making of Texas, 1836–1986* (Austin: University of Texas Press, 1987), 13–99. For more on Tejanos in leadership roles before, during, and after the Revolution, see *Tejano Leadership in Mexican and Revolutionary Texas*, ed. Jesús F. de la Teja (College Station: Texas A&M University Press, 2010). To focus more on Tejanas, see Jane Dysart, "Mexican Women in San Antonio, 1830–1860: The Assimilation Process," *Western Historical Quarterly* 7 no. 4 (Oct. 1976): 365–375.

20   Matovina, "Between Two Worlds," 75–76; Jesús F. de la Teja, "Seguin, Juan Nepomuceno," *Handbook of Texas Online* (http://www.tshaonline.org/handbook/online/articles/fse08), accessed April 17, 2011. Published by the Texas State Historical Association.

21   Montejano, *Anglos and Mexicans*, 34–35.

22   Matovino, "Between Two Worlds," 81–85.

23 For more on the increase of slavery and racial attitudes in Texas, see Randolph B. Campbell, *An Empire for Slavery: The Peculiar Institution in Texas, 1821–1865* (Baton Rouge: Louisiana State University Press, 1989).

24 The Declaration with Plan and Powers of the Provisional Government of Texas (1836), Article VI, VII. For English common law regarding the status of women, see St. George Tucker, *Blackstone's Commentaries with Reference to the Constitution and Laws of the Federal Government of the United States and the Commonwealth of Virginia* (Philadelphia: William Birch Young and Abraham Small, 1803; repr. New Jersey: Rothman Reprints, 1969), 1:418–445; Marylynn Salmon, *Women and the Law of Property in Early America* (Chapel Hill: University of North Carolina Press, 1986); Jean Stuntz, *Hers, His, and Theirs: Community Property Law in Spain and Early Texas* (Lubbock: Texas Tech University Press, 2005), 99–107.

25 Bexar Archives Translations (BAT) microfilm Reel 3, vol. 17, 1–6.

26 Ibid., reel 7, vol. 48, 16–23, 27, 32, 38–39, 65.

27 Ibid., reel 2, vol. 10, 51–55. For more explanation on Spanish laws of inheritance, see Joseph W. McKnight, "Spanish Law for the Protection of the Surviving Spouse," *Anuario de Historia del Derecho Espanol,* tomo 57 (1987): 373–395.

28 *Debates of the Texas Constitution* (Houston, 1836), 10–11, 53–55, 417–426, 453–462, 505–508, 598–601; Constitution of the State of Texas of 1845, Title 7, Sections 19 and 20. For more on how these Spanish laws were used in the Republic and state of Texas, see Stuntz, *Hers, His, and Theirs,* 133–169.

Soldaderas

Mexican Women and the Battlefield

John M. Belohlavek

FOR MANY AMERICANS, THE CLOUD OF Anglo-Saxon superiority floated triumphantly over the conquest of Mexico. An inferior race limited by an ancient Spanish culture and a corrupt Catholic Church, Mexicans should have been grateful for the opportunity to become enlightened. The antiwar poet James Russell Lowell caustically expressed those views in *The Bigelow Papers*, where Birdofredum Sawin, a fictional Massachusetts volunteer under the command of General Caleb Cushing, vents his frustration and disillusionment with the war.

Afore I come away from hum I had a strong persuasion

Thet Mexicans worn't human beans,—an ourang outang nation

A sort o'folks a chap could kill an'never dream on t'arter

_____

It must be right, fer Caleb sez it's reg'lar Anglo-saxon

_____

Thet our nation's bigger 'n theirn an' so its rights air bigger,

An' thet it's all to make 'em free that we air pullin' trigger,

Thet Anglo-Saxondom's idee's abreakin' em to pieces;

An thet idee's that every man doos just wut he damn pleases.[1]

Apparently, "wut he damn pleases" spilled over into the exploitation of young Mexican women. As US forces occupied a city, officers employed locals to perform the basic domestic tasks of cooking and cleaning. Samuel Chamberlain, of Massachusetts, claimed that "all the Americans quartered in town, kept house with a good-looking señorita." Indeed, Chamberlain maintained a young married girl, Carmeleita Veigho de Moro, whose husband later had her raped and murdered for comporting with a Yankee. When an American doctor named Morton departed Chihuahua, his mistress dressed as a man and followed him to his new home in Saltillo, where she was observed living in his tent "in the most public manner."

How do we define the image of these women? Are the terms *collaborator, camp follower,* and *victim* fair designations? Many women interacted with the Americans because of economic need or opportunism; they washed clothes and sold food to soldiers in the marketplace. In the minds of many Mexicans, such fraternization with the enemy, which perhaps also included providing "female companionship," sparked predictable resentment. Assuming that every relationship between a Mexican girl and an American soldier had a sexual dimension would be highly presumptive, since engaging in questionable behavior with young Hispanic women would be taboo in both the northern and the southern society. Still, the line seems to have been crossed with disturbing ease.[2]

The Mexican Army

The idea of the United States' racial and cultural superiority played out in many ways in Mexico, largely on the battlefield, where Americans expected their skill, size, courage, and ethnicity to triumph. The Anglo perception that dark-skinned, diminutive Mexican men were more effeminate and therefore inferior tore at the scab of a country trying to heal its national wounds. The Mexican soldier, typically an illiterate peasant impressed into service, too often had little loyalty or commitment to the state, which was riddled by political factionalism and revolution. Only a quarter century from independence, there was a struggle between those Mexicans who envisioned a centralized union and those who envisioned a federal one. In many ways, it was not unlike the situation the Founding Fathers faced in Philadelphia during the summer of 1787 and in the following decades.[3]

The historian Mark Wasserman contends that three factors—a chronic lack of funds, inadequately trained soldiers, and poor leadership—led to the defeat of Mexico. The Mexican government attempted to provide uniforms and arms to equip a substantial military, and did so with Napoleonic-era surplus weapons purchased from Great Britain. The armaments were obsolete and substandard, the Americans owning a particular advantage in terms of artillery. Too many men were conscripted. Pay was poor (a few centavos a day), instruction minimal, and discipline uneven. No wonder. The officer corps, made up of Creole social and economic elites, relished their privilege and status. They habitually neither identified with their men nor generally cared about their well-being. Caught up in the turmoil that could affect their power and position, officers monitored the politics of the capital as closely as they did the movements of the American forces. The scholar David Clary maintains that "the Mexican officer corps was unschooled, corrupt, incompetent and heavy with generals." Wasserman agrees: "The officers, Santa Anna in particular, were irresolute, inconsistent, and often distracted by personal vindictiveness and political scheming, which at crucial times led to costly mistakes in battle."[4]

Their harsh estimation of the officers may spark debate among historians, but certainly the question of the leadership and character of the president and commanding officer, Antonio López de Santa Anna, prompts heated controversy. Self-styled as the Napoleon of the West, the fifty-two-year-old general had fought Mexico's enemies, including the rebellious Texans, for more than a decade and lost a leg in resisting the French in 1838. The severed limb later received an elaborate burial in Mexico City. Elected president initially in 1833, Santa Anna would be in and out of power for the next twenty years. Timothy J. Henderson deems him "the indispensable man of his generation," while struggling to explain his survival in Mexican politics. "Vain, corrupt, incompetent and untrustworthy," Santa Anna was also a genuine hero, dashing, dynamic, and charismatic with an unrivaled personal flair. K. Jack Bauer suggests that he "had difficulty separating opportunism from love of country." His wealth and roguish lifestyle, including an unabashed affection for gambling and women, blended with an image of decisiveness and serious sense of purpose that inspired confidence. While he was no friend of democracy or the masses, the nation repeatedly turned to him in a crisis—and the American invasion posed such an emergency.

In August 1846, Santa Anna returned to Mexico from exile in Cuba. Utilizing his own financial resources and drafting his peons into service, the general rushed to assemble a fighting force to hurl back the Yankees. Clearly, the Mexican forces already in the field seemed unprepared. Lieutenant Manuel Balbontín bewailed the condition of the men in his command in July as they marched to confront Zachary Taylor in northern Mexico. "The state of drunkenness of the troops and the teamsters was unbearable." Predictably, morale among the rank and file suffered.[5]

Numerous historians remark that the Mexicans did possess one area of superiority—the band. Common soldiers carved wooden flutes for camp enjoyment, while every army had its own large brass band, prepared to play everything from Indian pueblo melodies to songs from *The Barber of Seville*. Soldiers fatalistically embraced an old whimsical tune, "La cucaracha" (The cockroach), as the comic symbol of unsympathetic superiors: "La cucaracha, la cucaracha, ya no puede cambiar" (The cockroach, the cockroach, it can never change).[6]

The *Soldaderas*

The soldiers' cynicism was well placed. For the average *soldado,* forced to march hundreds of miles, often with minimal food and water, music, gambling, and *pulque,* a thick juice fermented from the agave plant, offered the major avenues for entertainment and vice. With virtually no organized quartermaster corps to deliver sustenance or medical corps to provide balm for injury, the military relied upon an essential element of every Mexican army—the *soldaderas*. Unlike the Americans, who made limited use of women in their camps, typically as laundresses, the Mexicans traditionally embraced the concept of women in the capacity of critical support. The historian Donald Frazier refers to them as "a shadow army" and "the supply system" of the Mexican military. In the villages and towns, and especially on the march, hundreds, sometimes thousands, of wives, girlfriends, mothers, and sisters assembled their worldly possessions, as well as their children, to trudge along behind the troops. They functioned as nurses, cooks, and laundresses, as well as foraging and providing vital services to family members. Their role was critical. A decade earlier, as many as fifteen hundred *soldaderas* and their children had accompanied the army of Santa Anna on his campaign into Texas. While only three hundred women had reached San Antonio, many dying or simply dropping out of the column, the strength of the women and their cause became legendary. Efforts to end the custom proved fruitless, and the generals grudgingly accepted the invaluable contributions of the women in providing comfort and deterring desertion. Where the officers failed their men, the *soldaderas* supplied essential needs and boosted the morale of their loved ones.[7]

Whether in the city or the countryside, the women suffered along with their men. After the fight for Matamoros in June 1846, a US soldier could not but notice "a most disagreeable stench" emanating from a house. He entered to find "on the floor lying without covering ... fifty Mexicans wounded in the late engagements, attended by some 10 or 12 women. The smell of the place was insufferable and I had to leave it. The next door was the same and so on for about 20 houses."[8]

On the road, blistering heat, sandstorms, and drought could quickly change into enervating cold, rain, or snow. Rarely possessing adequate food or water, the *soldaderas* tramped on, "dead with fatigue and with their killing burdens of wood." After the action at Cerro Gordo in April 1847, John Peoples, of the *New Orleans Bee*, rode along the five-mile column of paroled Mexican prisoners and their entourage. He took particular interest in the camp women, those "devoted creatures" who trailed their men through good times and bad. Peoples referred to them as "slaves" of affection and grieved to see them "worn down with fatigue, moving at a snail's pace, with their heavy burdens almost weighing them to earth." He described a scene painful to witness yet somehow filled with an admirable loyalty and devotion. Struggling with bedding and clothing on their backs, the women carried food and the utensils to prepare the meals. The reporter acerbically pointed to the exhausted women cooking dinner while their unworthy mates slumbered. "The woman of sixty or more years—the mother with her infant wrapped in her rebosa—the wife ... the youthful señorita frisking along with her lover's sombrero upon her head; even the prattling girl who had followed padre and madre to the wars." The verb *frisking* connoted an innocent moment, while Peoples accurately described their lives of daily drudgery.[9]

The sterner reality of the plight of the *soldaderas* was reflected in the forced march of hundreds of miles of Santa Anna's army in February 1847 to confront Taylor at Buena Vista. With few rations, shabby clothing, and inadequate weapons, the Mexican Army, numbering more than twenty thousand, departed San Luis Potosí on a brutal trek that would cover almost three hundred miles of desert in just three weeks. Bitter winter weather, freezing temperatures, exhaustion, and starvation took a heavy toll. No firewood was available to warm either the troops or their women. Almost a quarter of the Mexican Army failed to report for roll call on the eve of the contest. Before firing a shot, Santa Anna had lost five thousand soldiers. Many dispirited men simply faded into the night. Others suffered a more tragic fate on a road lined with "dead men and women feasted on by coyotes, along with broken wagons, dead livestock, and deserters scattered in the brush."[10]

On February 22, Santa Anna's exhausted army commenced the attack on Taylor's vastly outnumbered force near Saltillo. The wooden-legged Napoleon of Mexico had traveled in a chariot driven by eight mules, accompanied by "a bevy of wanton women" and a baggage train that included his fighting gamecocks. Lacking in elegance but not preparation, Taylor's five thousand soldiers held their ground. After two days of fighting, the Americans claimed victory. Santa Anna likewise declared himself the winner, then hurried off to attend to the renewed political chaos in the capital. In what can most judiciously be labeled a costly stalemate, Mexican casualties reached sixteen hundred, not including an inexplicable eighteen hundred missing. The Americans suffered about seven hundred killed and wounded. Santa Anna left the *soldaderas* to explore the devastated field, hoping to find the form of their family member intact. A Mexican observer noted, "Here a woman sobbing over the body, now lifeless, of her husband, and there, another ministering to hers, tortured with his wounds."[11]

After the encounter on February 24, Taylor detailed a dozen men, including Samuel Chamberlain, to approach Santa Anna's camp with a flag of truce. Chamberlain's portrayal of the Mexican site revealed the horror of war: stench, filth, dead men and animals everywhere. The men found themselves surrounded by a large party, many "almost witchlike" women, "old, bleary eyed, skin a mass of wrinkles, the color of oak bark." These "fearful hags" thought that the Americans were prisoners and, taking pity, offered them handfuls of rice. Chamberlain realized that the "poor wretches possess the true woman's heart." Though starving themselves, they evidenced kindness toward the enemy. Recognizing their generosity, the Americans opened their haversacks and distributed what supplies they had brought with them to the women. Chamberlain commented with admiration on the burdens and self-sacrifice of the *soldaderas,* who carried on without praise, rations, or pay and endured the severe treatment of their "indolent husbands."[12]

Tragically, not only did the Mexicans withdraw from the field at Buena Vista but the retreat across recently traveled ground marked the deaths of thousands more. The wounded unable to walk, as well as uncounted women and children, abandoned to the animals, endured putrid food, brackish water, and the bone-chilling cold. So extensive was the disaster of the campaign that residents of the town of San Luis Potosí decried the devastating "disappearance" of so many of its women.[13]

The agonizing outcomes repeated themselves in Winfield Scott's campaign on the road to the capital in the summer of 1847. Incompetence and rivalry among the Mexican generals led to the additional slaughter of their troops. The proximity of the women to combat, the chaos of cavalry assaults, and the air filled with bullets and artillery shot yielded a foreseeable outcome. Following one clash, an American officer described the revulsion of burying too numerous *soldaderas* who had died with their soldiers. A Mexican reporter bemoaned the "chaos and terror" of another encounter in which "screaming women ran back and forth like furies. United States cavalry charged through the terrified masses, slaughtering left and right." An American trooper moaned, "The most distressing of all was the sight of hundreds of dead *soldaderas* scattered among the bodies of their men."[14]

The Angel of the Battlefield

While the careful derogation of Mexican men did occur, especially *off* the battlefield (there is little glory in defeating an unworthy opponent), the place of the Mexican woman was quite another matter. Not only their beauty and their plight but their courage and sacrifice emerged as common themes in both letters and the popular literature. Perhaps the most well known and most heartrending image of a Mexican woman materialized from the engagement at Monterrey. The tragic scene was first depicted in a letter written by a soldier on October 7, 1846, sent to the *Louisville Courier,* and then republished for a wide readership in a December issue of Baltimore's *Niles' National Register.*

The missive recounted the clash on September 21 and the actions of a young woman moving about the ground that evening, carrying bread and water to the wounded of both armies and binding their injuries with articles of her own clothing. She returned to her cottage and reappeared on the field later that evening to continue her mission of mercy. Then, the soldier continued, "I heard the report of a gun and saw the poor innocent creature fall dead! I think it was an accidental shot that struck her. I would not be willing to believe otherwise. It made me sick at heart, and turning from the scene, I voluntarily raised my eyes towards heaven, and thought, great God, and *is this war?* The next day her body still lay where it had fallen, with the bread and a few drops of water in a gourd beside her. As the cannon shot and grape continued to fly around them, the American soldiers buried 'the angel of Monterrey.'" Only a few months into the conflict, newspapers far and wide, large and small, recounted this tale of a woman's courage and self-sacrifice under headlines such as "The Horrors of War: A Sad Case" and "A Mexican Woman: Her Noble Conduct and Sad Fate."[5]

The antiwar press, especially in New England, rallied to a vision of the senseless demise of a compassionate woman who only moments earlier had been "holding her pitcher of cooling drink to the feverish lips of the dying." Verse and song quickly followed. In January 1847, the accomplished McConnelsville, Ohio, poet Frances Gage, described as "one of the most gifted daughters of our Buckeye state ... who has written much, and acquired for herself a reputation high amongst the first female writers of our age," crafted her tribute to the "angel," published along with the account of the incident in the *Ohio Statesman*. The paper noted that the piece would be "read with interest by every admirer of good poetry and correct sentiment." After retelling the maid's brave deeds, Gage's poem concluded with these lines:

> Thy horrors war—oh! who shall tell?
>
> Struck by a random ball or shell;
>
> That brave, that noble woman fell
>
> None died that day more gloriously.
>
> _____
>
> Genius will sing the soldier's name
>
> And give his daring deeds in fame,
>
> For her a holier meed we claim,—
>
> The heart shall shrine her memory.

"Correct sentiment" indicated that due deference should be granted the courage of the soldier; however, a higher place in the heart and heaven would be the reward of the brave maiden. Victorian Americans established a special elevated emotional station in both literature and reality for the fair, blonde, virginal woman, although exceptions could be made for the heroic darker-tressed woman. Should her virtue or honor be threatened or, worse, taken from her, death was to be preferred. Those women who positioned themselves in harm's way or sacrificed for spouse, family, or humanity writ large by performing acts of kindness as designated within the proper women's sphere were memorialized in poem and song.[16]

In this vein, the Episcopal minister the Reverend James G. Lyons composed "The Heroine of Monterey," which was quickly put to music for voice and piano accompaniment. The four-verse song became increasingly more graphic and creative as the angel ministered amid booming shot and flaming shell "thick as winter's driving sleet." Lyons crafted a final scenario for the martyred maid:

> They laid her in her narrow bed, the foemen of her land and race;
>
> And sighs were breathed, and tears were shed, above her lowly resting place—
>
> Ay! glory's crimson worshippers wept over her untimely fall,
>
> For deeds of mercy, such as hers, subdue the hearts and eyes of all.[17]

Politicians seized upon the tragedy. In February 1847, Senator Thomas Corwin delivered his powerful speech attacking the morality of the war and the image of the United States among the Christian nations of the world. The "bloody hands" passage, however, overshadowed his remarks about the "angel of Monterrey." Corwin also recalled the benevolence and "robust courage" of the young woman who delivered water to the parched lips of the dying "amid the falling houses and shrieks of war." Suddenly, as an American officer looked upon her, "a cannon ball struck her and blew her to atoms." Clearly, by the time the story of the "angel"'s actions reached antiwar circles in Washington, the story of her death had taken on more dramatic dimensions and varied markedly from the account in the original Louisville letter.[18]

After the war, the legend still would not die. The New York native John Hill Hewitt gained fame as a composer of minstrel ditties, songs of the South, and in the Civil War era, ballads such as "All Quiet Along the Potomac." In 1851, however, Hewitt made his mark with a song for voice and guitar entitled "The Maid of Monterey." The music was up-tempo, and the lyrics created a very different scene for the maid. As dusk fell and quiet encompassed the bloody ground, she went about her acts of mercy. Hewitt wanted his audience to be aware of her sacrifice, but appears to have been uninterested in the maudlin nature of her death or burial.

For tho she loved her nation, and pray'd that it might live

Yet for the dying foemen, she had a tear to give

Thus here's to that bright beauty, who drove death's pang away

The meek-eyed señorita, the maid of Monterey.

Some thirty years after the war, the maid was granted a more interesting rebirth in the mind of Luis P. Senarens, the son of a Cuban tobacco merchant and an American mother, who wrote fantasy fiction for teenage boys. In 1886, Senarens created a short story entitled "Old Rough and Ready, or The Heroine of Monterey," which rekindled the image for a younger generation.[19]

From campaign to campaign, "angels" abounded thereafter. The Charleston, South Carolina, *Southern Patriot* reported an incident involving the wanderings of an American soldier, Gwin Bernard of Illinois, after the Battle of Buena Vista. Suffering from fractured ribs and separated from his mates, a feverish and starving Bernard stumbled upon a shack made of reed, mud, and leaves. He entered, desperate, only to find a young woman grieving with her rosary over the body of a family member recently killed. Bernard explained that while her eyes flashed with hatred, the tender nature of her gender and race ultimately prevailed. She provided him with water and a few kernels of parched corn and bound his wounds. Her poverty and dark complexion signaled that nothing more would come of their encounter; "her swart features were beautiful in their ruggedness by an air of fervent devotion." She wept bitterly, but the soldier had no words of consolation as he departed the cottage. He realized, however, that he had been saved by his own angel.[20]

Americans seemed consumed with the anthem of the tender, tragic Mexican maid providing nourishment and relief. Several possible explanations can be offered for the fascination. The heroic woman, whether martyred on a humanitarian mission or on the field of combat, confirmed the Anglo concept that Mexican women were more patriotic, more fearless, and more steadfast than their male counterparts. Gwin Bernard's nameless savior exemplified the depth of compassion of the Mexican woman who in her time of grief and despair afforded comfort and nourishment to her enemy. For the war's survivors, common decency, at least among women, still prevailed. This was in sharp contrast to the bluff and bravado of politicians, generals, and their supporters, who justified the fight as extending the boundaries of liberty and civilization.

An added prompt emanated from the war zones, so far removed from everyday existence for Americans, which gave few Anglo women the opportunity to contribute or sacrifice.

Inserting the gender dimension certainly humanized the conflict by demonstrating that actions fought around villages, towns, and cities could well endanger the lives of Mexican women and children. The resultant deaths, the individual woman senselessly shot down by a single bullet or a family crushed by the walls of a falling building, provided fodder for those who saw the killing of Mexican civilians as a barbaric product of a needless quarrel.

The antiwar poet John Greenleaf Whittier seized on the theme in his widely heralded "The Angels of Buena Vista," published in the *National Era*. Whittier took aim at the American political and military leaders who had dragooned the nation into an unholy contest. His sympathies went to the innocents on both sides of the Rio Grande. Inspired by the sentiment of earlier poems and songs of Monterrey, Whittier penned a lengthy, moving scenario of "sisters" witnessing the bloody American victory in February 1847 and hastening onto the field to tend to the wounded with a sip of water and a prayer:

Whispered low the dying soldier, pressed her hand and faintly smiled;

Was that pitying face his mother's? did she watch beside her child?

All his stranger words with meaning her woman's heart supplied;

With her kiss upon his forehead, "Mother!" murmured he, and died!

And as the day ended,

The noble Mexic women still their holy task pursued

Through that long, dark night of sorrow, worn and faint and lacking food.

Over weak and suffering brothers, with a tender care they hung,

And the dying foeman blessed them in a strange and Northern tongue.[21]

Several weeks later, in March 1847, Major John Corey Henshaw came across yet another real-life "angel" near Veracruz. As his command moved through a wooded area, Henshaw soon discovered a dead woman, about twenty-eight years old, dressed in white. She had been shot through the right breast and apparently died without a struggle, evidently the target of an American rifleman. In each hand she tightly held a small basket containing provisions, which she obviously had hastily thrown together. Probably, he opined, she was in the act of escaping to the forest "when the messenger of death arrested her flight." Henshaw concluded with the dispassion of a veteran, "Her clothes and body were completely crimsoned with her blood."[22]

Not surprisingly, the Mexicans propagated several of their own "angels of Monterrey." Yolanda García Romero suggests that María Josefa Zozaya was a composite figure. The initial version of her story, published in 1848, has Zozaya engaged in activities, albeit courageously, that seem acceptable to traditional cultures in both Mexico and the United States. Interestingly, however, she was most certainly *not* the "angel of the Monterrey" bringing succour to all the afflicted, but a bona fide Mexican patriot who moved nimbly about the rooftops of the city aiding her countrymen with much-needed food and munitions. A young woman, "as beautiful as the protective goddesses sculpted by the Greeks," she taught her compatriots "how to despise danger" and gave them the pluck necessary to face the challenge of the invading Yankees. The second depiction portrays Zozaya as a much older woman leading on the battlefield and dying in combat. Yet another version, which the historian Elizabeth Salas endorses, parallels the story related in the American press: Zozaya brings relief and comfort to men of both armies until felled by a bullet. While her identity remains obscured in legend, Mexicans seemed to prefer Zozaya as an active patriot, while the "angel" image resonated north of the Rio Grande.[23]

Women in Combat

Women traditionally constituted a key support element of the army, but their emergence in the line of fire, while not unknown, had been unusual. Precedents did exist. In the nineteenth century both Latin and American cultures held a restricted view of women in the public sphere. However, traumatic events in a nation's history sometimes demand the exceptional, and the crucible of war creates unusual heroes. For the United States there was a composite figure called "Molly Pitcher," first bringing water to parched Revolutionary War soldiers and then, when her husband fell, taking his place by his cannon. Almost a century later, Barbara Fritchie, an octogenarian resident of Frederick, Maryland, defied the Confederate general "Stonewall" Jackson to "shoot if you must this old grey head, but touch not your country's flag." In Mexico, the figures of María Zozaya and Doña Jesús Dosamentes make up a critical component of Mexican legend.

When Monterrey fell to the Americans in September 1846, Zachary Taylor allowed his defeated opponent to withdraw from the city in rank order. Two American officers commented on the unfolding drama. Abner Doubleday watched the procession and derisively recorded seeing "the Mexican forces file by in all their disgrace. They were accompanied by a perfect army of females on horseback." Daniel Harvey Hill also took note of the scene, praising the appearance of the Castilian-looking officers, while demeaning the regular soldiers as "inferior looking men." A large number of women on horseback, apparently officers' wives, followed the army, and trailing behind on foot trudged a host of women carrying packs. "I did not see a good looking woman among them all," he remarked, offhandedly describing their appearance rather than their burden.[24]

A Scotswoman, Frances Calderón de la Barca, observing a similar formation in Santa Anna's army some years earlier, in 1841, concurred with Hill. While remarking about the Indian *soldaderas* following the army, carrying the shoes and clothing of their husbands, de la Barca focused with scorn on a body of "masculine women with serapes or mangas, and large straw hats tied down with various colored handkerchiefs." These "mounted Amazons," she sniffed, "looked like very ugly men in semi-female disguise." Elizabeth Salas rebuts that such disparagement typifies the emergent Victorian view in the West regarding the proper place for women in warfare. Women in a dangerous supportive role most certainly did not meet with the approbation of de la Barca or her peers, who failed to understand both the culture and the needs of the Mexican Army.[25]

Indeed, the environment appeared desperate in 1846, when the Joan of Arc of Mexico first made her appearance, documented in both US and Mexican sources. On September 19, 1846, General Pedro Ampudia, commander of the forces in defense of Monterrey, wrote a short and most unusual letter to the minister of war. A young señorita, Doña Jesús Dosamentes, had reported to him dressed as a captain "and mounted to fight the unjust invaders." Ampudia seized the moment. Recognizing the impact that her audacity might have on the army, rather than brushing the presumptuous woman aside, he received her with the affection "that her heroic behavior deserves" and sent her out to ride the line and inspire the troops. She carried an order from him, however, "so that all would show the respect due to her."

Ampudia dispatched his Joan of Arc to the Third Brigade, where Colonel José Uraga savvily comprehended his part and how the army might utilize its new enthusiastic volunteer to best advantage. He knew that such an opportunity was "rare in the annals of history," and it "moved him to joy and enthusiasm." Before any fighting had occurred, Ampudia and Uraga referred to Doña Jesús as an "intrepid heroine" committed to repelling "the infamous usurpers." Uraga explained to her the dangers and privations, suggesting that a safer environment might be suitable. She remained steadfast. Doña Jesús wanted to be "where the enemy bullets will whistle first and where there will be more glory, even if greater risk." Uraga also wisely understood that he could employ her courage to great effect among his men and ordered that they accord "her all the deference due to her sex" and her patriotic conduct. Grateful that "this delicate señorita" was willing to die for Mexico, Uraga assured his superior that Doña Jesús's praiseworthy conduct would not be "buried in oblivion" and had tremendous potential to impact the morale and enthusiasm of the soldiers.[26]

Doña Jesús Dosamentes would have her Joan of Arc moment, and she would not disappoint her nation. Several months later, in a column for the New York paper *Spirit of the Times*, George Wilkins Kendall included part of a letter from a young Irish deserter from the US Army, "G de L," who had witnessed the lengthy contest for Monterrey. He described the tale of a young woman, known as Dos Amades, who, "seized with a patriotic spirit, unsexed herself and dressed in the full suit of a captain of lancers." She swore that she would drive the "Northern barbarians" from the land or shed her last drop of blood in the effort. Prior to leading a charge on September 21, Dos Amades rode along the line of her troops, exhorting their patriotism and challenging their manhood. The charge failed, and many of her lancers died that day, but the legend of Dos Amades was born. The Irishman praised the courage of the Amazon warrior and her lancers. "There's an example," he exclaimed, "of heroism worthy of the days of old. It has remained for Mexico to produce a second Joan d' Arc, but not, like her successful." Kendall postscripted these comments, declaring that rumors held the young officer to be the daughter of the former governor of Nuevo León. She continued to fight and was almost captured in the city by Texas Rangers. When Monterrey fell, a saddened Dos Amades put her uniform aside and returned to her family and temporary obscurity.[27]

The fact and mythology that surround both María Josefa Zozaya and Doña Jesús Dosamentes inform us about the role of certain Mexican women during the war. We know very little about either individual in terms of her background or fate following the actions during the Monterrey campaign. Doña Jesús was, importantly, the daughter of a high-ranking government official, upper class, and light skinned. It seems unlikely that a poor peasant girl would have access to the tent of the commander of the Army of the North and demonstrate the impudence of demanding a role in the field. When General Ampudia consented to the notion of this female warrior, he clearly saw the inspirational possibilities, but did he indeed envision a martyr or an ongoing symbol? We may never know.

Certainly, less-heralded women risked life and limb defending their country and their men. The Spanish-born writer Niceto de Zamacois stirred and incited Mexicans with his short story published in October 1847 about the martyrdom of the twenty-eight-year-old patriot and intellectual Luis Martínez de Castro at Churubusco, near Mexico City. Zamacois embellished the tale of his doomed hero by creating a fictional love interest, sixteen-year-old Matilde. In the dramatic conclusion, as the Yankees stormed the heights, Mexican resistance stiffened and the valiant Martínez de Castro suffered a ball to the chest, prompting all but his faithful flag-bearer to abandon him. As the Americans closed in and were about to deliver a fatal saber blow, the flag-bearer removed his cap, allowing two long braids to fall, and proclaimed, "Wound, wound this unhappy woman from whom you have taken the only treasure she had in the world." Martínez de Castro recognized the voice and opened his eyes a last time to gaze on his beloved. Life without him had no meaning, however, and the girl soon died of spotted fever, which "came from her constant weeping and suffering." While Martínez de Castro's sacrifice marked "the true way to glory," his friends protested that the romance compromised the actions and the character of the real man.[28]

In December 1846, the US colonel Alexander Doniphan's command of five hundred men had its first skirmish at Bracito, near El Paso. In the brief encounter, a Mexican force of nearly twelve hundred unsuccessfully attacked Doniphan, resulting in no loss of American lives and perhaps a few dozen Mexican casualties. As the Americans sifted through the residue of the melee that remained on the field, a soldier reported with considerable glee, "The Mexican women were gloriously represented in this fight." The rumor abounded that two women had crewed a cannon and that a rifle ball had struck one in the forehead, instantly killing her. Her friend had bravely carried her off the field. "I do not doubt it," the soldier explained, "the women have much more courage and even sense than the men." Another source reported, however, that Missouri volunteers had actually found the woman beside her cannon.

A skirmish at Taos had a more positive ending. As an American dragoon contemplated slaying a Mexican soldier, she managed to save her own life "by an act of the most conclusive personal exposure." Outside Mexico City, US soldiers stumbled upon the tombstone of Doña María Vicario de Quintana. The inscription subtly noted that "she preferred to leave her convent and join the standard of her country, under which she performed many feats of valor." These snippets of patriotism offer insight into what were likely broader, unrecorded sacrifices.[29]

Whether in front leading the soldiers or behind in support, women remained highly visible to the army. That visibility cut both ways. Women expected their men to uphold the honor of the Mexican people and their nation. When American columnists and novelists derided the diminutive size and effeminate nature of Latin men, the women reacted strongly to such language and challenged their men. D. H. Hill observed that after the fall of Monterrey in September 1846, Mexican women, including his very patriotic landlady, doffed mourning garb and draped their houses in black for three days, as the church bells rang funereal tolls. The ladies then proceeded to paint pictures of Mexican officers engaged in sewing and other "feminine occupations," while American officers in full dress looked on.[30]

The indignation of Mexican women regarding the conduct of the war appeared early and expressed itself in broadsides and posters. Legend, hearsay, and reality commingled to create an image of Mexican women engaged in acts of heroism, danger, and self-sacrifice—as well as opportunism—during the contest. Some women emanated from the upper classes, and their deeds, while often real, were intended to inspire patriotism among the sometimes reluctant masses. The extent of their success is elusive, but their status in Mexican history is well established.

Mexicans remain conflicted about the role of women in their turbulent past. Certainly, some women did collaborate with Maximilian's French forces of occupation in the 1860s, as they had with those of Taylor and Scott. The numerous nameless *soldaderas* carry a particular burden, since their motives for collaboration or patriotism varied so dramatically. Many were simply forced into service. For others, money, employment, independence, marriage, or desperation provided the enticement. Salas blasts a minority as "parasitical camp followers." Far more, however, enacted the centuries-old responsibility of giving sustenance and support to their men and their country. Lacking any parallel within the national experience, Americans have too often marginalized their role or simply derogated the *soldaderas* as servants or slaves. Such harsh judgment fails to appreciate the impact they had on the army and what it reveals about gender and Mexican culture.[31]

Notes

1   James Russell Lowell, *The Bigelow Papers* (Cambridge, MA, 1848), 23–25. For an excellent analysis of Lowell's work and the disillusionment and loss of belief that accompanied the soldiers' experience in Mexico, see Jaime Javier Rodriguez, *The Literatures of the U.S.-Mexican War: Narrative, Time, and Identity* (Austin: University of Texas Press, 2010), 110–28; and Rodriguez, "The U.S.-Mexican War in James Russell Lowell's *The Bigelow Papers*," *Arizona Quarterly* 63 (Autumn 2007): 1–33.

2   Elizabeth Salas, *Soldaderas in the Mexican Military: Myth and History* (Austin: University of Texas Press, 1990), 32–33; Christopher Conway, "Ravished Virgins and Warrior Women: Gender and Literature of the U.S.-Mexican War," *Fronteras* 18 (Fall 2009): 3–4.

3   Donald Frazier, "Life in the Mexican Army," in *The United States and Mexico at War: Nineteenth-Century Expansionism and Conflict,* ed. Frazier (New York: MacMillan Reference Books USA, 1998), 28–29.

4   David Clary, *Eagles and Empire: The U.S., Mexico, and the Struggle for a Continent* (New York: Random House, 2009), 132; Mark Wasserman, *Everyday Life and Politics in Nineteenth Century Mexico: Men, Women, and War* (Albuquerque: University of New Mexico Press, 2000), 79, 82–83. For a detailed discussion of the nature and background of Mexican recruits, see Peter Guardino, "Gender, Soldiering, and Citizenship in the Mexican-American War of 1846–1848," *American Historical Review* 119 (February 2014): 23–46.

5   Christopher Conway and Gustavo Pellón, *The U.S.-Mexican War: A Binational Reader* (Indianapolis: Hackett, 2010), 78–80; Timothy J. Henderson, *A Glorious Defeat: Mexico and Its War with the United States* (New York: Hill & Wang, 2007), 76–81, 119, 162; K. Jack Bauer, *The Mexican War, 1846–1848* (1974; reprint with an introduction by Robert W. Johannsen, Lincoln: University of Nebraska Press, 1992), 393; Manuel Balbontín, *La Invasion Americana 1846 a 1848* (Mexico City, 1883), 12–18.

For a general discussion of the organization and effectiveness of the respective armies, see Henderson, *Glorious Defeat*; Clary, *Eagles and Empire*, 130–32; Richard Bruce Winders, *Mr. Polk's Army: The American Military Experience in the Mexican War* (College Station: Texas A&M University Press, 1997); and John D. Eisenhower, *So Far from God: The U.S. War with Mexico, 1846–1848* (New York: Random House, 1989).

6   Frazier, "Life in the Mexican Army," 28–29; Clary, *Eagles and Empire*, 135–38.

7   Donald Frazier, "Soldaderas," in Frazier, *United States and Mexico at War*, 391.

8   "The Corporal," writing for the *New Orleans Bee*, June 27, 1846.

9   Ramón Alcaraz, *The Other Side, or Notes for the History of the War between Mexico and the United States* (1850; reprint, New York: Burt Franklin, 1970); *Baltimore Sun*, May 13, 1847; *Constitution* (Middletown, CT), June 2, 1847; George Winston Smith and Charles Judah, eds., *Chronicle of the Gringos: The U.S. Army in the Mexican War, 1846–1848* (Albuquerque: University of New Mexico Press, 1968), April 28, 1847, 215–16; Tom Reilly and Manley Witten, *War with Mexico: America's Reporters Cover the Battlefront* (Lawrence: University Press of Kansas, 2010), 138–39; Salas, *Soldaderas*, 32.

10 Clary, *Eagles and Empire*, 271–72; William DePalo, *The Mexican National Army, 1822–1852* (College Station: Texas A&M University Press, 1997), 119–20.

11 Alcaraz, *Other Side*, 132–37. K. Jack Bauer contends that Santa Anna was solid at strategic conception but not execution. "He was not a good battlefield general." Bauer, *Mexican War*, 218.

12 Samuel Chamberlain, *My Confession: Recollections of a Rogue*, ed. William Goetzmann (Austin: Texas State Historical Society, 1996), February 24, 1847, 170–71.

13 Clary, *Eagles and Empire*, 282.

14 Ibid., 313, 351n26; James McCaffrey, *Army of Manifest Destiny: The American Soldier in the Mexican War, 1846–1848* (New York: New York University Press, 1992), 187.

15 *New Hampshire Sentinel* (Keene), December 9, 1846; *Niles' National Register* (Baltimore), December 19, 1846; *Maine Farmer* (Winthrop), November 26, 1846; *Ladies Repository and Gatherings of the West* (Cincinnati), April 1847; *Dwight's American Magazine and Family Newspaper* (New York), December 19, 1846; Smith and Judah, *Chronicle of the Gringos*, 90; Clary, *Eagles and Empire*, 199. The story remained critical to the narrative of the war and was retold a half century later in A. D. Hall's novel *Captain Impudence: A Romance of the Mexican War* (New York: Street & Smith, 1897), 13–14.

16 *Ohio Statesman* (Columbus), January 4, 1847.

17 "Heroine of Monterey," by James G. Lyons, Music for the Nation: American Sheet Music, 1820–1860, Library of Congress. The Americans spelled the city name Monterey, while the Spanish spelled it with an additional *r*, Monterrey. The latter form is used throughout.

18 Senator Thomas Corwin, speech, February 11, 1847, reprinted in *Niles' National Register*, February 27, 1847; Amy S. Greenberg, *A Wicked War: Polk, Clay, Lincoln, and the 1846 U.S. Invasion of Mexico* (New York: Alfred A. Knopf, 2012), 193.

19   J. H. Hewitt, "The Maid of Monterey," (1851), *Music for the Nation: American Sheet Music, 1820–1860*, Library of Congress (a very interesting version, sung by a woman, can be found on Youtube); Luis Senarens, *Old Rough and Ready, or The Heroine of Monterey* (New York: F. Tousey, 1886), available on microfilm at the University of Minnesota.

20   "Gwin Bernard, or the Escaped Soldier and the Dog," *Southern Patriot* (Charleston, SC), September 10, 1847.

21   "The Angels of Buena Vista" (1847), in John Greenleaf Whittier, *The Writings of John Greenleaf Whittier* (Boston: Houghton, Mifflin, 1892), 112–16; John H. Schroeder, *Mr. Polk's War: American Opposition and Dissent, 1846–1848* (Madison: University of Wisconsin Press, 1973), 102; Whittier, "Angels of Buena Vista," 173–76.

22   John Corey Henshaw, *Major John Corey Henshaw: Recollections of the War with Mexico,* ed. Gary Kurutz (Columbia: University of Missouri Press, 2008), 116.

23   Yolanda Romero, "María Josefa Zozaya," in Frazier, *United States and Mexico at War,* 490–91; Frazier, in a separate entry, ibid., 391, adopts Salas's argument, arguing that Zozaya, as the "Angel of Monterrey," was a *soldadera* who nursed Mexican soldiers and was killed by a bullet; Salas, *Soldaderas,* 31; Clary, *Eagles and Empire,* 199; Abner Doubleday, *My Life in the Old Army: The Reminiscences of Abner Doubleday from the Collections of the New York Historical Society,* ed. Joseph E. Chance (Fort Worth: Texas Christian University Press, 1998), 322n7.

24   Doubleday, *My Life in the Old Army,* 99; Daniel Harvey Hill, *A Fighter from Way Back: The Mexican War Diary of Lt. Daniel Harvey Hill, 4th Artillery, USA,* ed. Nathaniel C. Hughes Jr. and Timothy D. Johnson (Kent, OH: Kent State University Press, 2002), 27.

25   Salas, *Soldaderas,* 30–31.

26   General José Uraga, Monterrey, to General Pedro Ampudia, September 19, 1846, and Ampudia, Monterrey, to Minister of War, September 19, 1846, in Conway and Pellón, *U.S.-Mexican War,* 78–81; *Harbinger* (New York), November 13, 1847.

27   George Wilkins Kendall, "Irish Deserter and Mexican Joan of Arc," in *Spirit of the Times* (New York), January 2, 1847, reprinted in Chavez, *U.S. War with Mexico,* 104–5; William S. Henry, *Campaign Sketches of the War with Mexico* (New York: Harper Bros., 1847), 233–34. Kendall credits the remarks in his column to an Irish deserter. Almost concurrently, Henry, who was an officer in Monterrey in 1846, used the identical language to describe Doña Jesús in his memoir published in 1847. Clary, *Eagles and Empire,* 195, cites the Henry volume. Robert Johannsen, *To the Halls of Montezuma: The Mexican War in the American Imagination* (New York: Oxford University Press, 1985), 137–38.

28   Niceto de Zamacois, "Don Luis Martínez de Castro of the National Guard," in Conway and Pellón, *U.S.-Mexican War,* 188–90.

29   Frank S. Edwards, *A Campaign in New Mexico with Colonel Doniphan* (Philadelphia: Carey & Hart, 1847), 88; *Albion* (New York), November 27, 1847; McCaffrey, *Army of Manifest Destiny,* 158–59;

Eisenhower, *So Far from God,* 234; John Frost, *Pictorial History of Mexico and the Mexican War* (Philadelphia: Thomas, Cowperthwait, 1849), 418; Doubleday, *My Life in the Old Army,* 322n7.

30   Hill, *Fighter from Way Back,* October 16, 1846, 29–30.

31   Salas *Soldaderas,* 35.

DISCUSSION QUESTIONS

1. What was daily life like for Tejanas prior to the Texas Revolution?

2. What pushed Hispanics to join in the Texas Revolution?

3. How is Juan Seguín's life experience an example of the prejudice faced by Mexicans after the war?

4. In the years immediately following the war, how did intermarriage between wealthy Hispanic families and Anglo-Americans benefit both parties? Why was this short lived?

5. How did the Spanish and American law systems differ? How did the shift from the Spanish system to the American system impact Tejanas?

6. How did the role of women in the war differ between Americans and Mexicans?

7. What types of jobs did soldaderas perform?

8. How have Americans marginalized soldaderas? Why is this problematic?

Chapter 3

Mexican Lynching

Editor's Introduction

The theme of chapter 3 is Mexican lynching. Until recently, the history of lynching had largely ignored the experiences of minority groups other than African Americans. Even with growing scholarship on lynching, few textbooks—particularly in K–12—reflect these new studies and continue to enforce the idea that lynching was something that was essentially exclusive to African Americans. I have found that students are surprised to discover that other ethnic groups suffered the same fate. This chapter seeks to remedy that by highlighting the Mexican American experience.

"'This Community Will Not in the Future Be Disgraced': Rafael Benavides and the Decline of Lynching in New Mexico" sheds light on the practice of the lynching of Mexicans in the United States Southwest. Scholars William D. Carrigan and Clive Webb examine the last-known lynching that took place in New Mexico and explain how and why this particular lynching served as a turning point in the history of anti-Mexican violence. In this reading you will learn about Rafael Benavides, the details of his lynching, and its connection to the decline and end of mob violence against Mexicans.

This reading was chosen because Carrigan and Webb are two of the leading scholars on mob violence against Mexican Americans. Their research brings to the fore the long-overlooked history of the lynching of Mexican Americans. In the United States, lynching is almost synonymous with African Americans—other minorities are rarely acknowledged. This is especially problematic for Mexican Americans, who were the second-largest ethnic group to be lynched in the United States. Unlike most readings on American lynching that privilege the African American experience, Carrigan and Webb's reading analyzes the experience of Mexican American victims.

While African Americans were lynched in higher numbers, it is important to learn about other ethnic groups because it provides a more in-depth understanding of mob violence in the United

States. The driving forces of mob violence were not the same across the board—these forces differed based on one's ethnic background. By examining the Mexican American experience and placing it in the broader history of lynching, the reader gains a deeper understanding of the causes of mob violence and the ways in which individuals and groups sought to resist lynching and vigilantism (Carrigan and Webb, 2013).

Carrigan and Webb argue that there are three key reasons that the lynching of Rafael Benavides was a turning point for Mexican mob violence: (1) the growth of institutionalized legal systems; (2) a change in the climate of public opinion; and (3) the renewed power of the new Mexican government to protect its citizens both within its own borders and on American soil. The authors want the readers to understand that the Benavides lynching did not magically convince everyone in the state that lynching was wrong and should be abandoned. However, the lynching *did* decisively tip the balance of public opinion toward those in New Mexico who "favored due process solutions to problems of social order and away from those who favored informal methods of control such as vigilantism and mob violence." After 1928 it was generally no longer socially acceptable to commit mob violence against Mexican Americans and to take justice outside of established legal institutions.

"This Community Will Not in the Future Be Disgraced"

Rafael Benavides and the Decline of Lynching in New Mexico

William D. Carrigan and Clive Webb

At 11:15 on the morning of Friday, November 16, 1928, four masked men marched into the San Juan County Hospital in Farmington, a remote town in northern New Mexico. The men seized one of the patients, a Spanish-speaking sheepherder of Mexican descent named Rafael Benavides, and bundled him into the back of a pickup truck. Accompanied by a second vehicle carrying six other men, the kidnappers sped to an abandoned farm two miles north of town. There, they forced their victim to stand on the back of one of the trucks as a rope was tied around his neck and fastened to a locust tree. The vehicle then accelerated forward, snapping Benavides's neck as his body became suspended above the ground.

Less than twenty-four hours earlier, Benavides had been admitted to the hospital with a serious gunshot wound. The injury was inflicted when he attempted to escape a sheriff's posse pursuing him for an assault upon a local farmer's wife. According to the physicians who treated him, Benavides had only hours to live. In their words, the lynching "probably saved the criminal a good deal of suffering." Benavides was thirty-nine years old.[1]

In many respects the lynching of Rafael Benavides conforms to the broader patterns of mob violence throughout the American West and the larger world. The men responsible for his murder acted in open disobedience of the law and with the approval of elements of the community, and no member of the mob was ever brought to justice. A grand jury hearing on the murder occurred on December 4, 1928. Judge Reed Holloman issued a stern instruction to the jurors to set an example, so "that this community will not in the future be disgraced in the eyes of the state and the United States as it recently was." However, although more than fifty witnesses were called to testify, the jury failed to indict a single member of the mob. As one newspaper observed, the authorities had "run against a rock wall" in their efforts to secure a conviction.[2]

The Benavides case is nonetheless of crucial significance. The historian Robert Tórrez believes Benavides to be the last ethnic Mexican lynched in the state of New Mexico.[3] F. Arturo Rosales, one of the foremost experts on anti-Mexican violence, goes further, arguing that Benavides was the last ethnic Mexican lynched in the entire United States.[4] It is impossible to verify these claims for a variety of reasons, including the vexing question of how one defines lynching. Nevertheless, there is little doubt that no later U.S. mob executed an ethnic Mexican with such a public disregard for legal repercussions. The Benavides murder, described by contemporaries as a lynching, therefore represents an important turning point in the history of anti-Mexican violence. Mob violence against persons of Mexican descent was a widespread phenomenon in the American Southwest after the U.S.-Mexican War. Such violence was often committed with the implicit support of law officers and, in many instances, with their direct participation. Benavides was taken by masked intruders from a public place and hanged in broad daylight. The men responsible for the crime were not prosecuted despite the fact that their identities were well known. Although such a series of events had been common in the preceding eight decades, the pattern of mob violence changed after the Benavides lynching. Mexicans continued to live with the danger of mob violence after 1928. However, any attacks against them took place surreptitiously rather than in open defiance of the law, and mobs received more public censure than support.[5]

This [reading] places the Benavides lynching both in the context of lynching in New Mexico and within the broader framework of the decline and end of mob violence against Mexicans. The collective, extralegal killing of Mexicans was a common occurrence in the borderlands, but patterns of mob violence differed dramatically from region to region, from state to state, and even from country to country. Lynching in New Mexico contrasted sharply with mob violence even in nearby states such as Texas, California, and Arizona, and the United States was far from the only nation to have its legal authorities circumvented by mobs. Many recent Mexican immigrants to New Mexico had experienced mob violence within Mexico, especially during the turbulent decade of the Mexican Revolution. While the local context is crucially important, the Benavides case also provides insights into the larger regional decline of mob violence against Mexicans.

By 1928, northern New Mexico had been firmly controlled by the United States for many decades. However, in the previous century, the sovereignty and control of New Mexico was much in dispute. Spanish-speaking settlers arrived during the seventeenth century. Initially, they entered a region at least partially controlled by Native Americans. Whether under Spanish rule (until 1821), as residents of an independent Mexico (until 1836) or a disputed territory claimed by Mexico and Texas (until 1848), as American citizens living in a U.S. territory (until 1912), or as residents of the state of New Mexico (after 1912), the lives of those Spanish speakers living in and around present-day Farmington changed very little. They raised sheep and saw themselves as "Hispanos" or "Nuevomexicanos," no matter the ruling government of the moment. When Anglos arrived in large numbers at the end of the nineteenth century, they often identified the region's longtime residents as "Mexicans," even though the term was resented by Nuevomexicanos, who were American citizens by virtue of the Treaty of Guadalupe Hidalgo (or by birth after that date).[6]

As for the town of Farmington itself, settlers began to congregate on the future location of the town—some 150 miles north of Santa Fe and 20 miles south of the Colorado border—as early as 1876, but the community was not incorporated as a town until 25 years later. The local economy was based principally upon ranching and agriculture. Limited commercial and industrial development restricted population growth during the early days. By 1910 there were still only 785 people in the town. Although the discovery of oil during the interwar era caused the hurried purchase of land by oil companies, by the late 1920s Farmington had not become a boom town. By 1930, the entire population of San Juan County was only 14,701.[7]

Although the population remained small, there were important differences among the peoples of the region. Some were obvious. The Anglo immigrants were recent arrivals, spoke English, and were Protestant, whereas the Nuevomexicano families had settled earlier, spoke Spanish, and were Catholic. While both groups were principally ranchers, Nuevomexicanos grazed sheep, while the majority of New Mexican Anglos raised cattle.

Yet there were also forces unifying the two groups. Local farmers of both ethnic groups sold their produce to mining camps across the border in Colorado. While the two groups did not identify with each other, they also saw themselves as landowners and distinct from their Navajo neighbors and more recent Mexican immigrants who were contracted as herders and laborers by both Anglo and Nuevomexicano ranchers. And perhaps most important, both groups had experience with disregarding legal procedures and inflicting mob violence.

Lynching-like violence was not something new, and it had not just been brought in by the Anglo settlers who arrived in the region. Spanish speakers, first in the Mexican North and then in the American Southwest, had experience of mob violence, which was, after all, a tool for frontier settlers throughout world history. In 1836, vigilantes in Los Angeles executed Gervasio Alipás for the murder of Domingo Félix, "a great ranchero" whose wife had been seduced by Alipás.[8] Mexican-on-Mexican mob violence did not cease with American conquest in 1848. In 1852, a California mob reported to include "principally Mexicans" hanged three of their countrymen near Santa Cruz for horse theft.[9] In 1871, an Albuquerque mob of masked Spanish speakers hanged Diego Lucero for the murder of Manuel Garcia y Gallegos.[10] In 1893, in Las Vegas, New Mexico, a mob hanged a Mexican outlaw leader for the murder of a ranch hand. According to the *Las Vegas Daily Optic*, the "mob was said to number 1000 with 900 being Hispanic."[11]

What contribution did Anglo-American settlers make, then, to the tradition of mob violence that already existed among Spanish speakers in the American West? Like others throughout the world, Spanish speakers both in Mexico and in the United States adopted the word *lynching* from their Anglo-American neighbors. Initially the literal "ley de lynch" was common, but quickly the words *linchar* (to lynch), *linchado* (lynched), and *linchamiento* (lynching) developed in the Spanish-language press. The term entered the Spanish language at least as early as the 1850s and was so commonplace by the 1890s that it could appear alone in a newspaper's column heading with no need for explanation. Editors and others used these new Spanish words to describe certain acts of mob violence no matter whether the mob was composed of English or Spanish speakers. Yet, at the same time, there also seemed to be a connotation that Americans were more prone to commit "linchamientos" than other groups and that when they did, they were more likely to target ethnic Mexicans. For example, the California editor Francisco P. Ramirez creatively coined the term "linchocracia" (lynchocracy) to condemn and describe Anglo-orchestrated anti-Mexican mob violence in the 1850s.[12] Throughout the late nineteenth and early twentieth centuries, numerous individuals echoed Ramirez's protests of the targeting of Mexicans and Mexican Americans by Anglo mobs. Such protests had failed to end such mob violence, but this [reading] argues that the "linchamiento" of Rafael Benavides proved a turning point. Emphasis is placed on three particular factors: the growth of institutionalized legal systems, a change in the climate of public opinion, and the renewed power of the new Mexican government to protect its citizens both within its own borders and on American soil.

Given the long history of mob violence against Spanish speakers both by other Spanish speakers and by Anglo mobs, the execution of Rafael Benavides could not have been surprising to the residents of the small and relatively remote community of Farmington. Benavides himself, like most victims of lynching, remains largely unknown to historians. Little is known of his life. He was born into an apparently impoverished family in Salazar, New Mexico, in 1889. His birth in an American territory made him an American citizen, though many Anglos continued to perceive all persons of Mexican descent as "Mexican" outsiders, no matter their nativity.[13]

Regardless of his citizenship, with no formal education, Benavides was unable to read or write and therefore restricted to the life of a manual laborer. Although both a husband and father, he appears to have been separated from his family, who were living across the border in Mancos, Colorado, at the time of his death. The probable reason for the separation was Benavides's earlier conviction for a criminal offense, details of which will be revealed later. This would certainly explain the response of his wife when asked whether she wanted his body returned for committal. Her only words were "Bury him."[14]

The circumstances surrounding the lynching were established in some detail by contemporary newspaper reports. On the night of Wednesday, November 14, 1928, a drunken Benavides broke into the home of a Spanish-speaking family in the nearby town of Aztec and attempted to assault a young girl, only to be scared off by the screams of her sister. Benavides then became involved in a brawl when he attempted to force entry into another house. Eventually he made his way to the ranch of a prominent Anglo farmer, George Lewis. Although Lewis was away on a hunting trip, his wife was asleep at home. Awoken by Benavides, Mrs. Lewis attempted to defend herself with a shotgun, only to discover it was empty. Benavides physically assaulted the farmer's wife and then carried her to a remote hillside, where he left her naked and unconscious. The sixty-year-old woman sustained injuries to her face and chest, including boot marks where she had been furiously kicked. When she regained consciousness some hours later, she staggered to the nearest house, where an alarm was raised. Sheriff George Blancett assembled a posse, which pursued Benavides to the loft of an abandoned house near the Colorado border. When Benavides refused an order to surrender, the posse fired a series of shots into the house, one of which struck the fugitive in the abdomen. Benavides was then arrested and returned to Farmington.[15]

Informed that Benavides would not recover from his wound, Blancett withdrew an armed guard on the hospital. The masked men who abducted Benavides therefore faced no resistance. According to one rumor, Benavides himself struggled forcefully, "striking and biting his kidnappers." In his fearful rage he is reputed to have pushed one of his assailants out of the truck as it sped toward the abandoned farm. This story may account for the bruise above one of Benavides's eyes where the butt of a revolver struck him. At the same time, it seems improbable that a dying man who had been administered a powerful sedative should have summoned up such reserves of physical energy.[16] There is certainly no intimation of superhuman strength in the haunting image of Benavides captured by a local photographer. In the picture, the dead man hangs suspended from a tree limb, his head bowed to his chest, his hands tied behind his back.[17]

Before assessing the political repercussions of the Benavides lynching, it is important to place the case within the broader historical context of mob violence in New Mexico.[18] Between 1848 and 1928, our research suggests that at least fifty-four persons of Mexican descent in New Mexico met their deaths at the hands of lynch mobs. During the same time period, we calculate that at least 597 persons of Mexican origin or descent were lynched in all of the southwestern states.[19]

Identifying and counting victims of lynch mobs is an inexact science at best. We readily admit that our list of lynching victims is imperfect. There are undoubtedly victims of mob violence who do not appear in our data. Some whom we do include may not merit inclusion in the eyes of others. We claim only that we have been consistent according to our own understanding of lynching. In compiling the data, we have followed the lead of most scholars of mob violence and adopted the definition of *lynching* established by the National Association for the Advancement of Colored People (NAACP): a retributive act of murder for which those responsible claim to act in the interests of justice, tradition, or community order.

It should be noted that this definition was not universally agreed upon by lynching activists when it was proposed in 1940. Such a definition certainly did not govern the use of the word *lynching* by Anglos or Mexicans prior to 1940. The definition of the word varied according to the race, ethnicity, and class of the speaker. All of this is to underline the difficulties of using the word *lynching*, an American word that maintains an American connotation even when translated into other languages, for anyone interested in studying acts of extralegal violence, acts that history reveals are not limited to American mobs.[20]

In any event, numbers of ethnic Mexicans killed by mobs provide only a part of the story. Mob violence in New Mexico can be truly understood only in the broader context of racial and ethnic relations in the state and, in particular, in the process of cultural and political accommodation between the state's Anglo and Nuevomexicano elites. Anglos initially settled New Mexico in small numbers. As late as 1900, there were only 50,000 Anglos in the territory, compared with 125,000 Nuevomexicanos. As a result, many early pioneers intermarried with the Nuevomexicano population. By 1870, this situation was true of 90 percent of the married Anglo men in Las Cruces; in Mesilla, 83 percent; and in Doña Ana, 78 percent. This cultural interaction muted racial and ethnic tensions between the two peoples. The overwhelming size of the Nuevomexicano population also constrained Anglos from assuming hegemonic control of the political system. In many areas of the southwestern states during the nineteenth and early twentieth centuries, Mexican Americans were effectively disfranchised. By contrast, the Nuevomexicano elite in New Mexico wielded political power on a scale unparalleled in any other part of the American Southwest. Although Anglos attained control of the territorial legislature in 1886, Nuevomexicanos continued to hold elected office at all levels of government. As late as 1909, eleven of the twenty-one representatives in the New Mexico House of Representatives were Nuevomexicanos. Four Nuevomexicanos also served as governor in the years prior to Benavides's murder: Donaciano Vigil (1847–48), Miguel Otero (1897–1906), Ezequiel Cabeza de Baca (1918), and Octaviano Larrazolo (1918–19). A similar arrangement of racial power sharing operated within the criminal justice system. While Anglos monopolized the most eminent positions within the legal hierarchy, Nuevomexicanos controlled important elected offices such as sheriff. The active participation of Nuevomexicanos in the political and legal systems protected against the unrestrained power of Anglos and promoted racial and ethnic cooperation over conflict. As Charles Montgomery affirms, Anglos and Nuevomexicanos were "locked in a precarious balance of power, a sometimes cooperative though always suspicious relationship that redounded to all levels of New Mexico society."[21]

The ties between the Anglo and Nuevomexicano elites were also secured by the campaign to attain statehood for New Mexico. New Mexico remained a territory under federal jurisdiction until 1912. Congressional opposition to statehood rested on the racist assumption that only a white majority population could be entrusted with the responsibility of self-government. One pamphlet distributed in Santa Fe argued that the "Territory should not be admitted as a State because the majority of its inhabitants" were "catholic" and a "mixture of peons and Indians" and therefore "a people unworthy to live in the great American Republic."[22] The Nuevomexicano elite attempted to establish their claim to a white racial identity and the political privileges this bestowed by calling themselves "Spanish Americans," a name which invoked their common European heritage with Anglos. The Anglo elite supported Nuevomexicanos in their assertion of whiteness, since it represented the best strategy of securing statehood. In this and other respects, the elites shared common class and political interests that transcended ethnic antagonism.[23]

The cultural, political, and economic interaction between Anglo and Nuevomexicano elites affected the pattern of mob violence in New Mexico. In the southern states, the primary motivation of mob violence against African Americans was racial prejudice. Southern whites used terror and intimidation as a means of consolidating their control of the region. By contrast, lynching in New Mexico cut across racial and ethnic lines. Lynching protected the economic interests of the propertied classes, both Anglo and Nuevomexicano. The Nuevomexicano elite consciously distinguished itself from the majority Mexican population and was prepared to orchestrate acts of mob violence in defense of its socially and economically privileged status. In 1893, for instance, Cecilio Lucero, a member of a notorious gang, was arrested in Las Vegas for the murder of a ranch hand who had caught him stealing sheep. Members of the community seized Lucero from his prison cell and hanged him.[24] Although Mexican mobs lynched Mexicans in other parts of the Southwest, such intra-ethnic violence was far more common in New Mexico.[25]

There were nonetheless clear constraints to the extralegal force commanded by the Nuevomexicano elite. The power-sharing relationship between Anglos and Nuevomexicanos was not evenly replicated throughout New Mexico. In certain areas, English-speaking and Spanish-speaking elites joined forces to eliminate horse and cattle thieves regardless of their race or ethnicity. In other areas, competition over grazing rights often broke into ethnic conflict between Nuevomexicano sheepherders and Anglo cattlemen. These patterns were further complicated by the relative size of the two populations. In those areas of the territory where Anglos were a minority, it was essential that they reach some level of accommodation with the Nuevomexicano population. This acculturationist impulse had far less force in those regions where Anglo settlers assumed a majority status.

One region of intense Anglo-Mexican conflict was southeastern New Mexico, a region commonly known as "Little Texas" because of the large influx of Anglo settlers from that state in the post–Civil War era. Competition for economic resources created bitter ethnic rivalry in these newer areas of Anglo colonization. Texas cattlemen ruthlessly forced Nuevomexicano sheepherders from the land. Nuevomexicano retaliation fueled further Anglo aggression, creating a vicious cycle of violent retribution. In areas such as Little Texas where ethnic hostility was pronounced, vigilantism could easily transform into indiscriminate racial warfare. This is most clearly illustrated by the Horrell War. The Horrells were ranchers who had recently settled in New Mexico after fleeing Texas, where they had killed four officers of the pro-Republican state police. They wasted little time in getting into trouble in New Mexico. Driven by the desire to avenge the murder of one of their family members, the Horrells took arbitrary action against the entire Nuevomexicano community. On December 20, 1873, the Horrells murdered four Nuevomexicanos at a dance in Lincoln; later that month, they lynched five Nuevomexicano freighters fifteen miles west of Roswell. The Horrells also intercepted and killed Severanio Apodaca while he was transporting a load of grain to a local mill. In all of these cases, the ethnic identity of the victim appears to have been the only reason they were killed.[26]

Mob violence against Nuevomexicanos reached its pinnacle during the range wars of the 1870s and 1880s. The indiscriminate violence of the Horrells combined with more traditional acts of vigilantism against alleged horse and cattle thieves. In August 1884, the *Raton Comet* reported that a band of Mexican horse thieves was active in the local area. "Immediate flight is their only chance for safety, as their speedy extermination has been decided upon by a set of resolute, determined men, who have suffered by their depredations," the *Comet* reported.[27] Although the fate of these particular horse thieves is uncertain, the "speedy extermination" of Mexicans became common practice. In July 1889, for instance, a deputy sheriff in Socorro County was shot dead as he attempted to arrest Mexican cattle thieves. The suspects were apprehended and imprisoned in an empty house. On the night of July 21, a band of cattlemen stormed the house and then shot and hanged the inmates.[28] The conflict over grazing rights between Anglos and Nuevomexicanos and the more general impulse to punish criminals created an era of violence. During the 1870s and 1880s, mobs lynched at least forty-three Nuevomexicanos.

The area of New Mexico where Rafael Benavides lived lay outside the influence of Anglo and Nuevomexicano interaction. The demographic balance had clearly swung in favor of Anglos by the 1920s. Benavides lived in a community where Nuevomexicanos were socially, economically, and politically marginalized. A system of de facto segregation curtailed social interaction among Anglos and Nuevomexicanos. Physical separation in turn created a psychological distance between the two peoples. In the absence of any power-sharing relationship,

Anglos therefore came to regard Nuevomexicanos as a distinct and inferior racial other. Oral tradition suggests that several Nuevomexicanos were lynched in northwestern New Mexico in the late nineteenth and early twentieth centuries, but research into the surviving written records has only been able to verify one case, the 1882 hanging of Guadalupe Archuleta at Bloomfield, a settlement located just a few miles from Farmington.

Archuleta, according to his defenders, was in the midst of performing his duties as justice of the peace when he shot and killed an Anglo. The shooting and subsequent lynching of Archuleta further divided the town into a Nuevomexicano and an Anglo camp. Archuleta's killing no doubt provoked such division because of ongoing ethnic conflict between the two groups over grazing rights. The lynching occurred at a pivotal moment in this conflict. According to the historian Frances Leon Swadesh, Archuleta's lynching "effectively silenced all Hispano challenge to Anglo strong-arm tactics along the San Juan."[29] Memories of these early conflicts did not fade quickly, and ethnic tension between the two groups persisted well into the twentieth century. For instance, only four years before the Benavides lynching, the *Farmington Times Hustler* printed the call of one local citizen for the "organization of the whole state into active divisions of the KKK."[30]

It is difficult to imagine a situation any less dangerous than the one in which Rafael Benavides found himself.[31] Benavides's position as an illiterate laborer of the mestizo, or mixed-race, class afforded him little social protection from the violent prejudice of Anglos. In contrast to the Nuevomexicano elite, who claimed a pure European ancestry, lower-class Mexicans were perceived as a degenerate mongrel race who had assumed the worst characteristics of their Indian and Spanish ancestors. Anglos feared what they perceived as the moral depravity of the mestizo class and sought to protect themselves through the brutal enforcement of racial boundaries. The murder of an Anglo woman in particular incited the vengeance of the lynch mob. On May 5, 1893, a mob of seventy men stormed the jail in Las Lunas and seized three Nuevomexicanos arrested for the murder of two Anglo women. The three suspects—Victorio Aragon, Antonio Garcia, and Antonio Martinez—were all hanged.[32]

Benavides was a member of the despised mestizo class who committed the one offense most liable to arouse the violent retribution of Anglos. Although he did not murder Mrs. Lewis, his lynching must be attributed to the impulse of Anglo men to protect their wives and daughters from physical assault by what they believed to be morally degenerate Mexicans. Although Anglos perceived any assault upon a white woman as an implicit rape, there is no actual evidence that Benavides attempted to sexually assault Mrs. Lewis. Had there been the intimation that such an offense had occurred, it would almost certainly have been reported by the press. Newspaper accounts of lynchings often contained salacious details of the sexual crime committed by the victim. There is no evidence of this "folk pornography"[33] in press reports of the Benavides case, even after Farmington came under intense attack for permitting the mob violence. Nonetheless, the lynching contained an important element of ritual. The photograph of Benavides's corpse shows that the lynchers tied his bedgown above his waist so as to expose his genitals. Evidently, the mob was not content to murder Benavides but committed a deliberate act of public humiliation intended as a symbolic reassertion of Anglo male supremacy.

Despite the dramatic outburst of ethnic violence in Farmington, Rafael Benavides was the last Nuevomexicano to be lynched in New Mexico. This section and the ones that follow explore why Benavides's murder was such a turning point. A satisfactory answer will not be found solely by sifting through the details of the Farmington lynching. Public figures and forces condemning lynching were at work long before 1928 in New Mexico. And Benavides's lynching did not convince everyone in the state that lynching was wrong and should be abandoned. What Benavides's lynching did do was decisively tip the balance of public opinion toward those in New Mexico who favored due process solutions to problems of social order and away from those who favored informal methods of control such as vigilantism and mob violence. The result was that would-be lynchers after 1928 would no longer have the support of the majority of their fellow citizens. This mattered. Potential lynchers could no longer count on escaping arrest by the authorities. They would have to be careful with their identities and with the location of their planned murder. Ethnic and racial violence was clearly still possible after the lynching of Rafael Benavides, but potential lynchers who had previously been protected by a widespread belief in "rough justice" now found themselves dangerously isolated from majority opinion.[34]

During the late nineteenth and early twentieth centuries the New Mexico press shared a consensus of opinion in support of mob violence against Nuevomexicanos. Newspapers commonly restricted their reports of lynching to a factual recounting of events, and the absence of editorial opinion can be interpreted as an implicit endorsement of mob action. On occasion, the press also expressed more outspoken support. In 1881, the *Santa Fe Democrat* argued that the failures of the legal system justified mob violence. The editorial ran under the title "Let There Be More Hanging, and Less Sniveling."[35] In 1889, the *Socorro Chieftan* commented on a lynching in Kelly, New Mexico: "Horse thieves will be found scarce around Kelly and Magdalena after this. That juniper tree of justice out there is a court that grants no appeals." The newspaper gave no information about who committed the killings but instead speculated that the two Mexicans "came to their death by pulling their necks too hard against a rope."[36] In January 1890, a mob in the mining community of Georgetown seized a Mexican "desperado" from sheriff's officers and hanged him. The *Silver City Sentinel* published an editorial that openly encouraged such acts of retribution. According to the paper, the courts had failed to protect innocent citizens from the incursions of Mexican outlaws. The lynching was therefore a legitimate act of self-defense intended to discourage further criminal outrages. The editorial asserted, "It is high time that the citizens should awake to the importance of putting a stop to this promiscuous shooting. Let a few judicial hangings occur, and the shooter will give this county the go-by."[37]

Occasional muted condemnations of lynching can be found in New Mexico dating back to the nineteenth century. Even these editorials, so guarded in their criticism, make it clear that public support for vigilantism and lynching was widespread throughout the state. For example, in 1876, after reporting that "Judge Lynch had evidently been around last night," the *Albuquerque Review* commented: "We cannot but deprecate this action, yet taking all things into consideration, the parties concerned were not so much to blame."[38] Similar logic was displayed in the *Santa Fe New Mexican* in 1881. In January, authorities in Albuquerque arrested three Nuevomexicanos accused of the murder of Colonel Charles Potter. On the night of January 31, a mob estimated at two hundred in number seized the suspects from the county jail and hanged them. The editor of the *New Mexican* began by stating that "lynching in general is to be condemned" but then went on to defend the actions of local vigilantes. He believed that "in cases such as the cowardly and dastardly murder of Colonel Potter it is very doubtful whether justice can be too swiftly meted out." The editor went even further, encouraging similar action to purge the community of other dangerous criminals: "the sooner such a fate does overtake them the better will it be."[39]

Press support of vigilantism reflected and reinforced a broader community approval of the actions of lynch mobs. The Socorro Committee of Safety, which executed at least two Nuevomexicanos in the 1880s had, according to one observer, "the tacit endorsement of the highest territorial officials," being "composed of the reputable Americans of the town including in its membership, bankers, clergymen, merchants, ranchmen, miners, lawyers, doctors, and all others interested in the enforcement of law and order."[40] As a witness to the lynching of a Nuevomexicano in Las Vegas observed, there were many in the town "who viewed the actions of the Vigilantes as meet and proper."[41] In order to deter official inquiry, local citizens often enforced a conspiracy of silence. In 1953, Marietta Wetherill recalled her attempt forty years earlier to report the hanging bodies of two Nuevomexicanos that she had encountered on the road to Cuba, New Mexico. Wetherill was told that if she were smart, she would not report the lynching and that "she shouldn't know anything about it either." When she returned to the spot of the hanging four hours later, the bodies were gone. Wetherill concluded that "hanging wasn't a hard matter to do apparently at all."[42]

The silence surrounding this lynching and others like it effectively stymied investigation. Local authorities, even when in possession of specific information, usually made only the most cursory attempts to secure the arrest and imprisonment of mob leaders. Only once was anyone prosecuted for the mob murder of a Nuevomexicano. In August 1877, O. P.

McMains stood trial for the lynching of Cruz Vega in Colfax County. The case was eventually thrown out for lack of evidence.[43]

The lynching of Rafael Benavides received considerable sanction from the New Mexico press. Some individuals and newspapers emphatically endorsed the actions of the mob. According to a letter published in the *Farmington Times Hustler*, the men who abducted and murdered Benavides performed a "noble and patriotic service" because they protected the community from further criminal incursions. The *Durango Herald-Democrat* was more blunt, stating that "the degenerate Mexican got exactly what was coming to him."[44] Newspapers such as the *Herald-Democrat* made much of the fact that Benavides was a convicted felon. On September 5, 1914, Benavides was sentenced to a term of five to seven years in the New Mexico State Penitentiary for the rape of a ten-year-old Nuevomexicano girl.[45] Prison had apparently failed to reform him. In a blatant act of recidivism he had drunkenly assaulted an innocent woman and left her for dead. The failure of the penal system therefore forced the people of Farmington to take preventive action against any further criminal outrages Benavides might perpetrate. As the *Rio Grande Farmer* concluded, "He will commit no more crimes." The lynching of Benavides, it was believed, would also serve as a salutary lesson to other potential offenders. In the words of the *Mancos Times-Tribune*, "a more pronounced means of instilling fear into the hearts of the criminal class, was never resorted to."[46]

There was nothing surprising about such editorials. Newspapers throughout the southern and western states had for decades attempted to exonerate the actions of lynch mobs by emphasizing the supposed failure of the courts to protect innocent people from dangerously violent criminals. What is remarkable is that many newspapers, despite their acceptance of Benavides's guilt, denounced his lynching as unjustified even under these circumstances. A thorough analysis of press reaction to the Benavides lynching reveals that the public consensus in support of lynching had collapsed by 1928. The *Santa Fe New Mexican* is a potent illustration of this sea change in popular opinion. As noted above, decades earlier the paper enthusiastically endorsed the lynching of three Nuevomexicanos accused of murder. Yet in 1928, it led press reaction in an impassioned denunciation of mob violence. In a widely reprinted editorial, the paper condemned lynching as "a dangerous experiment" because it claimed innocent victims, and demanded a "thorough and searching investigation" of the incident. The *New Mexican* articulated the influence of Progressive politics on public discourse about law and order. Its publisher, Bronson M. Cutting, had moved to Santa Fe from Long Island, New York, in 1910. As a former chairman of the board of commissioners of the New Mexico State Penitentiary, Cutting had a clear interest in the promotion of the criminal justice system over the lawless behavior of the lynch mob. In 1927 Cutting had also been appointed as a Republican to the U.S. Senate following the death of the incumbent, Andrieus A. Jones. A year later, he won election in his own right. As the holder of such high political office, Cutting had to protect the reputation of his adopted state. However, he also had a reputation for actively promoting the political rights of Nuevomexicanos. These concerns informed the denunciation of the Benavides lynching in the pages of the *New Mexican*.[47]

How is this adverse press reaction to be explained? A number of interrelated social and political forces had by the late 1920s contributed to a decline in popular acceptance of mob violence. It is important to consider the impact of reformist impulses at state, national, and international levels.

In other southwestern states, protest against the lynching and murder of Mexicans assumed a confrontational character. In Texas and California, where mob violence was more endemic, Mexicans rose up in violent retaliation against their Anglo oppressors. The men who embodied this spirit of armed resistance have become folkloric heroes: Joaquín Murrieta, Juan Cortina, and Tiburcio Vásquez. Anglos refused to distinguish between general lawlessness and legitimate acts of resistance, indiscriminately labeling any challenge to their legal and political power as "banditry." Although some of these outlaws did engage in indiscriminate acts of robbery and violence, others pursued an explicitly political agenda. Scholars therefore commonly describe these Mexican outlaws as "social bandits."[48] The Texas outlaw Juan Cortina best illustrates the distinction between banditry and political resistance. Between 1859 and 1873, Cortina led a small army of outlaws against the U.S. military. Anglos considered Cortina a dangerously violent criminal. Cortina, by contrast, proclaimed that his purpose was to punish Anglos who murdered Mexicans and escaped prosecution because of the racism of the southwestern legal system. "There are to be found criminals covered with frightful crimes," roared Cortina. "To these monsters indulgence is shown, because they are not of our race, which is unworthy, as they say, to belong to the human species."[49]

New Mexico, like Texas and other parts of the borderlands, had a history of resistance and self-defense. In New Mexico, however, such resistance was not often directed at Anglo mobs. The most dramatic illustration of armed opposition to Anglo oppression in the state is Las Gorras Blancas, or the White Caps. By the late 1880s Nuevomexicano farmers in San Miguel County faced financial ruin as a result of the fenced enclosure of formerly communal lands. Las Gorras Blancas were a band of masked night riders who resisted confiscation of the pasture lands, tearing down fences, burning barns and haystacks, and destroying livestock. A handbill distributed by the riders in March 1890 declared: "Our purpose is to protect the rights and interests of the people in general and especially of the helpless classes."[50] However, Nuevomexicanos do not appear to have utilized similar tactics in the struggle against ethnic violence. Daring acts of physical resistance were confined to the issue of land enclosure, not the lynch mob. It should also be emphasized that Las Gorras Blancas was a class as well as an ethnic movement, since its raids were directed against both Anglo and Nuevomexicano property owners.[51]

Nuevomexicanos did mobilize in collective protest against ethnic prejudice. According to Phillip Gonzales, between the late 1880s and early 1930s Nuevomexicanos organized "mass meetings of indignation" on twenty-six separate occasions. Yet not one of these demonstrations was directed against lynching.[52]

The contrast between New Mexico and other southwestern states emphasizes distinct regional variation in the pattern of response to mob violence against Mexicans. In New Mexico, at least, neither vigorous protest by the Nuevomexicano elite nor acts of armed resistance can account for the demise of lynch law.

The institutionalization of a formal legal system had a more important impact on public opinion than did public protests by Nuevomexicanos. The Benavides incident appeared to belie the transition of the southwestern states from a remote frontier society to a more stable social order. During the early decades of western settlement, many observers believed that vigilantism fulfilled a vital function of the frontier. In the absence of a fully functional legal system, the preservation of public order became the responsibility of community-minded citizens. Although not sanctioned by law, these vigilance committees acted impartially and in the interest of the common good. As Ray Abrahams observes, contemporary accounts portrayed lynch law "in positive terms as fundamentally the cool-headed response of public-spirited citizens to an emergency in which life and property had become dangerously insecure."[53]

The historical record does not support this uncritical acceptance of vigilante committees. Far from acting in the interests of law and order, Anglo vigilantes lynched Nuevomexicanos in deliberate defiance of the authorities. This was especially the case in those areas where Anglos did not control the legal system. The actions of the Socorro Committee of Safety offer a telling example. In March 1881, three members of a wealthy Nuevomexicano family murdered an Anglo who had insulted them. Skeptical that the Nuevomexicano sheriff would arrest prominent members of his own community, Anglos independently organized a Committee of Safety. The committee seized one of the suspects, Onofrio Baca, from an arresting officer and hanged him. Some months later, the committee lynched another Nuevomexicano, this time for rape. The following day, further evidence was uncovered that established his innocence.[54] An assessment of New Mexico vigilantism by Montague Stevens reveals the dangers of mob violence: "Well, these cattlemen got together and made an association of Vigilantes. That part was all right but the trouble was that most of the Vigilantes were the worst thieves of the lot."[55]

Whether or not frontier justice had ever served a legitimate purpose, what was important was the perception that New Mexico no longer had need of vigilantes. By the late 1920s the establishment of an institutionalized legal system throughout the southwestern states undermined the legitimacy of frontier justice. An analysis of San Juan County court records between 1887 and 1928 demonstrates that the authorities commonly secured the indictment and conviction of serious criminal offenders.[56] The sentencing policy of the court appears to have been in part determined by the ethnic identity of the convicted felon, evidenced by the fact they handed down particularly harsh prison terms upon Nuevomexicanos. The minimum sentence for a Nuevomexicano convicted of rape was two to three years; the maximum sentence was life.[57] By contrast, the only Anglo convicted of the offense received a one-year sentence.[58] Lengthy prison terms were also imposed on Nuevomexicanos convicted of murder. Donaciano Aguilar was incarcerated for ninety-nine years in 1909 and Edumenio Meastas for fifty to sixty years in 1927.[59] Arturo Rosales also affirms that after 1910 the use of the death penalty in New Mexico assumed a more explicitly racial dimension. The disproportionate number of Nuevomexicanos executed during these years demonstrates that state authorities had to a certain extent supplanted the role of the lynch mob.[60]

Since there appeared to be indisputable evidence that Rafael Benavides committed an assault on Mrs. Lewis, the Anglo citizens of Farmington should have been confident of his conviction by a court of law. On November 27, the *Santa Fe New Mexican* affirmed that the actions of the mob therefore served no legitimate purpose. "In raw frontier communities where law was not yet established, Vigilantes were sometimes necessary. It is a question for San Juan county to decide as to whether she holds herself as a raw, lawless, frontier district," the paper observed. Although most newspapers accepted that Benavides was guilty of having committed a serious criminal offense, this did not in their opinion sanction the actions of the lynch mob. In the words of the *Alamogordo News,* Benavides was a "miserable wretch" who had committed an almost unspeakable crime. However, he had already been arrested and would no doubt have been convicted by a court of law had he lived. Other newspapers expressed a similar sentiment that the barbarity of Benavides's crime did not in itself justify the actions of the mob. According to the *Farmington Times Hustler,* Benavides was a "beast man," the "perpetrator of the most revolting crime ever committed in the county." But he was also entitled to be tried according to the due process of law. Lynch mobs, "however well-intentioned, are dangerous means for dispensing justice and when less well-intentioned are a most dangerous menace to life, liberty and property."[61]

The increased power of the state and the growing stability of the legal system also acted as a deterrent to potential vigilantes. The state was now more capable of protecting prisoners threatened by lynch mobs. Vigilantes also had reasons to be cautious about the newly strengthened legal system. If judges and juries determined to eradicate lynching, the courts would have been much more effective in doing so than in New Mexico's territorial period.

Given the strength of the legal system and the expanded power of the state, why had a band of outlaws resorted to vigilante violence? The lynching of Rafael Benavides seemed to be an aberration, an unwelcome reversion to an era when citizens ignored due process conventions for informal, community justice. The press acknowledged that racism had been the principal determining factor. Every one of the Nuevomexicanos convicted of a capital offense in San Juan County committed his crime on members of their own ethnic community. So long as this was the case, Anglos appear to have respected the due process of law. However, when a Nuevomexicano committed a criminal outrage against an Anglo, it inflamed a violent ethnic prejudice. The *Santa Fe New Mexican* astutely recognized this double standard. Had he survived his bullet wound, Benavides would have been tried and convicted by the authorities. Those men who dispensed frontier justice could claim to have upheld the law; the mob that murdered Benavides undermined it.[62]

Many New Mexicans would have been uncomfortable with the racism in the execution of Benavides in any event, but the shifting national perception of lynching in the interwar era made the episode even more troubling. The phenomenon of mob violence was in irreversible decline throughout the United States by the 1920s. According to the Tuskegee Institute, the peak lynching decade of the 1890s claimed the lives of 1,333 people. By the 1920s, the figure had fallen to 321. While still disturbing, and a sign of the continued tolerance of mob law in the United States, this amounts to a decline of 400 percent within a single generation.[63] The interaction of a number of forces shaped a new political climate less tolerant of the violent lawlessness of the mob. News reports of European atrocities in World War I caused a reconsideration of racial violence at home. The Red Summer of 1919 also intensified fears that mobs threatened the United States' own democratic order.[64] These events gave added political impetus to the antilynching campaigns of civil rights organizations. The NAACP launched an unrelenting political offensive against lynching in 1910. Less than a decade later, in 1919, the Commission on Interracial Cooperation mounted a regional campaign to mobilize southern liberal opposition to mob violence. The increasing political outcry encouraged Missouri representative Leonidas C. Dyer to introduce a federal antilynching bill to Congress in 1921. Although a southern filibuster in the Senate resulted in the defeat of the bill, the surrounding publicity stirred further popular outrage against lynch mobs. The federal government responded by assuming a more activist role in the arrest and prosecution of mob members.[65]

The Benavides lynching therefore threatened to place New Mexico outside the pale of national opinion. Newspapers across the country reported the incident. This unwelcome publicity tarnished the reputation of New Mexico and threatened its association in the popular imagination with the violent racial intolerance of the southern states.[66] Newspapers across the state branded the lynching an act of barbarism that disgraced the people of New

Mexico before the rest of the nation. According to the *State Tribune,* "The good name not only of the county but of New Mexico is at issue."[67]

Political pressures not only within the United States but without also explain the critical reaction to the case. The ink of the signatories to the Treaty of Guadalupe Hidalgo had barely dried before the Mexican government received reports of the violent mistreatment of its citizens within the United States. The diplomatic protests of the Mexican government had a powerful cumulative effect upon the course of mob violence. Federal authorities initially insisted that they had no jurisdiction to intervene in the internal affairs of individual states. By the last decade of the nineteenth century, however, Mexican demands proved too persistent to ignore. In unrelated incidents during the fall of 1895, Anglo mobs lynched two Mexican citizens, Luis Moreno and Florentine Suaste. Confronted by furious Mexican protests, the United States government sanctioned the payment of a two-thousand-dollar indemnity to the families of both victims.[68]

Mexican authorities continued during the interwar era to place unrelenting pressure on the U.S. State Department. Three episodes that occurred in the decade before the lynching of Rafael Benavides illustrate how the forceful diplomacy of the Mexican government fostered official intolerance of mob violence.

On September 13, 1919, a mob in Pueblo, Colorado, lynched two men for the murder of a local police officer. The victims, Salvador Ortez and José Gonzales, were both Mexican citizens.[69] The Mexican embassy in Washington immediately instructed the local consul, A. J. Ortiz, to launch an investigation. Although Ortiz did not discover the identities of the mob leaders, he did establish that the dead men were entirely innocent.[70]

While the Mexican government routinely investigated the murder of Mexican nationals in the United States, the degree of Mexican protest often fluctuated according to the political situation within Mexico and its international relationship with the United States. In 1919, Mexico's interest was energized by recent diplomatic tensions with the United States. Mexico understood that attention to the Pueblo lynching case would cause the American government acute embarrassment. In recent months the State Department had imposed increasing pressure on the Carranza administration for the protection of American citizens in Mexico. The failure to defend Mexicans from American mobs implied a blatant double standard. The *Houston Post* concurred with Mexican officials when they observed that the United States was in no position to claim the moral high ground in its diplomatic disputes with Mexico: "After the stern warnings our government has sent to Mexico against further outrages on our citizens, it is going to be humiliating in the extreme for our government to receive similar complaints from the Mexican government making charges against our people who have claimed to be so much higher in the scale of civilization."[71]

Mexican diplomatic protest therefore pressured the federal government to take remedial action against lynch mobs in an attempt to more purposefully fulfill the ideals of American democracy. On November 11, 1922, a mob in Weslaco, Texas, lynched a suspected murderer named Elias Zarate. Racial tension spread rapidly through the local region. Within hours, an armed mob marched through the streets of Breckenridge in an attempt to scare Mexicans out of town. Ambassador Manuel Téllez issued the State Department a demand for their protection. At the recommendation of Secretary of State Charles Evans Hughes, the governor of Texas sent a detachment of Rangers to safeguard against any further violence. The crisis soon passed.[72]

In 1926, Mexican diplomatic protest culminated in the arrest and conviction of Sheriff Raymond Teller. Teller and his fellow law officers had been implicated in the lynching of four Mexicans in Raymondville, Texas. According to the sheriff, the Mexicans had been arrested for the murder of two of his officers. Teller was taking the suspects from jail out into the countryside in search of their cache of arms when he was ambushed. The prisoners were killed in the resultant gunfight. Yet according to other testimony, Teller and his officers had themselves tortured and then shot the Mexicans. For decades the State Department had invariably taken the reports of local law officers at face value in its investigations of the murder of Mexicans. These reports repeatedly failed to identify those responsible for the lynchings, instead concluding vaguely that the victims had met their deaths at the hands of persons unknown. This case demonstrated a new determination to avoid diplomatic tensions with Mexico over the lynching of its citizens on American soil. Not only did the State Department reject the conclusions of the sheriff's report, but federal pressure upon state authorities was critical in ensuring that Teller and his fellow officers were tried, convicted, and sentenced to prison.[73]

New Mexican newspapermen and community leaders paid attention to the events in Texas and Colorado. They were no doubt unsurprised when Mexican authorities made similar remonstrations to secure the arrest and prosecution of those responsible for the lynching of Rafael Benavides. When Ambassador Téllez undertook an investigation into the incident, Assistant District Attorney George Bruington immediately announced his intention to determine the nationality of the dead man. Bruington informed the press that the nurse who treated Benavides claimed he told her his father was an African American. The story received a strong emphasis in several newspapers, which described Benavides as "a Negro Mexican half-breed."[74] Although pure speculation on the part of the assistant district attorney, this appears to have been an attempt to attribute the criminal misconduct of Benavides by implication to his "blackness." The insinuation of a racial hierarchy that elevated Mexicans above African Americans may also have been a means of defusing diplomatic protest. Ambassador Téllez was in any event obliged to abandon his investigation.

Although the racial identity of Benavides's father could not be determined, the district attorney conclusively established that he was a citizen not of Mexico but the United States. The publicity in part generated by Mexican protest did, however, adversely affect state authorities. An editorial in the *Farmington Times Hustler* reflected the determination not to allow any further outbreaks of mob violence. "It will take San Juan County a long time to live down the bad name received by this lawless act," observed the paper. "The outside world will long remember the lynching but will forget the terrible crime that caused it."[75]

Protest of the lynching of Rafael Benavides by the Mexican government and condemnation of the episode by local and state newspapers and community leaders were important developments in the evolution of New Mexican attitudes toward vigilantism and extralegal violence. But the newspapermen and diplomats who criticized Benavides's lynching did not change attitudes toward lynching in New Mexico by themselves. Rather, these critics of lynching succeeded in preventing future lynchings because the values they upheld were now more widely internalized among the people of New Mexico. Residents of New Mexico, like citizens of the United States in general, underwent a slow, gradual transformation in their attitudes toward lynching. In the nineteenth century, most New Mexicans had supported lynching as a necessary evil because of the frontier condition of the territory and the weakness of its courts. As those courts improved, however, attitudes toward lynching evolved. By the twentieth century, more and more New Mexicans had come to believe that justice should be meted out not by vigilantes but through the legal system in a deliberate and formal manner that emphasized due process rights and procedures. The lynching of Rafael Benavides did not reinvigorate the older tradition in New Mexico. Instead, it forced New Mexicans to evaluate what they thought about lynching and vigilantism. The arguments and criticisms put forward about the Benavides lynching, both within New Mexico and without, helped New Mexicans understand why they were now so uncomfortable with extralegal violence. In the end, the lynching of Rafael Benavides confirmed and accelerated a change in attitude that had been taking place in the previous quarter century. The murder of Benavides tipped the balance of public opinion in favor of those opposing mob violence and thus became the last lynching of its kind.

Notes

Originally published in the *New Mexico Historical Review* 80, no. 3 (summer 2005): 265–292. © 2005 by the University of New Mexico Board of Regents. All rights reserved. Reprinted by permission.

1   *Farmington Times Hustler,* November 23, 1928.

2   *Farmington Times Hustler,* December 7, 1928; *Santa Fe New Mexican,* December 5 and 6, 1928.

3   Robert J. Tórrez, "New Mexico's Last Lynching," *'Round the Roundhouse* (November 11–December 9, 2003): 6.

4   F. Arturo Rosales, correspondence with authors, August 5, 2002.

5   Although Benavides was the last identifiable Mexican to be murdered in such a public manner by a mob, Mexicans certainly continued to suffer other forms of group violence. The Los Angeles Zoot Suit Riot of August 1943 is a stark illustration of continued conflict between Anglos and Mexicans. Although anti-Mexican violence continued after 1928, Benavides's lynching coincided with a subtle but decisive shift in Anglo attitudes. According to our research, in the years that followed, would-be mob members were discouraged by the threat of public condemnation and prosecution by the courts after 1928. *Los Angeles Times,* October 11, 1933; *New York Times,* October 11, 1933; Mauricio Mazón, *The Zoot-Suit Riots: The Psychology of Symbolic Annihilation* (Austin: University of Texas Press, 1984); Carey McWilliams, "The Los Angeles Riot of 1943," in *Violence in America: A Historical and Contemporary Reader,* ed. Thomas Rose (New York: Random House, 1969), 168–80.

6   On resentment of the term *Mexicans,* see Brian Michael Jenkins, "The Border War: A Study of the United States–Mexico Relations during the Mexican Revolution, 1910–1920," (master's thesis, University of California, Los Angeles, 1965), 8.

7   Miriam Taylor, "San Juan County: Farmington," unpublished paper, Farmington Public Library; Hartsill Lloyd Clark, "A History of San Juan County, New Mexico" (master's thesis, University of Tulsa, 1963), 69–80, 91–98; Bureau of the Census, *Abstract of the Fifteenth Census of the United States* (Washington, DC: Government Printing Office, 1933).

8   Mrs. Fremont Older, *California Missions and Their Romances* (New York: Van Rees, 1938), 67–68; Frank Shay, *Judge Lynch: His First Hundred Years* (New York: Ives, 1938), 64–65.

9   *Los Angeles Star,* August 7, 1852; *Sacramento Daily Union,* July 28, 1852; *Nevada Journal,* August 7, 1852; Hubert Howe Bancroft, "Popular Tribunals—Volume I," in *The Works of Hubert Howe Bancroft* (San Francisco: History Company, 1887), 36:477; Ken Gonzales-Day, *Lynching in the West, 1850–1935* (Durham, NC: Duke University Press, 2006), 210.

10 *Albuquerque Republican Review,* April 15, 1871; *Santa Fe Weekly New Mexican,* September 25, 1871.

11 *El Nuevo Mexicano,* June 3, 1893; *Las Vegas Daily Optic,* May 31, 1893, 2; *El Boletin Popular,* June 1, 1893; Carlos C. de Baca, *Vicente Silva: The Terror of Las Vegas* (Truchas, NM: Tate Gallery, 1968), 38–39; Mitchell C. Sena, "Third-Rate Henchman of a First-Rate Terror," *True West* (February 1979): 28–29, 40–44.

12 For Ramirez's editorials and reports, see *El Clamor Publico,* April 25, 1857; November 14, 1857; January 23 and June 19, 1858; January 29 June 5, 11, and 18, and September 17 and 24, 1859. "Linchamiento," "linchar," and "linchado" were used in a wide number of Spanish-language newspapers from the 1850s (Los Angeles's *El Clamor Publico* and San Francisco's *El Eco del Pacífico*) to the 1890s and beyond (Santa Fe's *El Boletin Popular* and *El Nuevo Mexicano*). See,

for example, *El Nuevo Mexicano,* February 11 and June 3, 1893. For an indispensible discussion of Ramirez and his criticism of American democracy and lynching, see Coya Paz Brownrigg, "Linchocracia: Performing 'America' in El Clamor Publico," *California History* 84, no. 2 (Winter 2006): 40–53.

13   Ironically, Roger Taney's infamous *Dred Scott* decision guaranteed Benavides's citizenship rights. Although Taney did not mean for these rights to apply to nonwhites, his interpretation that constitutional rights followed the flag into the territories still prevails. See *Scott v. Sandford,* 60 U.S. 393 (1857).

14   Department of Corrections, Penitentiary of New Mexico, Record Book of Convicts, #3384, New Mexico State Archives, Santa Fe; *El Paso Times,* November 18, 1928.

15   The events surrounding the shooting and arrest of Rafael Benavides were widely reported in the press: *Farmington Times Hustler,* November 16 and 23, 1928; *Albuquerque Journal,* November 16, 1928; *Aztec Independent,* November 16, 1928; *Roswell Morning Dispatch,* November 16, 1928; *Roswell Daily Record,* November 16, 1928; *El Paso Times,* November 17, 1928; *La Prensa* (San Antonio), November 17, 1928; *Las Vegas Daily Optic,* November 17, 1928; *Santa Fe New Mexican,* November 17, 1928; *Raton Daily Range,* November 17 and 20 1928; *Alamogordo News,* November 22, 1928; *Santa Rosa News,* November 23, 1928; *Roy Record,* November 24, 1928.

16   *El Paso Times,* November 17, 1928; *Farmington Daily Times,* October 13, 1928; *Raton Daily Range,* November 17, 1928.

17   Vertical file, Salmon Ruins Museum, Bloomfield, New Mexico.

18   Most of the scholarship on lynching and mob violence in New Mexico focuses on specific localities. One recent overview for the territorial period is Nancy Gonzalez, "Untold Stories of Murder and Lynching in Territorial New Mexico" (master's thesis, University of New Mexico, 2003).

19   This essay arises from a larger study of the lynching of persons of Mexican origin or descent throughout the United States. For a fuller discussion of the statistics presented here, see William D. Carrigan and Clive Webb, "The Lynching of Persons of Mexican Origin or Descent in the United States, 1848–1928," *Journal of Social History* 37 (2003): 411–38.

20   Some of these lynching victims were naturalized American citizens, while others were Mexican nationals resident in the United States. It is not always possible to determine the citizenship of a particular individual. In the interest of linguistic simplicity, when referring to the broader southwestern states, we use the word *Mexican* to describe all persons of Mexican origin or descent. The Mexican community of New Mexico is also known by a number of terms, including *Spanish American, Nuevomexicano,* and *Hispano.* We use the term *Nuevomexicano* when referring expressly to the Mexican population of New Mexico. This term has been chosen over the other alternatives for its parallel with state-specific terms for Mexicans in other states such as Texas ("Tejanos").

The definition of lynching is open to interpretation, so it is important to explain the criteria used to calculate our statistics. In describing and analyzing mob violence, historians use words such as *lynching, vigilantism,* and *rioting.* It is often difficult to distinguish between these different forms of violence, both in the writing of historians and in the historical record itself. The key characteristics that distinguish one type of mob violence from another are the level of community approval and the degree to which premeditation and deliberation preceded the killing. On the one hand, historians see vigilantes as organized and controlled. Vigilantes choose their victims carefully, usually for some alleged crime or specific violation of the moral order. They also enjoy significant, if not universal, community approval and support. On the other hand, and at the opposite extreme, historians place rioters, whose acts of violence are generally not approved by the community and whose victims are likely to be chosen indiscriminately. The use of the word *lynching* has changed over time. Early in the twentieth century, *lynching* and *vigilantism* were nearly synonymous. Neither word was to be applied to a mob killing unless it exhibited both widespread community support and a certain level of discrimination on the part of the mob. During the twentieth century, however, the definition of lynching slowly changed to embrace almost any conceivable form of mob violence. Those who calculated lynching statistics were no longer bound to prove community approval, and they also began to include certain cases in which individuals were killed indiscriminately by riotous mobs. The NAACP formalized this new, expanded definition of lynching in 1940, and in the last half century, most historians of lynching, including the authors, have used this definition. For further insight on the shifting classification of lynching, see Christopher Waldrep, "War of Words: The Controversy over the Definition of Lynching, 1899–1940," *Journal of Southern History* 66 (2000): 75–100; and Waldrep, *The Many Faces of Judge Lynch: Extralegal Violence and Punishment in America* (New York: Palgrave Macmillan, 2002).

21   Charles Montgomery, "The Trap of Race and Memory: The Language of Spanish Civility on the Upper Rio Grande," *American Quarterly* 52 (2000): 488–89; Darlis A. Miller, "Cross-Cultural Marriages in the Southwest: The New Mexico Experience, 1846–1900," *New Mexico Historical Review* 57 (1982): 341; Juan Gómez-Quiñones, *Roots of Chicano Politics, 1600-1940* (Albuquerque: University of New Mexico Press, 1994), 329–30, 354; Laura E. Gómez, "Race, Colonialism, and Criminal Law: Mexicans and the American Criminal Justice System in Territorial New Mexico," *Law & Society Review* 34 (2000): 1129–1202; Charles Montgomery, "Becoming 'Spanish-American': Race and Rhetoric in New Mexico Politics, 1880–1928," *Journal of American Ethnic History* 20 (2001): 60.

22   *Republican Review,* March 11, 1876, quoted in Gonzalez, "Untold Stories," 8.

23   John Nieto-Phillips, "Spanish American Ethnic Identity and New Mexico's Statehood Struggle," in *The Contested Homeland: A Chicano History of New Mexico,* ed. Erlinda Gonzales-Berry and Daniel R. Maciel (Albuquerque: University of New Mexico Press, 2000), 97–142; Montgomery, "Trap of Race and Memory," 480.

24 *El Nuevo Mexicano,* June 3, 1893; *Las Vegas Daily Optic,* May 31, 1893; *El Boletín Popular,* June 1, 1893; de Baca, *Vicente Silva,* 38–39; Sena, "Third-Rate Henchman."

25 In February 1885, Jose Trujillo Gallegos was lynched in San Miguel County by a mob of men led by Cresensio Lucero. Gallegos, it was alleged, had murdered his family. In 1893, a mob of Nuevomexicanos hanged Ireneo Gonzalez for attempted murder. *Santa Fe New Mexican Review,* February 23, 1889; *El Nuevo Mexicano,* February 11, 1893; *Albuquerque Democrat,* February 7, 1893; *Santa Fe New Mexican,* February 7, 1893.

26 *Santa Fe New Mexican,* January 2, 1874; Maurice G. Fulton, *History of the Lincoln County War,* ed. Robert N. Mullin (Tucson: University of Arizona Press, 1968), 21–24; Robert N. Mullin, *A Chronology of the Lincoln County War* (Santa Fe, NM: Press of the Territorian, 1966), 11; P. J. Rasch, "The Horrell War," *New Mexico Historical Review* 31 (1956): 228; Ann Buffington, Lincoln County Historical Society, and New Mexico Federal Writers' Project, *Old Lincoln County Pioneer Stories: Interviews from the WPA Writer's Project* (Lincoln, NM: Lincoln County Historical Society, 1994), 1–3.

27 *Raton Comet,* August 10, 1884.

28 *Santa Fe New Mexican,* July 25, 1889. See also Fulton, *History of the Lincoln County War,* 29, 66; and Mullin, *Chronology of the Lincoln County War,* 12–13.

29 Frances Leon Swadesh, *Los Primeros Pobladores: Hispanic Americans of the Ute Frontier* (Notre Dame, IN: University of Notre Dame Press, 1974), 94–95; *Santa Fe Daily New Mexican,* November 1, 1882; Philip Rasch, "Feuding at Farmington," *New Mexico Historical Review* 40 (1965): 229.

30 *Farmington Times Hustler,* February 13 and 20, 1924, quoted in Robert W. Duke, *San Juan County Roars in the '20s* (Flora Vista, NM: San Juan County Historical Society, 2000).

31 Benavides may or may not have known about the lynching of Guadalupe Archuleta. Those Nuevomexicanos in the area who did remember might have warned Benavides that the man Guadalupe Archuleta killed was named John Blancett. One of the leaders of the lynch mob that killed Archuleta was also a Blancett. On the eve of Benavides's crime, the sheriff of San Juan County was George Blancett.

32 *Santa Fe New Mexican,* May 6, 1893; *El Boletín Poplar,* May 11, 1893.

33 Jacquelyn Dowd Hall, *Revolt against Chivalry: Jesse Daniel Ames and the Women's Campaign against Lynching* (New York: Columbia University Press, 1979), 150.

34 For a convincing discussion of the cultural struggle between those who favored "rough justice" and those who favored due process throughout the United States, see Michael Pfeifer, *Rough Justice: Lynching and American Society, 1874–1947* (Urbana: University of Illinois Press, 2004).

35 *Santa Fe Democrat,* January 3, 1881, quoted in Gonzalez, "Untold Stories," 8–9.

36 *Socorro Chieftan,* July 27, 1889.

37 *Silver City Sentinel,* quoted in *Santa Fe New Mexican,* January 9, 1890.

38 *Albuquerque Review,* June 24, 1876, quoted in Gonzalez, "Untold Stories," 19.

39 *Santa Fe New Mexican,* February 4, 1881. The three men lynched by the mob were identified as Miguel Barrera, Escolastico Perea, and California Joe.

40 Charles Potter, "Reminiscences of the Socorro Vigilantes," ed. Paige W. Christiansen, *New Mexico Historical Review* 40 (January 1965): 25.

41 Miguel Antonio Otero, *My Life on the Frontier,* 1864–1882 (New York: Press of the Pioneers, 1935), 192–93. Otero referred to the lynching of Manuel Barela. Although it was reported in a number of sources, there is some uncertainty as to the precise date of the lynching, which occurred either in 1879 or 1880. See Milton W. Callon, *Las Vegas, New Mexico: The Town That Wouldn't Gamble* (Las Vegas, NM: Las Vegas Daily Optic, 1962), 71, 94; and F. Stanley, *The Las Vegas Story* (Denver: World, 1951), 163–64.

42 Marietta Wetherill Oral Interview, MSS 123 BC, Pioneers Foundation Oral History Collection, Center for Southwest Studies, University of New Mexico, Albuquerque.

43 Colfax County District Court Records: Criminal Cases #351–70, New Mexico State Archives; Lawrence R. Murphy, *Philmont: A History of New Mexico's Cimarron County* (Albuquerque: University of New Mexico Press, 1972), 119–22; Morris F. Taylor, *O. P. McMains and the Maxwell Land Grant Conflict* (Tucson: University of Arizona Press, 1979), 39–55.

44 *Farmington Times Hustler,* November 30, 1928; editorial, *Durango Herald-Democrat,* republished in *Santa Fe New Mexican,* November 26, 1928; and *Farmington Times Hustler,* December 7, 1928.

45 Department of Corrections, Penitentiary of New Mexico, Record Book of Convicts, #3384.

46 Editorial, *Rio Grande Farmer,* republished in *Santa Fe New Mexican,* November 27, 1928; editorial, *Mancos Times-Tribune,* republished in *Farmington Times Hustler,* November 30, 1928.

47 *Santa Fe New Mexican,* November 17, 1928. For more information on Cutting, see Richard Lowitt, *Bronson M. Cutting: Progressive Politician* (Albuquerque: University of New Mexico Press, 1992).

48 This influential concept was initially conceived by Eric Hobsbawm in his book *Bandits* (London: Weidenfeld and Nicolson, 1969).

49 For further information on the life and career of Juan Cortina, see Charles W. Goldfinch and José T. Canales, *Juan N. Cortina: Two Interpretations* (New York: Arno, 1974); and Jerry D. Thompson, ed., *Juan Cortina and the Texas-Mexico Frontier,* 1859–1877 (El Paso: Texas Western Press, 1994).

50 Howard Bryan, *Wildest of the Wild West: True Tails of a Frontier Town on the Santa Fe Trail* (Santa Fe, NM: Clear Light, 1988), 211. The story of Las Gorras Blancas is told in Andrew Bancroft Schlesinger, "Las Gorras Blancas, 1889–1891," *Journal of Mexican American History* 1 (Spring 1971): 87–143; Robert W. Larson, "The White Caps of New Mexico: A Study of Ethnic Militancy in the Southwest," *Pacific Historical Review* 44 (May 1975): 171–85; and Robert J. Rosenbaum, *Mexicano Resistance in the Southwest* (Austin: University of Texas Press, 1981; reprint, Dallas: Southern Methodist University Press, 1998), 99–124.

51 Fabiola Cabeza de Baca, *We Fed Them Cactus,* 2nd ed. (Albuquerque: University of New Mexico Press, 1994), 89–90.

52   Phillip B. Gonzales, "La Junta de Indignación: Hispano Repertoire of Collective Protest in New Mexico, 1884–1933," *Western Historical Quarterly* 31 (2000): 161–86.

53   Ray Abrahams, *Vigilant Citizens: Vigilantism and the State* (Cambridge: Polity, 1998), 53–54.

54   Manuel Maria de Zamacona to James G. Blaine, April 19, 1881, Notes from the Mexican Legation in the United States to the Department of State, 1821–1906, National Archives, College Park, MD; Erna Ferguson, *Murder and Mystery in New Mexico* (Albuquerque: Merle Armitage Editions, 1948), 21–27; James B. Gillett, *Six Years with the Texas Rangers, 1875–1881* (1921; reprint, Lincoln: University of Nebraska Press, 1976); *El Paso Times*, April 8, 1881.

55   Montague Stevens, Pioneers Foundation Oral History Collection, tape 351, reel 5, Center for Southwestern Studies, University of New Mexico.

56   The observations that follow are based upon a systematic study of the county civil and criminal record books for the years 1887 to 1928: San Juan County District Court Criminal Docket no. 1, New Mexico State Archives; San Juan County District Court Criminal Docket no. 2, San Juan County Courthouse, Aztec, NM.

57   Criminal Docket no. 1, case 379: *State of New Mexico v. Teodoro Martinez* (1914); Criminal Docket no. 2, case 150: *Territory of New Mexico v. Prudencio Trujillo* (1904).

58   Criminal Docket no. 1, case 177: *Territory of New Mexico v. Joseph Palen* (1902).

59   Criminal Docket no. 1, case 299: *Territory of New Mexico v. Donaciano Aguilar* (1909); Criminal Docket no. 2, case 516: *State of New Mexico v. Edumenio Maestas* (1924). Our conclusions about the institutional bias of the legal system against Nuevomexicano defendants are commensurate with a broader territorial study by Donna Crail-Rugotzke, "A Matter of Guilt: The Treatment of Hispanic Inmates by New Mexico Courts and the New Mexico Territorial Prison, 1890–1912," *New Mexico Historical Review* 74 (1999): 295–314.

60   F. Arturo Rosales, *¡Pobre Raza! Violence, Justice, and Mobilization among México Lindo Immigrants, 1900–1936* (Austin: University of Texas Press, 1999), 141. Robert Tórrez notes that Spanish speakers were not executed in disproportionate numbers during the territorial period. He does note, however, that Mexican nationals were more likely to be put to death than Anglos or Spanish-speaking citizens of the United States in this period. Robert Tórrez to William D. Carrigan and Clive Webb, December 31, 2002, correspondence in possession of authors.

61   *Alamogordo News*, November 22, 1928; *Farmington Times Hustler*, November 16, 1923; November 23, 1928.

62   *Santa Fe New Mexican*, November 27, 1928.

63   "Lynchings: By Year and Race," http://www.law.umkc.edu/faculty/projects/ftrials/shipp/lynchingyear.html.

64   Philip Dray, *At the Hands of Persons Unknown: The Lynching of Black America* (New York: Random House, 2002), 235, 254, 256–57, 258.

65   W. Fitzhugh Brundage, *Lynching in the New South: Georgia and Virginia*, 1880–1930 (Urbana: University of Illinois Press, 1993), 248–49, 251. See also Robert L. Zangrando, *The NAACP Crusade against Lynching*, 1909–1950 (Philadelphia: Temple University Press, 1980).

66   Newspapers outside of New Mexico that reported the lynching included the *Montgomery Advertiser*, November 17, 1928; *New York Evening Post*, November 17, 1928; *Atlanta Constitution*, November 18, 1928; and *Norfolk Journal and Guide*, November 24, 1928.

67   *New Mexico State Tribune*, quoted in *Farmington Times Hustler*, November 30, 1928.

68   U.S. House of Representatives, document no. 237, 55th Cong., 2nd sess. (3679), 1–3; U.S. Senate, report no. 1832, 56th Cong., 2nd sess. (4064), 28–30.

69   *Des Moines Capital*, September 14, 1919; *Delaware Herald*, September 15, 1919; *New York Call*, September 15, 1919; *New York Sun*, September 15, 1919.

70   *New York Times*, September 16, 1919; *Denver Post*, September 20, 1919.

71   *Houston Post*, September 18, 1919. An editorial in the *New York Globe* of September 16, 1919, also noted the apparent hypocrisy of U.S. diplomatic protests: "When two Americans are killed in Mexico, even though it be in a section of the country remote from any city and notoriously infested with bandits, a roar for intervention goes up throughout this country. When two Mexicans are killed in a civilized American city by a mob it is regrettable, to be sure; but, after all, they look somewhat like Negroes, and everyone knows what we do with the latter."

72   *El Heraldo de Mexico* (Los Angeles), November 17 and 18, 1922.

73   Undated newspaper clipping, January 10, 1927, Oliver Douglas Weeks Collection, Rare Books and Manuscript Unit, Nettie Lee Benson Latin American Collection, University of Texas at Austin; undated newspaper clippings, George Coalson Collection, South Texas Archives, Texas A&M, Kingsville; *Houston Chronicle*, January 11–13, 1927; *La Prensa*, January 26, 1927; *El Cronista del Valle* (Brownsville, TX), September 9–11, 15, and 18, 1926; January 16, 22, and 27, 1927.

74   *Santa Fe New Mexican*, November 22, 1928; *Roswell Morning Dispatch*, November 16, 1928.

75   *Farmington Times Hustler*, November 23, 1928.

1. What can Benavides's physicians remarks reveal about their stance on the lynching?

2. How did Mexican mob violence change after the Benavides lynching?

3. What contribution did Anglo-American settlers make to the tradition of mob violence that already existed among Spanish speakers in the American West?

4. How did access to political power for Mexican Americans in New Mexico differ from the rest of the southwestern states? Why was this the case?

5. How did the pattern of mob violence in New Mexico differ from the rest of the southern states?

6. How and why was Benavides's lynching a turning point in mob violence history?

7. What change(s) contributed to the transformation of attitudes toward lynching in New Mexico?

Chapter 4

Immigration
The Bracero Program

Editor's Introduction

The topic of chapter 4 is immigration and the Bracero Program. The Bracero Program was established by the United States and Mexico in 1942 in an effort to fulfill a labor shortage that existed due to American men going off to fight in World War II. It was Mexico's way of showing their support for the Allied Powers. Mexico would export workers, marketed as "Soldiers of Peace," to the United States for short-term renewable contracts. The laborers were called *braceros*, after the name of the program itself, and referred to the Mexican manual laborers who came to work in the United States. On the one hand, the program offered access to economic resources unavailable to most rural Mexicans. On the other hand, some saw Mexico's pro-emigration policy as an affront to national dignity and a glaring reminder of Mexico's dependence on the United States.

Oral testimonies of braceros illustrate this mixed message as well. While some felt ashamed of their reliance on the United States and detested their experiences, others strongly defended the program, arguing that the hardships they faced did not outweigh the benefits that seasonal migration offered: significantly higher pay, decent treatment, and the opportunity to improve their families' lives upon return. To hear directly from braceros, I encourage readers to explore the Bracero Oral History Archive—a project of the Roy Rosenzweig Center for History and New Media, George Mason University, the Smithsonian National Museum of American History, Brown University, and The Institute of Oral History at the University of Texas at El Paso. There are hundreds of interviews available for listening in English and Spanish. It is important to remember the voices of the braceros themselves when studying this subject matter. The second reading in this chapter draws upon the negative experience of one bracero and its impact on his ancestors.

The readings in this chapter have been grouped together because they provide extremely varied perspectives on the Bracero Program. While one focuses on US imperialism and the political nature of the program, the other focuses on the human aspect of the program. Together they provide the reader with a broader understanding of what the program was, why it was successful, and how people were impacted both directly and indirectly by the bracero program.

The first reading, by Gilbert Gonzalez, is the introduction from a monograph entitled *Guest Workers or Colonized Labor?: Mexican Labor Migration to the United States*. It analyzes immigration, particularly the Bracero Program, through an imperialist lens. Gonzalez argues against perspectives that make it seem as though the United States and Mexico were on equal playing fields when negotiating the terms of the Bracero Program and other foreign policies.

This reading was chosen because it provides a unique perspective on a well-researched topic in Mexican American history. While there are many readings on the Bracero Program, few—if any—take such a firm imperialist stance. This reading provides both historical context on North American colonialism and an introduction to the complex power dynamics between Mexico and the United States. The reading is helpful in understanding foreign relations between the United States and their southern neighbor. Moreover, Gonzalez has been a leading scholar in Chicanx and Latinx studies for much of the late 20th and early 21st centuries. He has authored numerous books and more recently completed work on a documentary entitled *Harvest of Loneliness: The Bracero Program* (2010), which won four major awards; was broadcast nationally via PBS stations' played in 17 festivals in Europe, Latin American, and the United States; and was screened in over 50 venues in its first year.

Gonzalez emphasizes three key themes: (1) the neocolonialist economic relationship between Mexico and the United States; (2) the organized ongoing migration of laborers through the Bracero Program; and (3) Mexican migration through the lens of Mexico's neocolonial status rather than its frequent comparison to European migration. Gonzalez wants readers to understand that comparisons to European migration as a one-size-fits-all model for explaining Mexican migration to the United States is both inaccurate and misleading. He argues that the neocolonial status of Mexico was—and is—"the precondition for migration to the United States and for the subsequent Mexican immigrant experiences within the United States."

The second reading, "The Bracero Program as a Permanent State of Emergency," by Ana Elizabeth Rosas, is a fascinating look at one family's transnational history through photographs and a discussion of the Bracero Program. While the reading looks beyond the Rosas family history, their story demonstrates that not all braceros viewed the United States as the land of opportunity. In Manuel Rosas's case, it was quite the opposite—his tenure in the United States proved to him that illusions of the American Dream were unfounded and one should not romanticize the opportunities awaiting foreigners in the United States.

This reading was selected because it illustrates the human side of the Bracero Program rather than just the policy side. It provides the reader with an inside look at a former bracero's point of view on the program and the United States. The way Manuel Rosas chose to raise his family was a direct result of his experience as a bracero. His parenting and subsequent career decisions were made with his time as a bracero in mind. It is important to note, however, that not all braceros would describe their experience in a negative light. This is one point of view out of hundreds of thousands—but one that is likely shared by others.

Rosas's aim is to show how the Bracero Program itself created a permanent state of emergency for people of Mexican descent in both Mexico and the United States. She emphasizes that neither the US nor Mexican government officials wanted to acknowledge this reality because it was not in their best interests. As a result, the rights and dignity of immigrant workers and their families were not protected.

Introduction to Guest Workers or Colonized Labor?

Mexican Labor Migration to the United States

Gilbert Gonzalez

A LONG-STANDING CONVENTION EMPLOYED BY AMERICAN ACADEMICS specializing in Mexican migration, as well as by legislators concerned with migration policy affecting Mexico, maintains that U.S.-Mexico relations are normal relations, an expression of reciprocity, interdependence, and equality. The convention further holds that a hundred years of Mexican migration comprise one more migrant stream coming to America to struggle for and experience the mythological "American Dream." However, this commonly held perspective of U.S.-Mexico relations has not always been borne by Americans, particularly large-scale investors and corporate heads, who in the late nineteenth century deemed Mexico a colonial prize to be exploited for its natural resources as well as for its cheap and easily accessed labor.

Well into the twentieth century a widespread imperial mindset regarding Mexico mirrored an ongoing economic expansionism, or what amounted to a neocolonial strategy to systematically exploit Mexico's resources and labor. That international relationship, which assumed a central place in U.S. State Department policy going back to the late nineteenth century, bears the imprints of imperialist domination. The major social consequences of this U.S. imperialist domination—the mass uprooting of people from the countryside and the migration of that labor to the heart of the U.S. economy—will be the subject of the chapters that follow.

U.S. Imperialism and Mexican Migration

The U.S. imperialist agenda and, specifically, the labor policies contained within that agenda provide the context for this study. The analysis covers the long-standing American tradition by large-scale enterprises of employing temporarily imported Mexican workers, known today as "guest workers." Particular attention is accorded here to the bracero contract labor agreements lasting from 1942 until 1964, designed and initiated by U.S. agribusiness interests and signed onto by the Mexican government. By examining the bracero program (with attention to the 1917–1921 labor importation program and the current H2-A "guest worker" program), we can better understand the historic antecedents for the currently discussed guest worker agreements proposed by President George W. Bush (as well as those of then–Democratic presidential candidate John Kerry) and thereby more effectively evaluate current guest worker proposals.

The vast majority of commentary on the Bracero Agreements analyzes the program as if it were unique, no more than an agreement between two sovereign nations; indeed, none comes to mind that defines the program as a labor policy fitting an imperialist scheme.[1] In this book, however, the bracero program is understood to comprise a series of state measures designed to organize Mexican migration—measures that, in the period under discussion, conformed to an imperialist schema. Ample evidence demonstrates conclusively that, in many respects, bracero labor utilization paralleled traditional forms of colonial labor exploitation such as that practiced by the British and French colonial regimes in India and Algeria, respectively. In each case, workers were transported across borders as *indentured labor;* in other words, they were systematically placed under employer control (as well as state control), segregated, and denied the rights to organize, to bargain for wages individually or collectively, to protest, and to freely change residence or employer. Moreover, little if any oversight enforced rights and privileges legally accorded to the laborers.

Over the course of the bracero program, nearly a half-million workers were imported to the United States to work in agriculture and during the war on railroads, for wages—and in housing and working conditions—considerably less than the depressingly low standard for the period. Braceros who demonstrated "rebellious" tendencies or poor work performance faced a quick departure to Mexico and were placed on a blacklist. In their colonies the British and French commonly applied these practices as well.

More important, the bracero program operated within the context of an economic relationship between Mexico, which is an underdeveloped nation, and the economically powerful United States. Three fundamental themes related to this relationship underscore the present study. First, the economic relations between Mexico and the United States since the late nineteenth century have exhibited the classic hallmarks of neocolonialism.[2] Beginning in the 1880s, large-scale U.S. enterprises under the control of men of the Robber Baron era—such as J. D. Rockefeller, Jay Gould, William Randolph Hearst, and David Guggenheim, among others—sought to control significant sectors of the Mexican economy and accomplished that goal well before the 1910 Mexican Revolution. In the postrevolutionary period, U.S. capital not only maintained its dominance in several critical areas of Mexico's economy, including oil, mining, and agriculture; it strengthened its position.[3] U.S. capitalist interests expressed their power in ways other than through direct investment by entering into Mexico's banking and financing institutions. In the mid-1930s, for example, the Mexican government under Lazaro Cardenas established Nacional Financiera, Mexico's central financing body, and U.S. banking institutions occupied the leading position, holding a one-third stake in the institution's capital assets in the mid-1940s. It is therefore understandable that future economic programs ostensibly aimed at Mexico's economic development would follow the path established by the first wave of American investors during the late nineteenth century.

Another example is the construction of main highways in the northwest in the 1940s (largely funded by U.S. banks), which followed the blueprint of the U.S.-built railroads that were laid out in a north-south pattern. Building the roads in this fashion facilitated the export of goods, particularly natural resources, to the United States—and only second-arily were these roads connected with Mexico's economic heartland (an objective of British and French railroads in their colonies). In the immediate postwar period no fewer than 350 foreign-owned companies, most of them American, took advantage of the propitious investment climate and set up shop in Mexico. During the 1950s the American economic presence predominated in a number of areas, as pointed out in a 1953 *Yale Review* article:

> Many of our big corporations, like General Motors, General Electric, Ford, International Harvester, and Du Pont, have branches in Mexico. Current American investments in Mexico, which compose about 70 percent of all foreign investments there, are concentrating in industry, rather than in oil and mining, as they once did.[4]

One could add many more names to this "who's who" of major American corporations, including Monsanto, Anaconda, B. F. Goodrich, Westinghouse, Sears, Anderson Clayton, and banks such as Pan American Trust, Chase Bank, National City Bank, J. P. Morgan and Company, Bank of America, and the Export Import Bank.[5] Gradually, Mexico became a debtor nation, drawn into programs allegedly designed to develop Mexico economically but ultimately leaving it under the sway of foreign banks and investors.

A second theme concerns the bracero program itself, which expressed one variation of what then amounted to a half-century of Mexican migration and of the migrants' integra-tion as labor within the heart of the U.S. economy. The bracero program was established at the behest of the United States, and under its oversight, the two nation states managed and organized an ongoing migration. Elsewhere it has been argued that the continuing migration that began in the first decade of the twentieth century comprises one social consequence of U.S. economic domination.[6] Rather than viewing Mexican migration as a classic sup-ply-and-demand "push-pull" affair (the conventional model) as well as newer versions of push-pull, which hold that migration is "self perpetuating" based on "social networks that sustain it," migration here is explained through acknowledging the critical impact effected by U.S. imperialism upon the demography and social organization of the Mexican nation.[7] Explaining migration in this fashion is virtually unheard of today, even though the vocal critic of the bracero program, Ernesto Galarza, understood as early as 1949 the transnational forces leading to Mexican migration. He explained that the Mexican migrant "is forced to seek better conditions north of the border by the slow but relentless pressure of United States agricultural, financial, and oil corporate interests on the entire economic and social evolution of the Mexican nation."[8] These migrations, generated by the economic expansion of the United States into Mexico, manifested first as internal migrations that eventually continued into the United States and ultimately led to the ongoing formation of the modern ethnic Mexican community.

Finally, convention has it that the roots of Mexican migration are much like those of the majority of other migrations coming to the United States, most often compared to European migration. The heated rejoinders to the publication of Samuel P. Huntington's "The Hispanic Challenge" are a good case in point.[9] Huntington deplores what he contends is an emerging cultural divide in the United States between bilingual Hispanics and English-speaking America, and in response a chorus of critics counter that Mexican immigrants are undergoing experiences having much in common with previous European immigrants. Rather than using the European migrations to the United States as a "one size fits all" model for explaining Mexican migration to the United States, the present study emphasizes the neocolonial status of Mexico as the precondition for migration to the United States and for the subsequent Mexican immigrant experiences within the United States.

In addition to describing the bracero program as an expression of U.S. economic domination over Mexico, this study analyzes the marked similarities between colonial forms of labor and the bracero system. For example, several students of the bracero program have pointed out parallels with Spanish colonial forms of labor.[10] However, a more important comparison is that between the Indian and Algerian labor migrations (during their colonial periods) and the Mexican bracero program. That is, whereas the Spanish system evokes similarities, the British and French colonial labor systems and Mexican migration in its varied forms exhibit well-defined parallels, thus implying that Mexican migration is a manifestation of colonial labor migration rather than an independently spurred migratory flow similar to European migrations.

Interestingly, parallels with Roman imperial labor allocation have also been found. In their defense of bracero usage, agricultural entrepreneurs presaged by several decades the current imperialistic neoconservative outlook.[11] Indeed, many years earlier, at a 1958 congressional hearing on migratory labor, advocates of the bracero program were queried regarding the need for braceros. Their response, offered in a moment of unusual candor, ironically reflected the colonial character of the bracero program: "The same thing was true even in the Roman Empire. When they reached a stage of civilization they had to reach out to other areas where there was a lesser standard of living to bring in those people to do the menial tasks."[12]

Agriculture and Seasonal Harvest Labor

The vast majority of braceros worked in agriculture in a setting that had been well established for several generations before their arrival, and the heaviest users of bracero labor were Texas and California. Agriculture had developed to become the region's principal economic sector and one dominated by large-scale enterprises. Early in Texas's and California's agricultural development, a system evolved for securing labor through contractors hired by growers or grower associations to recruit a specified labor force. These contractors hauled workers to the work site for the harvest and performed the service of foreman. Growers seldom paid workers directly; instead, the contractors determined each worker's earnings and paid wages accordingly. Rarely if ever did workers come face to face with an employer or their representatives, and once the task was finished the labor force dispersed. With the next harvest, the cycle repeated, although workers were sometimes distributed to new farms from day to day. The only consistent factor in the organization of labor, and the main avenue available for farm workers to seek work, was the contractor system.

Throughout the history of southwest agriculture, tradition and sheer appropriation of power allowed growers to dictate wages, working conditions, work schedules, and standards in grower-supplied housing. That power secured the lowest wages in any industry and guaranteed extreme forms of poverty. Working and living conditions were abysmal, and health problems among farm workers and their families were common. It was into this historic context that braceros labored; the abilities and work habits accorded to braceros, as well as their placement in agriculture as seasonal labor, had been firmly established by two generations of Mexican laborers who, by then, had dominated the labor supply. The arrival of the braceros did not alter this historic legacy; indeed, the treatment that harvest labor had been subjected to fell upon the braceros with even greater intensity. Within this setting, braceros represented one variation on the theme of Mexican migration that entered into key sectors of the southwestern economy and society beginning in the early 1900s.

Reviewing the Bracero Contract Labor Program

Over the past several years the Bush and Fox administrations have engaged in highly publicized discussions over establishing a new guest worker program. Officials from both nations have met on numerous occasions to hammer out an agreement that has yet to bear fruit. However, the Fox-Bush discussions do not represent the first attempt at creating an international agreement to import Mexican labor. By reviewing the bracero program we can begin to understand the proposed Bush guest worker agreements. An estimated 450,000 Mexican males worked in the United States as temporary laborers under this program from

1942 until 1964—an export of labor considered by some observers to be one of the largest mass movement of workers in history. Under the auspices of a binational agreement, men (and only men) were recruited, processed, and transported from dirt-poor farming villages in remote sections of Mexico and, to a lesser extent, from urban centers to work as cheap, controlled, reliable, experienced, and easily-disposed-of laborers.

During the war, braceros were employed mainly in agriculture but also as railroad maintenance workers. Upon the termination of the contract, which lasted from six weeks to eighteen months, the men were immediately returned to Mexico. The war's end did not signal the end of the program as agriculturalists lobbied successfully for annual extensions without recourse to allegations of "labor shortage." After a series of extensions, a new formal agreement was negotiated and Public Law 78 was signed in 1951. This legislation, which codified a temporary labor importation program exclusively for agriculture, continued with minor modifications until the bracero program ended in 1964.

Over the course of the bracero agreements, the United States served as a labor contractor, Mexico served as the labor recruiter, and both worked for the employers: large-scale agricultural interests. The bracero program provided a huge subsidy for agriculture by supplying ideal labor at taxpayers' expense. Braceros were readily available and disposable, effortlessly controlled and efficient, and, best of all, cheap. As if that was not enough, braceros lowered the wages of the nonbracero workforce and in some areas, such as the citrus industry, virtually eliminated the domestic labor force. Perhaps more important for agribusiness, the program provided a formidable obstacle to the formation of agricultural labor unions. Throughout the twenty-two-year span of the bracero program, no labor union ever seriously threatened agricultural interests.

Administered over the years by various Washington agencies and their regional affiliates, the program was publicly and loudly celebrated by administrators—particularly by the same agricultural corporations that grew to depend on seasonal imported labor. Proponents lost no opportunity to reiterate alleged benefits to Mexico, declaring that the program contributed to Mexico's economic development and that the men were returning with pockets overflowing with dollars, sporting not only new apparel but also the wisdom that comes with modern ideas. Over the life of the program, the bracero program was said to be of a piece with the Good Neighbor Policy, the Point Four Program, the Alliance for Progress, and even the Peace Corps. Bracero program advocates (like the proponents of globalization forty years later) contended that the program lifted all boats equally, although in relation to Mexico no evidence ever appeared to buttress such contentions.[13] However, those who chose to critique the program faced the combined opposition of growers and of federal and state authorities charged with managing the program. Two prominent examples illustrate the clear linkage of economics with political power. (1) Ernesto Galarza, in his opposition to the program, researched and authored a severely critical overview of the bracero program, *Strangers in Our Fields*, which prompted grower associations to lobby federal officials to prohibit its publication.[14] Fortunately for Galarza and opponents of the bracero program, the growers' efforts were unsuccessful. And (2) UC Berkeley researcher Henry Anderson lost his position at the university after California growers learned of his critical opinions regarding the bracero program.[15]

The Contemporary Migration Phase

With the end of the bracero program in 1964, the demand for Mexican labor in the United States continued and, contrary to some prognostications, mechanization failed to decrease the required labor in agriculture. Consequently, the flow of undocumented labor filled the places formerly held by braceros and by the end of the century comprised one-half of all agricultural labor in California. Subsequently, with the disastrous decline of the Mexican economy that began in the early 1980s and nose-dived after the implementation of the North American Free Trade Agreement (the archetypal expression of the neoliberal model), the flow of undocumented and documented labor reached epic proportions in the 1990s. During this period of unrelenting migration a chorus of voices in opposition to undocumented migration resulted in such programs as the Clinton administration's Operation Gatekeeper, California's Proposition 187, and Arizona's Proposition 200—the latter two intended to deny public-welfare benefits for the undocumented.[16] Nonetheless, the conditions driving migration worsened.

While undocumented laborers are blamed for causing drug trade, crime, and poor public education and accused of poaching welfare funds, the free investment policy that goes by the innocuous acronym NAFTA has resulted in the mass desertion of vast areas of rural Mexico and the placement of hundreds of thousands of people on the migratory trail, a migration that began in the early twentieth century. To this day, U.S. economic expansionism into the heart of the Mexican economy continues to tear Mexico's society apart. Farmers cannot compete with the "open door" to imports of U.S. corn, soy, beans, rice, beef, pork, chicken, and much more, which have come to dominate the Mexican marketplace since NAFTA lowered the bar to U.S. imports and, taking advantage of cheap labor, vastly increased the numbers of maquilas (foreign-owned manufacturing plants located mainly along the U.S.-Mexico border) to produce goods for consumption in the United States.[17] Today, Mexico has lost its ability to feed itself, a fundamental tenet of national sovereignty. Sociological studies have found that thousands of people—farmers and their families—leave the countryside annually and move to cities, many arriving at the border seeking poverty-guaranteeing jobs at maquila plants where women comprise nearly 70 percent of laborers.[18]

The countryside is being abandoned across Mexico. Between 1995 and 2000, 1 million people or more migrated from Mexico's central and southern sections to the northern border towns, which are growing at a record pace and where 80 percent of maquilas are located. In the 1990s, Tijuana, for example, increased its population by nearly 7 percent annually; 56 percent of the city's population were born elsewhere, many comprising a floating population intending to cross the border.[19] The maquila plants, which offer employment, are little more than export platforms disconnected from the rest of Mexico's economy and therefore have no "spin-off" effects; they are islands of U.S. production on Mexico's soil. If migrants cannot find a maquila job, they find a route across the increasingly dangerous border—with or without a *coyote* (smuggler). People displaced by the actions of U.S. imperial capital will seek work, legally or illegally, across the border regardless of guest worker agreements, Operation Gatekeeper, or Proposition 187. Not even the extreme dangers of border-crossing (several hundred migrants die each year) deter men and women who have no other options.

The bracero program is a strategy designed to transport indentured labor from an underdeveloped country to the most powerful nation in history and, as such, comprises a labor policy whose contemporary parallels can be found in colonial labor systems such as those implemented by the British in India and the French in Algiers. The same parallel can be drawn with respect to the currently proposed guest worker agreements between the United States and Mexico, a system of state-controlled migration of cheap labor that replicates the bracero program in its fundamental details. If we are to understand the various guest worker proposals put forward during and shortly before the 2004 presidential elections, we need go no further than a thorough analysis of the former "guest worker" agreement and the currently tendered proposals for such worker agreements.

Policies falling under the mantle of free trade have not borne the benefits promised; if anything, conditions in those countries undergoing neoliberal reforms, including the United States, have moved backward.[20] Poverty throughout the Third World has increased rather than decreased since the onset of free trade, and the distance between the First and Third Worlds is growing steadily. Mexico is an example of free trade that has lowered the standard of living for peasants, workers, and even the middle class, and official prescriptions to solve poverty seldom go beyond promoting "guest worker" emigration to the United States, remittances, and more free trade.[21] On the other hand, Mexico's farmers, students, workers, and teachers have taken actions against NAFTA in street demonstrations, even stopping shipments of U.S. goods that compete with small Mexican producers.[22] Such demonstrations against free-trade policies have taken place throughout Latin America—in Ecuador, Bolivia, Colombia, the Dominican Republic, Argentina, and Peru. A battle line is being drawn within nations and across continents. The people versus free trade and its varying identities—such as free markets, globalization, the Washington Consensus, and neoliberalism—has emerged as a key political battle of the twenty-first century.

Ernesto Galarza was the first to identify the actions of U.S. capital as the cause of conditions leading to continual migration from Mexico; but his suggestions for resolving the crises that spur migration need to be heard again. In particular, he argued that

> [u]ntil Mexico can offer a far larger degree of economic security to its people, thousands of them will seek relief by migrating over the border, legally or illegally. Thus it becomes of primary importance to determine whether the economic policy of the United States is fostering or hampering the chances for creating a Mexico able to employ, feed, house, clothe, and educate its workers on a rising standard of living. To ignore this basic premise is to overlook the roots of the problem.[23]

Galarza addressed this very issue when in the same essay he pointed to the actions of U.S. capital as a principal cause of Mexican migration. Unfortunately, his prescription for initiating a review of the actions of U.S. capital and its relation to the migration question has been long overlooked; yet the first step in understanding Mexican migration requires that we, too, address this issue. Galarza further contended that the bracero program was "a palliative, a national narcotic" that postponed the great need for a fundamental alteration of Mexico's political and economic institutions. Exported labor only concealed the fundamental economic problems facing the nation, which could be resolved through a revolutionary change that eliminated Mexico's "reactionary elements, who perpetuate the bracero program."[24] Thus two objectives were foremost in Galarza's mind for explaining Mexican migrations: first, that we identify the social consequences of U.S. economic expansionism, which in itself is the cause of migration; and, second, that we recognize the Mexican elites' collaboration with that economic domination by promoting migration.

This study explores the actions of U.S. capital in relation to migration—the bracero program, in particular—from a perspective in which the United States is acknowledged as a quintessential expression of imperialism. The imperialist character of U.S.-Mexico relations and its significance for explaining Mexican migration and, hence, Chicano history remain on the margins in academia and among liberal reformers. By examining the Bracero Agreements within a context of imperialist domination, we can engage more realistic explanations regarding the U.S.-Mexico relationship and its offspring—migration—and thereby establish valuable approaches to the more important aspects of Chicano history. Simultaneously, we can explain the political struggles now taking place domestically (the anti-WTO demonstrations in Seattle and Miami come to mind) and internationally (Cancun and Genoa) against the very policies that have led to migration. This study seeks to contribute to that objective.

Notes

1   See, for example, Erasmo Gamboa, *Mexican Labor and World War II: Braceros in the Pacific Northwest, 1942–1947,* Austin: University of Texas Press, 1990; and Barbara Driscoll, *The Tracks North: The Railroad Bracero Program of World War II,* Austin: University of Texas Press, 1999.

2   John Mason Hart, *Empire and Revolution: The Americans in Mexico Since the Civil War,* Berkeley: University of California, 2002; Robert Freeman Smith, *The U.S. and Revolutionary Nationalism in Mexico, 1916–1932,* Chicago: University of Chicago Press, 1972; and Gilbert G. Gonzalez and Raul Fernandez, *A Century of Chicano History: Empire, Nations and Migration,* New York: Routledge, 2004.

3   Smith, *The U.S. and Revolutionary Nationalism in Mexico,* p. 34.

4   David L. Graham, "The United States and Mexico: A Reluctant Merger," *Yale Review,* vol. 43 (December 1953): 238.

5   Hart, *Empire and Revolution,* pp. 414–415.

6   Gilbert G. Gonzalez and Raul Fernandez, "Empire and the Origins of Twentieth Century Migration from Mexico to the United States," *Pacific Historical Review,* vol. 71, no. 1 (2002).

7   On the "self perpetuating" model for explaining Mexican migration, see David Jacobson, *The Immigration Reader: America in Multidisciplinary Perspective,* Malden, Mass.: Blackwell Publishers, 1998, p. 11; Robert S. Leiken, "Enchilada Lite: A Post-9/11 Mexican Migration Agreement," Center for Immigration Studies, available online at http://www.cis.org/articles/2002/leiken.html; David M. Reimers, *Still the Open Door: The Third World Comes to America,* New York: Columbia University, 1985; and Douglas Massey et al., *Worlds in Motion: Understanding International Migration at the End of the Millennium,* Oxford: Clarendon Press, 1998. Massey and his cohorts write: "[T]he absence of well-functioning capital and credit markets creates strong pressures for international movement as a strategy of capital accumulation. The manifold links between various market failures and international migration are illustrated by the following examples" (p. 22); these include crop insurance markets, futures market, unemployment insurance, and retirement insurance. In short, the sending countries do not have what the receiving countries have, a gap that migrants seek to close by migrating. It all sounds very much like "push-pull" in new dress.

8   Ernesto Galarza, "Program for Action," *Common Ground,* vol. 10, no. 4 (Summer 1949): 31.

9   Samuel P. Huntington, "The Hispanic Challenge," *Foreign Affairs* (March-April 2004).

10   In particular, see Henry Anderson, *Harvest of Loneliness: An Inquiry into a Social Problem,* Berkeley: Citizens for Farm Labor, 1964, ch. 4; and Richard Hancock, *The Role of the Bracero in the Economic*

and Cultural Dynamics of Mexico, Stanford, Calif.: Stanford University Hispanic American Society, 1959.

11   See, for example, Greg Grandin, "The Right Quagmire: Searching History for an Imperial Alibi," *Harper's Magazine* (December 2004).

12   Ernesto Galarza, *Merchants of Labor: The Mexican Bracero Story* (Boston: Houghton Mifflin, 1964, p. 259.

13   See, for example, Verne A. Baker, "Braceros Farm for Mexico," *Americas*, vol. 5 (September 1953). The author writes: "At the start it may have seemed to Mexico that the U.S. employers were the principal beneficiaries of the international hiring plan, but now it turns out that Mexico is the long-term winner" (p. 4). And later: "So the agricultural improvements introduced by the workers who went north legally on contract may in the long run be a big factor in solving the problem of their unauthorized fellow migrants" (pp. 4–5). See also the following: J. L. Busey, "The Political Geography of Mexican Migration," *Colorado Quarterly*, vol. 2, no. 2 (Autumn 1953); D. S. McClellan and C. E. Woodhouse, "The Business Elite and Foreign Policy," *Western Political Quarterly*, vol. 13, no. 1 (March 1960); A. R. Issler, "'Good Neighbors' Lend a Hand," *Survey Graphic*, vol. 32 (October 1943); and Richard H. Hancock, *The Role of the Bracero in the Economic and Cultural Dynamics of Mexico: A Case Study of Chihuahua*, Stanford, Calif.: Stanford University Hispanic American Society, 1959.

14   Ernesto Galarza, *Strangers in Our Fields*, Washington, D.C.: Joint United States-Mexico Trade Union Committee, 1956.

15   In an interview conducted by Henry Anderson for his study, which was summarily terminated by the University of California (and discussed in Ch. 4), Anderson found that others beside himself were victimized for criticizing the bracero program. His interviewee stated: "A friend of mine back East had prepared a manuscript in which he was highly critical of the Department of Labor. His treatment was critical, but fair. He said a number of things that badly needed saying by someone. He submitted the manuscript to a publisher—one of the national magazines. Would you believe it? The editor sent the manuscript to the Department of Labor for evaluation! My friend has never been able to get the darn thing published." See Anderson, *Harvest of Loneliness*, p. 718.

16   Richard Marosi, "Arizona Stirs Up Immigration Stew," *Los Angeles Times*, November 6, 2004.

17   On the failed promises of NAFTA and its negative consequences for Mexico, see John J. Audley et al., *NAFTA's Promise and Reality: Lessons From Mexico for the Hemisphere*, New York: Carnegie Endowment for International Peace, 2004; Michael Pollan, "A Flood of U.S. Corn Rips at Mexico," *Los Angeles Times*, April 24, 2003; Hector Tobar, Sam Howe Verhovek, and Solomon Moore, "A Scourge Rooted in Subsidies," *Los Angeles Times*, September 22, 2003; and Victor Quintana, "The Mexican Rural Sector Can't Take It Anymore," in Gilbert G. Gonzalez et al., eds., *Labor Versus Empire: Race, Gender and Migration*, New York: Routledge, 2004.

18 See Alexandra Spiedoch, "NAFTA Through a Gender Lens: What 'Free Trade' Pacts Mean for Women," *Counterpunch* (December 30, 2004); Carlos Salas, "The Impact of NAFTA on Wages and Incomes in Mexico," in Economic Policy Institute, *Briefing Paper* (Washington, D.C., 2001); and Juan Gonzalez, *The Harvest of Empire: A History of Latinos in America,* New York: Viking Press, 2000, ch. 13.

19 San Diego State University Institute for Regional Studies of the Californias, Tijuana, Basic Information, available online at http://www-rohan.sdsu.edu/~irsc/tjreport/tj3.html(p. 1).

20 Paul Krugman, "The Death of Horatio Alger," *New York Times,* January 5, 2004; Aaron Bernstein, "Waking Up from the American Dream," *Business Week,* December 1, 2003; Jeff Faux, "NAFTA at Seven: Its Impact on Workers in All Three Nations," in Economic Policy Institute, *Briefing Paper* (Washington, D.C., 2001). Faux writes that maquila plants "in which wages, benefits, and workers rights are deliberately suppressed—are isolated from the rest of the Mexican economy. They do not contribute much to the development of Mexican industry or its internal markets, which was the premise upon which NAFTA was sold to the Mexican people" (p. 2).

21 Lisa J. Adams, "Fox Acknowledges Dire Poverty in Rural Mexico," *Orange County Register,* February 6, 2003; Solomon Moore, "Mexico's Border-Crossing Tips Anger Some in the U.S.," *Los Angeles Times,* January 4, 2004; Olga R. Rodriguez, "Mexico Failing to Slow Migrant Smuggling," *Orange County Register,* July 27, 2004; and Olga Rodriguez, "Book Called Aid to Illegal Entry," *Orange County Register,* January 6, 2005.

22 Susanna Hayward, "Thousands Protest Fox's Address," *Miami Herald,* September 2, 2004; Ginger Thompson, "Fox Vows to Pursue Genocide Charges," *New York Times,* September 1, 2004; Mark Stevenson, "Workers Protest Fox's Economic Policies," *Orange County Register,* September 1, 2004; Chris Kraul, "Mexico on Right Path, Fox Says," *Los Angeles Times,* September 2, 2004; and "Protesters Attack Fox's Car in Mexico City Border City," *New York Times,* October 22, 2004.

23 Galarza, "Program for Action," p. 35.

24 Quoted in Anderson, *Harvest of Loneliness,* p. 617.

The Bracero Program as a Permanent State of Emergency

Ana Elizabeth Rosas

T HE BRACERO PROGRAM WAS INITIALLY NAMED the Emergency Farm Labor Program, and it was announced as a measure to address a temporary state of emergency, namely US short-ages of agricultural crops and labor.[1] But in fact the program itself created a permanent state of emergency for people of Mexican descent in both Mexico and the United States. This chapter shows how neither the US nor the Mexican government officials entrusted to implement the program wanted to acknowledge this reality. It draws on assessments of the program by Mexican men, as well as a report by the US Department of Labor's Children's Bureau, to reveal emergency conditions that the US and Mexican governments neglected for their convenience and for the sake of promoting the US agricultural industry's need for a labor surplus.

Silencing Braceros

The US and Mexican governments were negligent in protecting the rights and dignity of immi-grant workers and their families. As labor activist Ernesto Galarza explained in his personal papers, the Bracero Program had been presented to recruits and to US and Mexican society as an honorable emergency wartime program, based on friendship between allied nations, that braceros should embrace in the spirit of transnational patriotism, even at their own and their families' expense.[2] As Galarza recalled the rhetoric of the US and Mexican governments, "On the present conditions of emergency, patriotism must be imposed with preference to any other consideration. America is in danger. Mexico is in danger. Therefore, no effort is too small and no risks should be disdained. The workers, the farmers, the professionals, the press, the industrial and commercial classes, all must gather around the glorious banner of friendship."[3]

Because of this indoctrination, braceros who met with exploitation and injustice that neither government attempted to remedy felt pressured to keep their true assessment of the program and its consequences to themselves. As a result, they felt deeply alienated and kept an unbear-able silence. They themselves took on responsibility for the program as the government did not. In Galarza's words, "Before they leave Mexico, they are told that they are 'soldiers of the soil' whose job it is to help produce the food needed to defeat the Axis, that idleness or bad behavior will not be condoned, and that they will receive no sympathy in Mexico if they are repatriated for misconduct. As long as this attitude continues, hemispheric solidarity is strengthened at the expense of the bracero."[4]

Nevertheless, some Mexican citizens were bold enough to speak out about the program and assess for themselves its repercussions for the families who participated in it. In 1942, Manuel Ricardo Rosas, the repatriate in San Martin de Hidalgo [...] told his family and friends that the US and Mexican governments had failed to recognize that the emotional turmoil of consecutive repatriation and now the beginnings of the Bracero Program had created a permanent state of emergency for families throughout the Mexican countryside.[5] From 1929 through 1939 these governments had refused to admit the burdens on Mexican children and women caused by the abrupt repatriation of an estimated three hundred thousand Mexican American and Mexican immigrant children, women, and men from the United States to Mexico. Now the governments were not acknowledging the emotional and material costs incurred by the new wave of recruitment of Mexican immigrant men who were leaving their families in Mexico to labor for one to nine months at a time in the United States.[6] In Rosas's estimation, the persistent lack of adequate protections or specific information concerning braceros' citizenship rights and destinations had the makings of a dangerously permanent state for children, women, and men that was exacerbated by these governments' reluctance to acknowledge or take responsibility for it.

Rosas and other former repatriates in San Martin de Hidalgo frankly assessed the effects of unceasing migration of desperate, emotionally exhausted, hardworking, ill-prepared, impoverished, and poorly treated undocumented Mexican immigrants of all ages to the United States and their failure to thrive on either side of the US-Mexico border.[7] Rosas in particular took a daringly transnational approach to raising his own family and alerting others about how best to face this often overlooked reality.

Parenting Toward an Informed Future

Rosas's emotional investment in protecting his children from the hardships of the permanent state of emergency in the Mexican countryside inspired him to instruct them not to idealize the United States. His own experience and continued exposure to the US and Mexican governments' racialized mistreatment of Mexican children, women, and men as inferior to whites informed his decision to instill in his children the habit of questioning migration to and labor in the United States as an avenue toward a promising future. Like Veneranda Torres, Rosas staged and used photographic family portraits to craft and share a transnational family history with his children that would discourage them from migrating to the United States for work and would instead encourage them to settle permanently in Mexico. His own family's documentation of their history in the form of personally meaningful family portraits had given him courage when before and during his labor in the United States he had been required to answer personal questions from government officials or employers, and when he had to cope with being repatriated to San Martin de Hidalgo with only the clothes on his back.

Manuel understood the resourcefulness of his own parents, Jose and Agapita Rosas (figure 4.2.1), in acting upon the anxiety they felt when he chose to labor for years in the United States. They urged him to view their family portraits before his 1925 departure as a way of instilling in him an unforgettable sense of himself and his relationship to his family. The spirit of these photographs revealed that whatever the outcome of his migration to the

FIGURE 4.2.1   Jose Manuel Rosas and Agapita Rodriguez de Rosas, 1925.

United States, he had the potential and the family support to thrive in Mexico. Reflecting upon his parents' way of being supportive, Manuel understood that they wanted to make sure that he did not underestimate the moral character, education, work ethic, and relationships at his disposal, should he need to recover and rebuild from the emotional toll of migration.

The portraits from his family history that helped Manuel most were those of his parents Jose and Agapita celebrating their marriage and of himself after completing his first year of college in Mexico City (figure 4.2.2), a portrait he used to process his application for legal authorization to labor in the steel industry of Chicago. While laboring thirteen-hour workdays in the snow-covered windy city, he was comforted by these images of his parents wearing elegant attire as they posed together and of himself wearing one of his favorite three-piece suits that he had been able to purchase after saving his wages from delivering merchandise throughout the Mexican countryside. So empowered, he did not doubt his emotional and physical ability to complete an arduous employment schedule for a poor wage of at most twenty cents an hour, or to give up on his larger goal of eventually earning and saving enough US wages to return to his family and thrive—ideally wearing the suit he had worn to take the self-portrait used to process his government-issued documents. He could fondly recollect his parents' refinement, moral character, and marriage and his own education, work ethic, and personal sacrifice to purchase and wear suits that had made his completion of demanding employment and school schedules before his departure to the United States worthwhile. This eased the emotional and physical burden of laboring under conditions that in 1932 resulted in severe injuries to his hands and his resulting repatriation to Mexico. Hardly anybody, least of all the Mexican and US governments, objected to employment conditions that overexposed Mexican immigrant workers to on-the-job injuries. It was more convenient to repatriate physically compromised men back to Mexico than to investigate and address their susceptibility to physical injury and other dangers while they were on the job in the United States.

FIGURE 4.2.2   Manuel Ricardo Rosas, 1929.

During his time in the United States, Rosas had to travel on foot, bicycle, and train. He helped construct and maintain railroads in inclement weather for poor wages. When he was injured, he recovered in a US hospital where medical personnel refused to provide him with adequate information concerning his hands' injury. He returned to San Martin de Hidalgo in a railroad boxcar without restrooms, seats, or windows alongside at least two hundred other repatriated children, women, and men. Yet these experiences did not demoralize him completely because he embraced the optimistic spirit that had made each of the moments featured in his family's portraits possible. Focusing on what he had been able to share with his family and on what he had achieved in his employment history and a year of a college education at a time when most Mexican immigrant men had barely completed an elementary education motivated Rosas to endure the emotional and physical suffering that labor in the United States entailed. The qualities that his parents had instilled in him informed Rosas's spirited resistance against being treated as a disposable, illiterate, and undesirable Mexican immigrant. Each of the portraits his family had shared with him fueled his determination to overcome such hardships and to dedicate himself to finding employment opportunities and relationships that would not make him unrecognizably foreign to himself and his family.

These photographs helped keep Rosas from idealizing or settling in the United States under terms that would make his relationships, education, and other types of experience in Mexico irrelevant. Denied desirable employment opportunities, transportation, housing, and relationships, Rosas found it difficult to excel in the United States as a man who had completed one year of college, had once wore tailored suits on special occasions, had assisted business owners in their management of their enterprises, and had benefited from the support of dedicated and ambitious parents. The toil and invisibility of physically demanding and poorly paid US railroad construction had not afforded him opportunities to capitalize on his command of the English language, his college education, or what his college professors and employers had indicated was his gift for communicating well with others in person and in writing. Fortunately, these were qualities that his family photographs made readily accessible to him wherever he found himself.

Throughout his seven-year stint in the United States, Rosas had at best been able to labor alongside fellow Mexican immigrant men who, like himself, were losing sight of their identity, talents, and potential. All his work in the United States had amounted to his being able to finance only the medical expenses he had incurred there. The alienating experience of living as a man of Mexican descent in the United States made Rosas feel that who he had become in the United States failed to resemble the person he was raised and wanted to be. His family photographs emboldened him to remember that his failed migration was not the entirety of his lived experience and should not continue to define his identity and goals. A humble lifestyle was not new or foreign to him. Laboring tirelessly alongside his parents to keep their grocery store and other shops thriving throughout his adolescence and until his migration to the United States had already exposed him to working long hours. Nonetheless, being reduced to a "dirty Mexican" as he labored, traveled, or ate a diner meal in the United States made his experiences of working and socializing with his family and friends under far more personally satisfying conditions seem distant and foreign.

The disjunction between the photographs his parents had given him and the alienation he experienced as a migrant worker highlighted for Rosas that the United States was not receptive to who he was and wanted to become as part of his larger vision of a fulfilling day-to-day life and promising future. This introspectively and defiantly honest assessment of what had proven most restorative to him as he transitioned out of his own failed migration to the United States and into a new life back in Mexico led him to organize photographs of his children into a transnational family history in an informed attempt at inspiring them to take heart in what they had been able to achieve together—without having to experience firsthand the alienation of struggling to migrate and labor in the United States.

A Transnational Family History

On his return, Rosas took on the lifelong project of crafting, collecting, sharing, and preserving a transnational history of the family for his children. Rather than overburden his wife,

Josefina Gomez Rosas, with additional work, he first financed family portrait sessions in professional photography studios and eventually took photographs of the children himself. He wanted to give his children images that would show them that, even in the most challenging moments, thriving in Mexico was possible and preferable to migrating to and laboring in a foreign land.

One of the most personally meaningful photographs framing Rosas's transnational family history showed his children posing together after the family had completed the renovation of their home in 1955 (figure 4.2.3). Thirteen years into the Bracero Program, he enlisted a professional photographer to take this picture of his three eldest children—Cesario, Juventina, and Manuel Rosas Gomez—at ages eight, five, and seven, respectively, posing in front of a photo studio's painted landscape modeled after their town's plaza. The image shows that the family had saved enough to pay for not only a professional portrait but household fixtures and to begin living under improved conditions that would include decorating their home's freshly painted living room walls with this photograph. At a time when most of their extended family and friends were pooling their earnings in support of relatives laboring under the Bracero Program, the photo provided the children with an enduring reminder of their parents' dedicated commitment to permanent settlement in Mexico.

FIGURE 4.2.3   Studio portrait of Cesario Rosas, Juventina Rosas, and Manuel Rosas Jr., 1955.

This photograph was the first photograph of them together, as well as the most difficult to pay for. Manuel was determined that it would feature his children wearing new overalls and dresses, shoes, and impeccably ironed shirts—all purchases that confirmed his ability to simultaneously provide for them and complete recent additions and fixtures to their family home without having to join the Bracero Program. Financing these expenditures with their mother's support was meant to convey to the children that sharing their day-to-day life, working alongside and for those who meant most to them, could help them resourcefully forge a personally fulfilling future without their having to cross the US-Mexico border. Commemorating how the children had helped their parents raise and sell livestock and make cheese and other dairy products, and how the family's combined labor had provided them with a home and with portraits that would become formative to the children's upbringing, was meant to instill in their children a desire to pursue a future together without the separations required by immigration. Not allowing the Mexican and US governments' promotion of the promise of US wages to obscure the potential of working with one's children by one's side, Rosas used this photograph to write a responsibly defiant transnational family history.

In July 1956, photographs of their daughters Juventina at age six and Abigail Rosas at age five in rooms where Manuel and Josefina had made difficult decisions concerning their family's future were used to provide these children with glimpses of their influence during challenging moments in their family's history. During the summer of 1957, Juventina insisted on being at Manuel's side as much as possible, especially when her father was hard at work writing letters for the wives and parents of braceros who had not returned. She had such a calming and helpful presence that he failed to recognize how difficult this work was for a six-year-old child to understand or experience. The pain endured by these families had to a varying degree seeped into every family household. It was unavoidable. Sharing this important work with his daughter at such a young and impressionable age became his way of guiding her through the pain of the family separation she had encountered when interacting with relatives and friends. Sharing with her yet another form of responding to the permanent state of emergency facing fellow families throughout the Mexican countryside was Manuel's way of preparing his daughter to respond to such pain responsibly.

Beyond providing Manuel with an extra envelope, a pen, a sheet of paper, or a glass of water as he wrote letters on behalf of women and men in search of answers from their bracero relatives, Juventina was instrumental to his not giving up on writing these letters altogether. He suspected that the US and Mexican governments could be intercepting these letters, for families often told him that despite their not having received any letters in response from their bracero relatives it was emotionally comforting to write them anyway. His daughter's presence reaffirmed for him the importance of dedicating hours to writing letters twice weekly on behalf of families requesting information or providing updates on the status of ongoing family affairs. He never charged a fee for this service, although his family could have financially benefited from that or from his laboring at their family store instead of writing these letters. Juventina's mature presence during what felt more like counseling sessions of sorts—as these women and men came to their home's indoor patio overwhelmed by sadness and doubt—influenced Manuel to dedicate himself to helping these families pose important questions or share helpful information with their absent bracero relatives. His daughter's constant and considerate presence made it difficult for him to ignore the most promising result of writing these letters: the likelihood that those who would benefit most from these letters were the children whose parents and other Mexican immigrants were separated from them on the other side of the border. Making an effort to reach out to bracero relatives could at some point materialize into response letters containing emotionally reassuring information.

The family's photograph of Juventina wearing one of her favorite dresses and posing in their household's indoor patio where she helped Manuel write these letters was meant to reflect the diversity of ways in which their family had come together. It marked as well their support of each other in efforts to assist other families weathering the permanent state of emergency that the Mexican and US governments continued to ignore, even years into the Bracero Program (figure 4.2.4). A candid portrait not staged or posed before her father's desk or in his company reinforced that from the time Juventina was very young her labor crossed borders and was valued by the family. Rosas similarly took and used photographs of his youngest daughter Abigail to make clear to his children that they had been raised to actively participate in their family's work and that this orientation toward family life had been foundational to their welfare.

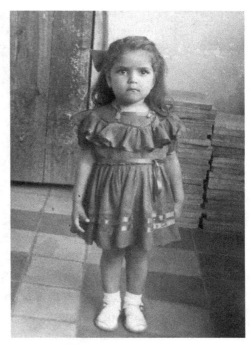

FIGURE 4.2.4 Juventina Rosas in the Rosas family's home patio, 1957.

Abigail's closeness with Manuel and Josefina made her family-supporting work easy to document. From the age of five, she had been interested in helping them with their organization of receipts and other accounting tasks that kept her at her parents' side as they drew up their weekly budget. Rather than discourage her or exclude her from this undertaking, they welcomed her initial efforts to organize into neat stacks their expense receipts, written requests for merchandise, and payment stubs for customers paying for their milk and cheese products as part of their installment plan.

Even though Abigail did not understand the specific details or issues framing Manuel and Josefina's discussions of their family's financial future, her willingness to carefully help them organize documents that were a part of this conversation, and eventually to learn how to maintain meticulous records of their expenditures and revenue, made her among the most reliable of their children. She would emerge as the most dedicated to ensuring that their business was being administered properly. At her extremely young age, her presence during these evening meetings also prevented them from arguing over their differences regarding maximizing their business revenue. Out of concern for her, they tried to avoid disagreements. This attitude often worked to Josefina's benefit. It left Manuel with no other choice than to discuss their family's business affairs with a receptive attitude toward her insights, concerns, and recommendations. Throughout the years, their daughter's continued participation in these conversations would prove an important example of the positive impact of sharing as much as possible with each other.

The photograph of Abigail before the chair in which she rested while Manuel and Josefina organized their family's finances, often well into the wee hours, records her influence on their careful management of delicate and important family investments (figure 4.2.5). Decisions made during these meetings had a strong bearing on the family's ability to finance living together in Mexico. Hence, taking this photograph of their daughter in a room that their children grew up in, and specifically the space where important family conversations occurred, signaled that, irrespective of their age, the children's proactive participation under their parents' supervision was valued. This photograph documents the children taking active interest in affairs that could foreshadow their interests as adults. Manuel's decision to use this photograph of Abigail to celebrate what he anticipated would mark her introduction to the demands of running a business was his way of classifying the children's every gesture toward being a part of this process as invaluable, as well as formative, to their own personal interests and goals. He intuited that their daughter had gravitated to them most when they were handling business receipts and discussing business-related issues because even at such a young age she was personally intrigued by the exchange and purposefulness of receipts and money, as well as the different people that money management would draw to their business. Without their having to encourage Abigail, her persistence at proactively participating in these meetings would only grow.

All this does not mean that Rosas took and displayed these photographs on the family's living room walls solely to instruct the children on the importance of

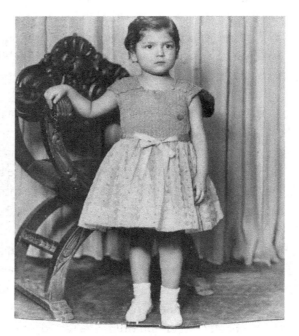

FIGURE 4.2.5   Studio portrait of Abigail Rosas, 1957.

defying repatriation, the Bracero Program, and the intensification of undocumented Mexican immigration to the United States. Rather, he used these and a series of other photographs that included those of their sons celebrating their completion of a hard day's work or sharing a good time together inside and outside their home to hold conversations with them that centered on their attitude toward their future. Throughout their transition into and out of the different stages of their lives and as women and men coming into their own, he used these photographs to portray their alternatives in Mexico and the United States as worthy of careful consideration, a defiantly responsible response to the continued underestimation and racialized mistreatment of people of Mexican descent in Mexico and the United States.

When the children were making decisions concerning their education, their employment, their romantic relationships, and especially their location of permanent settlement, Manuel would use these photographs to encourage them to reflect on the hardships and resilience behind each picture. The photographs reflected what a determined pursuit of their goals could make possible without migration to the United States. It was Manuel's way of at least stressing to his children that even in the most challenging of circumstances much could be and had been achieved in Mexico. Thus these photographs became an integral component of Manuel and Josefina's parenting.

By the summer of 1976, thirty-four years after the Bracero Program's inception, Manuel's transnational sensibilities toward raising his children became especially evident. His documentation and discussion of the transnational context framing their family's history, coupled with their own assessment of the alienation endured by family and friends laboring in the United States, motivated all but two of their eight children to permanently settle in either San Martin de Hidalgo or Guadalajara. Their informed consideration of the stakes involved in attempting to make a life in the United States, as well as their pursuit of college or trade school education, paved the way for a variety of careers: Cesario ran his own candy shop in San Martin de Hidalgo, Manuel Junior entered a series of businesses that combined the distribution and purchase of food products throughout Guadalajara, Miguel became involved in the production and distribution of textiles, Jesus thrived as a managing supervisor in the transportation of chemicals, Juventina dedicated herself to perfecting her skills as a seamstress and raising her family, and Abigail continued to excel as a savvy and enterprising businesswoman until she tragically died in a car accident at the age of thirty-eight (figure 4.2.6). Only Gerardo and Francisco opted to defy their father's counsel and, in some ways, their transnational family history: in search of their future, they migrated to San Antonio, Texas, and Los Angeles respectively.

His sons' decision to pursue their future in the United States was a source of great emotional pain for Manuel. Wary of losing them to the alienation of laboring in the United States, he would write them regularly to ensure that at least he knew the details of their whereabouts.

Although he reminded them to learn from the history of Mexican and US governments' border enforcement and immigration policies, Francisco found it too much information to deal with. His decision not to follow in his older siblings' footsteps by getting an education or working in San Martin de Hidalgo or Guadalajara led him to pursue what not only his father but most of his brothers and sisters, except for Abigail, dismissed as a reckless course of action.

Having little in the way of savings and only an elementary education, Francisco ignored most of the family's disapproval and counsel against going

FIGURE 4.2.6   Abigail Rosas and Josefina Rosas Gomez celebrating Abigail's graduation from her trade school program in accounting, 1972.

to the United States as an undocumented Mexican immigrant. Confident that in time he would earn sufficient US wages to determine whether he should settle in Mexico or the United States, and that in this way he would finally make a responsible decision, he set out for the United States anyway. In 1984, eight years after migrating to the United States, Francisco would take and use a photograph of his youngest daughter, Abigail Rosas, in his attempt to honor the lessons his father had worked so hard to instill in him as well as to assert his own defiantly responsible choice to seek his future in the United States (figure 4.2.7). He recognized the permanent state of emergency that his father had described and that he had experienced since childhood. As an adult and parent in the United States he used this photograph of his daughter, which had been years in the making, to communicate to his father that even in the United States he had not forgotten the value of continuing to document, share, and derive inner strength from their family's transnational history.

Francisco began to come into his own after laboring as an undocumented Mexican immigrant for a year. He had endured firsthand the pressure of working in a furniture company without even a three-minute break in a nine-hour work shift. He learned to take comfort in his earnings, which made it possible to support himself and a family of his own. In 1977, after returning briefly to San Martin de Hidalgo, Francisco married Dolores Graciela Rosas Medina and a year later reunited with her in Los Angeles. Afraid to risk giving birth to their first child while crossing the US-Mexico border, she had postponed her migration to the United States. Once together, Francisco and his wife worked for five consecutive years assembling furniture and sorting used clothing, as well as catering food for friends hosting family celebrations of baptisms, birthdays, weddings, and wedding anniversaries. Working long hours and pooling their earnings made it possible for them to save enough to purchase their first home in Guadalajara, Jalisco, Mexico, and to take and send a photograph of their daughter to Francisco's parents as a way of continuing Manuel's writing of their family's transnational history. The photograph recorded Francisco's transition into what he anticipated to be a promising future—in ways that met some of his father's expectations.

FIGURE 4.2.7   Abigail Rosas, Manuel Ricardo Rosas's grandaughter, 1984.

It was not a coincidence that Francisco took and shared a photograph of his daughter, Abigail, wearing a beautiful dress to celebrate her first birthday and posing in the living room of their apartment. In this space, he and his wife met with women and men to settle the details of their catering needs, as well as to set up play areas for Abigail. Manuel's example of taking and sharing photographs that documented his children's influence on him, in rooms where especially meaningful interactions had taken place, influenced Francisco's commemoration of this important transition and effectively shaped his own family's history. The living room's use both for negotiating the terms of their catering services and for interacting closely with their infant child made it the ideal space to take a photograph of her as they celebrated her birthday and their purchase of a home of their own in Mexico. Earning enough to raise a family as well as purchase a family home in which Francisco and his family would be able to settle should the alienation they experienced as undocumented Mexican immigrants in the United States become too unbearable or result in their deportation was meant to ease Manuel's anxiety concerning some aspects of Francisco's future. It was intended to resonate as a defiantly responsible reaction to the Mexican and US governments' management of immigration, as having this home in place allowed him and his wife to feel that unless they were deported they could choose for themselves whether to remain in the United States or return to Mexico. Thinking and acting to maximize what was accessible in both countries was Francisco's way of making amends toward his father and family of origin, while responding with his own family's welfare very much in his mind and heart.

The photograph of Francisco's daughter Abigail resembles the childhood portraits of his older sisters, Juventina and Abigail, in rooms where their parents had completed important tasks supporting families who faced the challenges of the permanent state of emergency that migration policies had created. The resemblance was meant to reflect that Francisco had indeed learned from and valued recording family history and had the transnational sensibilities of his father. This photograph brought Manuel to tears. He was relieved and overjoyed to learn that despite his anxiety concerning his son and his family's exposure to the alienation of life in the United States, his son had not idealized such day-to-day hardship but rather had responded to it as best he could, and with a sensibility tempered by his hard-earned experience and his own family's journey. Manuel respected Francisco's cautious approach to migration with the worst-case scenario in mind as a promising first step toward making other transitions as he forged his permanent settlement.

Despite the power of this photograph and its transnational transmission—it had enabled Francisco and Manuel, father and son separated by the US-Mexico border, to reconnect with each other on far more harmonious terms—Francisco was silent for many years about the Bracero Program and its enduring influence on him. This photograph may have made it easier for Manuel to accept his son's migration to the United States, but the issue remained painfully delicate. Francisco ultimately did not get to share much more time with his father. In 1985, the elder suffered a fatal stroke. Francisco never quite forgave himself that he had been away for years and had returned only for his father's funeral, with the result that he found it hard to discuss with his own children his decision to ultimately settle permanently in the United States.

I know this because Francisco Rosas is my father. It was his unwillingness throughout my childhood to answer why, unlike my friends, I could not visit my grandparents, aunts, or uncles on weekends or holidays that would later inform my historical investigation of the emotional depth and range of the transnational configuration of our family—most importantly, the enduring silence. The most my father brought himself to share with me was that if I wanted to understand why he had migrated to the United States but our extended family had not I would first need to learn more about and from my grandfather, whom my mother lovingly remembered and referred to as Don Manuel. My father's spirited efforts in support of my attempts to do so—through my visiting and listening to our extended family and, in Mexico, through his and my grandfather's documentation of our transnational family history—paved the way to my learning more about and from my grandfather through the stories behind each of the photographs my grandfather had carefully organized into stacks of photo albums.

When in the comfort of their family homes, in each other's company, or on their own, Manuel and other Mexicans of his generation dared to draw on their own immigrant experiences to identify the Bracero Program as the cause of a state of emergency for families of Mexican descent and varying legal status still recovering from the earlier dislocations of repatriation. Ultimately, that situation led to a permanent state of emergency for all families of Mexican descent. The program persuaded financially vulnerable Mexican families to endure separation in anticipation of receiving US wages, but those wages, earned under inhumane conditions, ended up being too low, in most cases, to allow the family ever to successfully reunite either in Mexico or in the United States. Manuel was among those who diagnosed and confronted the governmental neglect of enduring and ongoing family turmoil as a permanent state of emergency in large part born out of the governments' enforcement of the US-Mexico border. He leveraged this awareness to raise his own family in the Mexican countryside without idealizing the United States.

The Real Emergency

Historians have been reluctant to investigate the full implications of the Bracero Program for children, women, and men of Mexican descent.[8] Because the program followed on the heels of the massive repatriation of the 1930s, it extended the state of emergency that repatriation had begun, but historians have resisted seeing the program in this context. Instead, they have presented it solely as a wartime program intended to provide US agriculture with Mexican immigrant contract laborers to replace male and female citizens of Anglo, African, and Mexican descent who had left the fields to work in factories in US cities or to join the military.[9]

The crises unfolding simultaneously with the Bracero Program that have attracted the most attention from historians have been the indignities endured by *pachucas* and *pachucos,* the young Mexican American women and men who spoke a hybrid English-Spanish slang dialect, wore zoot suits, and tried to assert a personally meaningful style, forge friendships, and create a day-to-day social life and world.[10] In the Sleepy Lagoon incident, twenty-four Mexican American *pachuco* youths were arrested and charged with having beaten Jose Diaz to death, and despite insufficient evidence nine of them were convicted of murder (their convictions would later be reversed). They were mistreated while held in custody, denied due process during their legal proceedings, and inflammatorily portrayed in newspaper coverage. Hysteria over the murder led to a police roundup of six hundred zoot suiters, as well as the Zoot Suit Riots, in which servicemen and civilians attacked young Mexican American women and men while they were frequenting theaters, riding streetcars, and walking along the streets of downtown areas in Los Angeles and outlying neighborhoods.

Such injustices are important, but they reflect a more general reluctance on the part of the US government to protect its citizens because of their class, racial, and ethnic background and gender identities. The government neglected the state of emergency among people of Mexican descent while wholeheartedly serving the interest of agriculture, which it positioned as undergoing a real and consequential emergency. Similarly, historians have been hesitant to consider that around the same time as the Bracero Program inflicted hardship and separation on Mexican families, the internment of children, women, and men of Japanese descent in camps as a result of the December 7, 1941, bombing of Pearl Harbor similarly disrupted and tore apart Japanese American families within the United States. In a time of war, both were moves by the US government to assert and enforce its national security and its borders. The US government ignored the citizenship status of many Japanese American children, women, and men in order to address what it deemed a true emergency—containing this population's alleged threat to US national security.[11]

In the case of Mexicans and Mexican Americans, reports by the US Department of Labor's Children's Bureau show that the US government's pursuit of border enforcement measures often violated the rights of the very people it had been established to protect.[12] This agency documented for the US government a most urgent and real emergency, and its report asserted a transnational, humane perspective. But it could not compete with the American Farm Bureau Federation, the Vegetable Growers Association of America, the Amalgamated Sugar Company, the National Cotton Council, and other US agricultural interest groups that successfully persuaded the government to import a surplus of Mexican immigrant contract laborers to harvest much-needed crops as cheaply as possible.

The Migration of the Child Citizen

In April 1943, the Children's Bureau appealed to the US government to reconsider its continuation of the Bracero Program. The agency worried that the program, after being in place for eight consecutive months without any discussion of when it would end, had expanded to the point that the labor being imported was far greater than the wartime need. Although it did not describe the situation as a permanent state of emergency, it dared to point out that the implementation of the program hinged on the US and Mexican governments' separation of families of Mexican descent across the US-Mexico border at a time when the bureau was still struggling with the family dislocation caused by repatriation.[13]

In 1941, the problems attendant on repatriation had energized the agency to publish the first of a three-year series of reports, entitled *The Children's Bureau and Problems of the Spanish Speaking Minority Groups,* that extensively documented the US government's reluctance to consider the crisis already occurring—that of US citizen children as young as twelve years old crossing daily into the United States from Mexican border towns to labor in support of their parents in Mexico.[14] Because the bureau was entrusted with investigating and managing cases in which children were found laboring under unlawful conditions and terms in the United States, it identified and helped these children transition out of illegal work and into healthy family situations in the United States. Upon learning that US citizen children of recently repatriated Mexican immigrant parents were laboring as babysitters, maids, and shoeshine boys and girls in Mexico and the United States, this agency expressed its concern at the government's reluctance to acknowledge the situation as an emergency highly worthy of its attention and resources.

In the 1941 report the Children's Bureau had tried to appeal to the government by describing the lengths to which the most cooperative US elementary and middle schools throughout Arizona, California, Texas, and Nevada were going to accommodate US-born children aged five to sixteen, of recent repatriates into their schools. Noticing that they were without parents and at best accompanied by guardians who explained that their repatriated parents had not been able to finance these children's education in Mexico, the school administrators and teachers welcomed the students without requiring them or their guardians to submit the forms required for school enrollment. In Nogales, Arizona, school administrators' concern over "these children having drifted back to the United States, particularly older children, living from hand to mouth, and some having barely found sleeping space with friends or relatives and getting their living by fair and foul means—shining shoes, peddling, begging, and stealing," informed their decision to be as accommodating to these students as possible.[15] They deemed it the least they could do to keep the children from entering into lives of petty crime. The school administrators and the social workers heading the bureau had the disconcerting sense that the US government was not doing enough for these children as US citizens caught in a situation that their parents had not been able to protect them from. They argued that even under the best of circumstances these children still needed the US government to do more to care for them and their families.

Some US school administrators were, out of their own volition and concern for the welfare of these displaced children, doing their best to confront the ongoing consequences of repatriation. By identifying those administrators, the Children's Bureau report portrayed to the US government the accountability that those exposed to the plight of these students on a day-to-day basis had been moved to assume. The bureau devoted much of its report to describing the involvement of repatriated parents of Mexican descent in the lives of their children as posing a serious challenge to their handling of these children's cases. These parents were in such desperate emotional and financial straits that they would enter the country as undocumented immigrants to drop their children off in their child welfare department offices and ask that the staff look after their "American born 'orphan' children."[16] In Santa Cruz, Arizona, the greatest number of child welfare cases were US citizens who had been dropped off by their repatriated parents on the understanding that their being US citizens entitled them to social agencies' care. They feared that without any money or employment in Mexico they could not afford to be their parents for much longer. The feeble physical state of these children had moved social workers at these offices to accept custody of them as orphans so that they could pursue placing them in foster homes throughout the United States.

The bureau explicitly described what repatriated US citizen children had been doing in the United States, before being taken into its custody, to financially support their repatriated parents and siblings in Mexico. It used its report of repatriated children's activities to warn the US government that the new separations of the Bracero Program would similarly result in the migration of undocumented Mexican immigrant children from Mexico in search of their bracero fathers to the United States.

Repatriated twelve-year-old girl US citizens were reported as being taken into the bureau's custody after being found laboring as child caretakers, housemaids, and waitresses in the United States. Upon being interrogated in the processing of their case, these children admitted to laboring in order to send remittances to their repatriated parents and siblings in Mexico, and some had sought out the assistance of the bureau as a result of the exploitation endured at the hands of their US employers. One child, whose name was not provided, was described as laboring to support her nine-, six-, and five-year-old repatriated siblings in Mexico. Being the oldest child, and born in the United States, she was able to enter into the country to labor on their behalf. The department used these cases to emphasize for the US government the ongoing movement of US citizen children of Mexican descent, whose numbers, they feared, would increase if the program continued. New child laborers might migrate with the assistance of other children already doing so, then be exploited, and ultimately end up in the overburdened department's custody. The Children's Bureau tried its best to illustrate simultaneously that repatriated US child citizens were in desperate need of departmental services and that the department was unable to undertake more cases that might result from the US government's mismanagement of the border.

In anticipation of persuading the government to reconsider its pursuit of the Bracero Program's agricultural labor as the only emergency worthy of policy attention, the bureau report stressed that repatriated US child citizens were in emotional pain. It asserted that the US government had miscalculated in its implementation of repatriation and warned of the Bracero Program's impact on US citizen children and Mexican children, who would find themselves crossing paths with prospective braceros, undocumented Mexican immigrant men, and children who like themselves were journeying across the border in desperate search of US wages to support their families. It feared that their mutual and personal investment in providing for their families financially would lead more children to pick up bad habits from Mexican immigrant men and older children. According to the department's case records, US repatriation had resulted in a situation where US citizen children were "looking for things to take home" by stealing and committing other petty crimes for their families.[17]

Concluding its report with a thorough account of a case that had resulted in the death of a fourteen-year-old repatriated US citizen child in Nogales, Arizona, the bureau noted that the consequences of government enforcement of the border in the form of the Bracero Program could be fatal for the most vulnerable of populations. In this case, a repatriated father had asked his fourteen-year-old repatriated US citizen child to beg and "to work at anything he could find work in," resulting in the "child hauling garbage from a truck instead of going to school, jumping off the truck, the child falling under the wheels, and later dying as a result of his injuries."[18] Essentially, the US government had yet to develop a policy or program that could resolve or prevent the already dire and sometimes fatal consequences of repatriation and the Bracero Program.

In its efforts to acquire help in managing its caseload of repatriated US citizen children, the bureau requested that the government approve its efforts to locate these children in Mexico. This way, their repatriated parents could be afforded the choice of requesting their assistance in the raising of their children. The bureau guessed that these parents would prefer for their children to benefit from a stable family's care and an education in the United States rather than to starve, commit crimes, or migrate under dangerous conditions to and from the United States, even if this meant forfeiture of their parental rights. The bureau did not suggest reversing these parents' repatriation or allowing them to live with their children in the United States. Instead, it focused on what it considered best for the emotional and physical welfare of the children under its supervision. It did not advocate for any consideration of these children's parents and instead settled for urging the US government to do more to serve American children whose lives it had destabilized in unforeseen ways by repatriating their parents to Mexico—including going into the Mexican interior to find them and ensure that they had access to a childhood that did not center on laboring as an adult in Mexico or the United States.

The US government did not, however, approve of the bureau's expansion of its efforts to include locating and serving US citizen children of repatriated parents of Mexican descent in Mexico. The government also did not use the bureau's report when noting the potential drawbacks of continuing the Bracero Program. Instead, it carefully filed this report as part of its correspondence regarding the program with national departments under its administration. However, the report shows that at least one US department recognized the continuing emergency of destabilized and divided families that the US government had created and had neglected to address. The inadequate response to this report shows the US government's reluctance to hold itself accountable for the effects of its immigration measures and programs, even on its own citizens.

On November 13, 1948, the *Los Angeles Times* reported that thousands of braceros had been held in virtual slavery when working in the United States.[19] A group of them had been laboring for months without pay, hidden inside a packing plant and rarely afforded an opportunity to socialize with anyone but each other. They were locked inside barracks when asleep and restricted to their place of employment when awake. Such violation of their Bracero Program employment conditions had made them the subject of this news story, but nothing was done about it. Six years into the program, the US and Mexican governments' accountability for protecting children, women, and men continued to be, at best, dismal.

The US government was more concerned with shutting down El Escritorio Publico el Minutito ("The Quick Minute" Notary Public). Located in Mexicali, Baja California, Mexico, this notary public's office was derailing the US and Mexican governments' management of the Bracero Program. It dared to print and circulate flyers that offered prospective undocumented Mexican immigrants the "blanks for the necessary immigration documents, so that they obtain documentation needed to get an immigration visa even if the interested parties do not have in their possession a certificate of their Mexican military training or have been excluded from the United States before." This public notary office advertised that "no matter how difficult the immigration [situation] and red tape is, we can do it" and boasted that their fees were "fabulously low, $80 to $90 for each immigrant." It boldly advertised, "If you need any help to work, we can get it for you: mechanics, expert chauffeurs, specialized farm workers, servants, cooks, and any other kind of employee you may need. Some of them already have appointments to the consulate for their visa," which struck the US and Mexican governments as posing a challenge to their control over the routing of braceros and undocumented Mexican immigrants at their discretion.[20] These offers made the US government, with the assistance of the Mexican government, respond aggressively in prosecuting this notary office for knowingly violating US immigration laws.[21] Their response reveals that in the eyes of the government this affront, unlike the actual social emergencies occurring at the time, constituted an emergency warranting immediate prosecution.

It was this kind of awareness of the US and Mexican governments' penchant for neglecting the new and long-standing interconnected emergencies shaping Mexican immigrant family life in Mexico and the United States that made Desiderio Ahumada Medina decide against becoming a bracero.[22] Instead, he used his training as a police officer in Mexico City at the age of twenty-one and his business license in San Martin de Hidalgo to apply and obtain a Mexican tourist visa to travel throughout the United States (figure 4.2.8). He would travel throughout California, Arizona, and Texas, purchasing clothing items, sewing machines, and other household items to sell to the wives of braceros left behind in the Mexican countryside. His frank assessment that one should not rely on either the US or the Mexican government to protect one's citizenship rights or to provide one with opportunities or fair employment conditions motivated him to use whatever he had been able to achieve to establish the legal right to cross the US-Mexico border under terms that did not overexpose him or his family to labor exploitation and family dislocation in Mexico or the United States. He deemed it a most resourceful response to having witnessed the repatriation of his closest friends—among them, Manuel Rosas.

Desiderio and Manuel's conversations on the racialized mistreatment that characterized the experience of Mexican immigrants—bracero or nonbracero, documented or undocumented—emboldened them to respond resourcefully to what was in their estimation a most unfair permanent state of emergency. Desiderio would buy and sell household goods for five consecutive years until he was able to establish a thriving family business in the distribution and vending of grains and other animal food products used to raise livestock throughout San Martin de Hidalgo. Having

FIGURE 4.2.8   Desiderio Ahumada Medina's police academy graduation portrait, 1950.

exchanged with Manuel his thoughts on the risks of becoming invested in the United States, Desiderio had never taken seriously the idea of permanently settling in the United States. He did not trust that he could hold on to anything or that anything could be truly his in the United States.[23] Experience with the program would lead many other braceros to eventually come to the same conclusion.

Bibliography

Archives

Oviatt Library Special Collections and Archives, California State University, Northridge
Special Collections and University Archives, Stanford University

Oral Histories (Interviews by Author)

Arturo Buendia. March 2005, San Martin de Hidalgo, Jalisco, Mexico.

Gustavo Lopez. July 2005, Guadalajara, Jalisco, Mexico.

Dolores Rosas. 1996–2012, San Martin de Hidalgo, Jalisco, Mexico.

Newspapers

Los Angeles Times

Other Sources

Alamillo, Jose. *Making Lemonade Out of Lemons: Mexican American Labor and Leisure in a California Town, 1880–1960*. Urbana: University of Illinois Press, 2007.

Alanís Enciso, Fernando Saúl. *Que se queden allá: El gobierno de México y la repatriación de mexicanos en Estados Unidos (1934–1940)*. Tijuana: El Colegio de la Frontera Norte, 2007.

———. "Regreso a casa: La repatriación de Mexicanos en Estados Unidos durante de Gran Depresión, el caso de San Luis Potosí, 1929–1934." *Estudios de Historia Moderna y Contemporánea de México* 29 (2005): 119–48.

Alvarez, Luis. *The Power of the Zoot: Youth Culture and Resistance during World War II*. Berkeley: University of California Press, 2008.

Bacon, David. *Illegal People: How Globalization Creates Migration and Criminalizes Immigrants*. Boston: Beacon Press, 2008.

Balderrama, Francisco E., and Raymond Rodríguez. *Decade of Betrayal: Mexican Repatriation in the 1930s*. Albuquerque: University of New Mexico Press, 1995.

Cohen, Deborah. *Braceros*. Chapel Hill: University of North Carolina Press, 2009.

Fitzgerald, David. *A Nation of Emigrants: How Mexico Manages Its Migration*. Berkeley: University of California Press, 2009.

Galarza, Ernesto. *Merchants of Labor: The Mexican Bracero Story, an Account of the Managed Migration of Mexican Farm Workers in California, 1942–1960*. Charlotte, NC: McNally and Loftin, 1964.

Garcia, Juan Ramon. *Operation Wetback: The Mass Deportation of Mexican Undocumented Workers in 1954*. Westport, CT: Greenwood Press, 1980.

Garcia, Matt. *A World of Its Own: Race, Labor, and Citrus in the Making of Greater Los Angeles, 1900–1970*. Chapel Hill: University of North Carolina Press, 2003.

Gutierrez, David G. *Walls and Mirrors: Mexican Americans, Mexican Immigrants, and the Politics of Ethnicity*. Berkeley: University of California Press, 1995.

Lytle Hernandez, Kelly. *Migra! The History of the US Border Patrol*. Berkeley: University of California Press, 2010.

McWilliams, Carey. *Report on the Importation of Negro Labor to California*. Washington, DC: US Division of Immigration and Housing, 1942. Copy in box 1, Carey McWilliams Papers, University of California Special Collections.

Ngai, Mae M. *Impossible Subjects: Illegal Aliens and the Making of Modern America*. Princeton, NJ: Princeton University Press, 2004.

Pitti, Stephen. *The Devil in Silicon Valley: Northern California, Race, and Mexican Americans*. Princeton, NJ: Princeton University Press, 2003.

Ramirez, Catherine. *The Woman in the Zoot Suit: Gender, Nationalism, and Cultural Politics of Memory*. Durham, NC: Duke University Press, 2009.

Sanchez, George J. *Becoming Mexican American: Ethnicity, Culture, and Identity in Chicano Los Angeles, 1900–1945*. New York: Oxford University Press, 1993.

Spickard, Paul. *Almost All Aliens: Immigration, Race, and Colonialism in American History and Identity*. Oxford: Routledge Press, 2007.

US Department of Labor. Children's Bureau. *The Children's Bureau and Problems of the Spanish Speaking Minority Groups, Report Files, 1941*. Washington, DC: Government Printing Office, 1941. Copy in box 18, Ernesto Galarza Collection, Special Collections, Stanford University.

US Department of Labor. Children's Bureau. *The Children's Bureau and Problems of the Spanish Speaking Minority Groups, Report Files, 1943*. Washington, DC: Government Printing Office, 1943. Copy in box 18, Ernesto Galarza Collection, Special Collections, Stanford University.

Vargas, Zaragosa. *Labor Rights Are Civil Rights: Mexican American Workers in Twentieth-Century America*. Princeton, NJ: Princeton University Press, 2004.

Notes

1   Gutierrez, *Walls and Mirrors,* 134.

2   Ernesto Galarza, "Personal Writing of Ernesto Galarza," August 18, 1942, box 2, Testimony and Reports, Ernesto Galarza Collection, Special Collections, Stanford University.

3   Ibid.

4   Ibid.

5   Information about Manuel Ricardo Rosas's life and views was collected from oral life histories and archival documents provided by Francisco Rosas and Dolores Rosas in Guadalajara, Jalisco, Mexico, and Los Angeles, 1999–2008.

6   For more information on repatriation, refer to Alanís Enciso, *Que se queden allá* and "Regreso a casa"; Bacon, *Illegal People*; Balderrama and Rodríguez, *Decade of Betrayal*; Sanchez, *Becoming Mexican American*.

7   Arturo Buendia (oral life history, San Martin de Hidalgo, Jalisco, Mexico, 2005) and Gustavo Lopez (oral life history, Guadalajara, Jalisco, Mexico, 2005) were among the braceros who took part in these conversations.

8   I am thinking here of such works as Alamillo's *Making Lemonade,* Cohen's *Braceros,* Fitzgerald's *Nation of Emigrants,* Galarza's *Merchants of Labor,* J. García's *Operation Wetback,* M. Garcia's *World*

of Its Own, Gutierrez's *Walls and Mirrors*, Lytle Hernandez's *Migra!*, Ngai's *Impossible Subjects*, Pitti's *Devil in Silicon Valley*, and Var-gas's *Labor Rights*.

9   See, e.g., Spickard, *Almost All Aliens*, 304.

10   See Alvarez, *Power of the Zoot*; Ramirez, *Woman in the Zoot Suit*.

11   Spickard, *Almost All Aliens*, 317.

12   US Department of Labor, Children's Bureau, *Children's Bureau and Problems* [1941 and 1943]. See also McWilliams, *Report*, and a letter from Galarza to US consular officials at the US Consulate in Los Angeles, September 23, 1942, about the Children's Bureau's efforts and the emergency for children that they documented, in box 18, Ernesto Galarza Collection, Special Collections, Stanford University.

13   US Department of Labor, Children's Bureau, *Children's Bureau and Problems* [1943].

14   US Department of Labor, Children's Bureau, *Children's Bureau and Problems* [1941].

15   Ibid., 3.

16   Ibid., 5.

17   Ibid.

18   Ibid.

19   "Imported Laborers Held in Virtual Slavery," *Los Angeles Times*, November 13, 1948.

20   "El Escritorio Publico El Minutito Advertisement," Subseries G, box 10, Julian Nava Papers, Oviatt Library Special Collections and Archives, California State University, Northridge.

21   Ibid.

22   Information about Desiderio Ahumada Medina's life and photograph was obtained from an oral life history interview with his daughter, Dolores Rosas, in Los Angeles in 2008.

23   Their resourceful and responsible response to repatriation and the program earned Desiderio and Manuel a reputation as daringly thoughtful men with regard to their attitudes toward the United States. Hence, when I was conducting the research for this book, friends of Desiderio and Manuel welcomed my interviewing them for this historical investigation of their family experience. Desiderio is the father of my mother, Dolores Rosas, and, in turn, my grandfather. It was quite revealing to have all of the women and men I interviewed begin their oral life histories by expressing their profound respect for both of my grandfathers' frank and spirited assessments of what families needed and should do when facing the emergencies born out of repatriation and the Bracero Program. Actually, my mother and uncles were most invested in describing my grandfather, Desiderio, as a big dreamer and risk taker who believed that venturing to the United States should be a journey in which one would travel throughout the country to as many states as possible in search of experiences and business models that would make the wear and tear of being in the United States as a Mexican immigrant worthwhile. According to my uncles, my grandfather took pride in having defied the spirit of the US and Mexican governments' vision of the Bracero Program by visiting the United States under terms personally meaningful for their

family and him. His enterprising spirit had eventually enabled them to live and thrive together in the Mexican countryside on the proceeds of a family business. Nonetheless, when reflecting on his work history, they felt most proud of my grandfather for having trained and served as a police officer in Mexico's capital. That he had prioritized undertaking a personally meaningful goal early on in his life—one that had required leaving the Mexican countryside for the city—struck them as reflective of their father's responsibly adventurous approach to life as a Mexican man. Hence, an oil-painting replica of his police academy graduation portrait adorns the living room of each of his children's family homes. After his passing and upon my undertaking of this historical research, my uncles opted for my mother to keep the original portrait of this very special moment in our family's transnational history (see figure 4.2.8). They insisted that with my research I had earned our family the honor of having this cherished portrait as part of our family home in South Central Los Angeles. The spirit of this portrait and its meaning would keep us emotionally connected across the US-Mexico border.

1. Describe the contractor system that evolved early in Texas's and California's agricultural development. How did it work?

2. What did proponents of the Bracero Program argue were the benefits to Mexico?

3. Why are people abandoning the Mexican countryside in favor of cities and the northern border towns?

4. According to Gonzalez, who do the *maquilas* benefit? Why is this the case?

5. Do you agree with Gonzalez that the Bracero Program was a strategy designed to transport indentured labor from an underdeveloped country? Why or why not?

6. Why does Gonzalez argue that conditions in countries involved in free trade have moved backward? How has NAFTA impacted Third World countries?

7. How did Rosas use the photographs of his children to inform them about their potential in Mexico? How did he use the same photographs to sway them away from looking toward the United States for opportunities?

8. How did the Bracero Program impact U.S. citizen children of Mexican descent and Mexican children?

9. What did the report issued by the Children's Bureau demonstrate about the U.S. government?

10. What are the positive and negative aspects of the Bracero Program?

Chapter 5

Education

Editor's Introduction

This chapter focuses on the theme of Mexican American education. It particularly emphasizes Mexican American education in the early-to-mid 20th century, where the topics of education and segregation go hand in hand. In US history textbooks, segregation has often been synonymous with the African American experience and it is rarely acknowledged how it impacted other minority groups such as Asian Americans, American Indians, and Mexican Americans. Their experiences are distinct and each reveal a deeper understanding of race and ethnic relations in the United States. While the readings in this chapter do not dive into the specifics of all minorities, they provide the reader with a detailed look at Mexican American segregation and briefly discuss how Asian Americans and American Indians were impacted by segregationist laws. This illustrates the far-reaching effects of US segregation.

These readings have been grouped together because they build off of each other—the first reading by Gonzalez provides a sweeping overview of education and segregation and the second reading by Strum examines the groundbreaking *Mendez v. Westminster* court case. Gonzalez discusses the *Mendez* case briefly in his overview, but Strum's reading sheds light on the details of the case and the conditions that made its success possible. Both readings have similar goals of highlighting how the Mexican American story is an integral part of United States segregation history.

The first reading is a selection from Chicano scholar Gilbert G. Gonzalez's monograph, *Chicano Education in the Era of Segregation*. This reading provides an introductory overview of Chicano education in the 20th-century United States. The reader will learn about four different periods of Chicano education and how each period can be characterized. Gonzalez provides a thoughtful exploration of the roots of inequality in education and how it has evolved over time. This reading was selected because it is helpful in providing the reader with a broad historical overview of

Mexican American education. It also emphasizes the political economy—and not merely racial oppression like most texts—as the key factor in shaping the social relations between the dominant and minority communities. This allows the reader to understand a wider range of forces impacting the oppression and segregation of Mexican American students.

Since this reading serves as the introduction to Gonzalez's book, the aim is to set the historical foundation for oppression, segregation, and education for the remainder of the book. Thus, while this reading does not get into the crux of Gonzalez's argument for *Chicano Education in the Era of Segregation*, it is perfect for readers who need an overview of the Mexican American educational experience. The main thing Gonzalez wants the readers to understand two-fold: (1) segregation grew out of policy decisions corresponding to the economic interests of the Anglo community; and (2) the Mexican community never accepted segregation.

The second reading in this unit is entitled "Our Children Are Americans: *Mendez V. Westminster* and Mexican American Rights" and is written by scholar Philippa Strum. It is part of a larger collection in *The Pursuit of Racial and Ethnic Equality in American Public Schools: Mendez, Brown, and Beyond* by Kristi L. Bowman. This reading details the landmark case *Mendez v. Westminster* and illustrates how the case was a stepping-stone toward overturning *Plessy v. Ferguson*, the Supreme Court case that established the legality of "separate but equal" facilities.

This reading was selected because it dives into a court case that was arguably as impactful for Mexican Americans as *Brown v. Board of Education* was for African Americans, yet it has received minimal attention in classrooms across the country. The *Mendez* case, decided in 1947, was the first occasion on which a federal court declared that, in education, "separate but equal" was not equal at all. It was spearheaded by the Mendez family, along with four other Mexican American families, and changed the course of Mexican American education in the United States.

Strum's aim is to not only demonstrate the importance of the *Mendez* case but also to show how Mexican Americans were activists long before the Civil Rights Movement. They actively fought oppression and made significant strides with this monumental case and the ones that followed. Strum's goal is to give Mexican American activism its proper place in US history.

Introduction

Background to Segregation

Gilbert Gonzalez

THE AMERICAN PUBLIC SCHOOL SYSTEM HAS treated Mexican-Americans differently from other Americans; the consequences have contrasted markedly with the proposed objectives of dominant educational policies and practices. To understand the full nature of this contrast, we must first begin by acknowledging that historically, political domination and socioeconomic inequality have dictated the course of educational policy in America. As a result, we find that various factors and conditions external to the Chicano community have shaped the educational experience of that community. This appears evident in the Southwest, for example, where regional agricultural economies relied heavily upon migrant family labor and where the seasonal nature of this type of work affected the schooling process for members of the entire region and for Chicanos in particular. This does not mean, however, that regional factors dominated educational policy as applied to Chicanos. To be sure, that policy originated in national theoretical and practical constructions such as mass compulsory education, intelligence testing and tracking, curriculum differentiation, vocational education, Americanization, and segregation. In part, such international conditions as World War II and the cold war also influenced the development of this policy. This educational process has resulted in the inequality in educational achievement between Chicano and Anglo populations, and, as a result, it has impelled Chicano political action to overcome it.

The twentieth-century history of Chicano education may be divided into four periods. The first period, 1900–1950, represents the era of de jure segregation. Although there were no laws that mandated the practice of segregation, educators did invoke the state power granted to school administrations to adapt educational programs to the special needs of a linguistically and culturally distinct community. Thus, for example, as early as 1919, the superintendent of the Santa Ana, California, School District referred to a state attorney general's opinion upholding segregation as a legitimate educational policy for meeting the "special needs" of Mexican children. During the initial forty years of this period, educational policies for Chicanos involved the application of principles of biological determinism. Throughout the period, the Mexican community participated to a high degree in the agricultural economy, although many took up residence in cities and adapted to an urban industrial environment.

During the second period, 1950–65, the pattern of segregation remained, but without the deliberate official sanction of Mexican schools. For the most part, this period witnessed an educational policy that adhered to the culture concept: that is, Chicano culture was recognized as an impediment to Mexican-American adaptation to Anglo-American culture. In keeping with this perspective, educational programs tended to emphasize the acculturation of Chicanos to the dominant American culture, while at the same time Chicano laborers experienced an increasing shift away from agriculture and toward urban employment.

The third period, 1965–75, marked the militant and reformist era. Not surprisingly, education received much of the attention of the Chicano movement during this period, and the mass demonstration of discontent and demands for change forced substantial reforms of the schooling process. Programs such as bilingual and bicultural education, affirmative action, integration, curriculum reform, special admission to higher education, and financial aid, provided a substantially modified educational atmosphere. The reform phase, short-lived and quickly subverted by a conservative retrenchment, constitutes the fourth period beginning in 1975. Marked by a political conservatism emphasizing reliance upon traditional individualism and the marketplace and de-emphasizing and questioning the effectiveness of state-sponsored reforms, this period has witnessed at least a halt and, in some instances, a rollback of the reforms enacted during the previous period.[1]

A comprehensive study of the educational history of the Chicano community has yet to appear. I hope to provide the beginning of such a study in this book by examining the education of Mexicans in the Southwest during the era of de jure segregation covering the first half of the century. My intent includes an interpretation of the roots of inequality in education. The few texts examining the history of Chicano education somehow do not explain oppression. On the other hand, they are long on factual evidence. My analysis emphasizes the political economy (and not merely racial oppression as in most texts) as the key factor in shaping the social relations between the dominant and minority communities. Thus, I focus on an examination of that oppression by dissecting it and holding it up for analysis. In addition, I will look at one of the key efforts to overcome subordination in the 1947 case, *Mendez* v. *Westminster*, one of the major desegregation court cases in U.S. legal history.

The Chicano struggle to overcome segregation in schools has had a long history, and as Guadalupe San Miguel has recently shown, the League of United Latin American Citizens (LULAC) was at the forefront of that struggle. Because this organization remained limited to Texas until the 1940s, its efforts resulted in a number of court cases that unfortunately had no major effect on segregation until the 1960s and 1970s when the Chicano movement made its impact felt. A key consequence of the *Mendez* v. *Westminster* case was the inspiration it provided for a renewed campaign to terminate segregation, which resulted in more positive consequences than previous efforts. This study will focus upon *Mendez* v. *Westminster* as one example (and a major one, I might add) of a rather widespread movement in the Chicano community to overcome educational oppression.

Before proceeding, I must raise three points. First, the terms *Chicano* and *Mexican-American* had not yet become popular in the period under study; therefore, all persons of Mexican nationality or descent living in the United States are referred to as "Mexican." Second, I concentrate primarily on those areas of the Southwest that had a substantial Mexican population. I exclude the New Mexican Hispano population because these communities were isolated and historically distinct from those formed by Mexican immigrants of the twentieth century, and because the Hispano educational experience should be examined in light of the peculiar economic institutions shaping Hispano life. New Mexican villages are islands of traditional institutions and, during the de jure segregation period, stood outside of the educational developments taking place in the Southwest. Events since World War II have made it quite appropriate to include New Mexico in any analysis of southwestern Mexican communities today, but the immigration that has woven New Mexico into the Mexican Southwest was not a factor during the period under study. Third, I focus upon public education and exclude all religious and church-sponsored institutions of learning. In an effort to narrow my topic to manageable proportions and to identify the main currents in this historical period, I have concluded that an analysis of de jure segregation in public schools is comprehensive, logical, and significant.

Finally, in my research I utilize written documentation expressing those educational ideas predominate during the era under study. This does not negate the significance of classroom practice, however. This study will report upon that educational ideology that directed educational practice. There is sufficient reason to expect that the overwhelming pedagogical unanimity extant during the era of segregation would significantly impact upon classroom practice. Consequently, in the examples of classroom practice that I draw upon, the reader will readily note the unity between theory and practice.

An understanding of school segregation is contingent on an examination of two key factors that condition the educational process: the national political economy and the socioeconomic position of Mexicans within a class society.

Political Economy and Educational Reform

Ironically, during the first half of this century, as the United States rose as a world power and as an industrial giant, its domestic social policy often proved to be oppressive and antidemocratic, especially toward minorities. Others have argued elsewhere that its supporters designed this broad social policy so as to insure the necessary internal social and political conditions for the realization of domestic and foreign policy objectives. Historian James

Weinstein has concluded that Progressive "liberalism incorporated the concepts of social engineering and social efficiency that grew up alongside industrial engineering and efficiency."[2] Consequently, as Clarence Karier notes, a pervasive social engineering significantly affected the educational program of the United States, and as it did so, it maintained the existing socioeconomic and racial hierarchy in society. According to Karier, "The important theme which appears in the educational literature of the first three decades of the century was social efficiency and managed social order ... the schools were used to standardize the future citizen as interchangeable parts for an intricate production and consumption system."[3]

The educational programs of the turn of the century fit the social conditions created by the growing corporate economy.[4] The reforms accomplished in the first few decades reflected new economic forces and social conflicts. An increasing concentration of production within large-scale enterprises and an industrial working class emerging on a national scale, were key factors leading to the rise of labor unions and labor-capital conflicts that threatened the social order.[5] Progressive reformism represented essentially the political face of the economic evolution of U.S. capitalism. By and large, schooling programs throughout the nation assumed the task of creating among minorities, the political consciousness and productive skills necessary for stability and growth in the economy.

The first item on the Progressives' agenda consisted of a critique of prevailing social theory and the presentation of alternatives that corresponded to new realities. It forecasted that as society became more industrialized and capital more concentrated, an "organic society" must be created. The organic society, the central concern of Progressivism, was posited in various theoretical ways by a number of social scientists and social philosophers, including the preeminent John Dewey.[6] The second item on the reformers' agenda expressed the need to inculcate the Progressive ideology of political culture in the population especially in the working class. Many reformers were academics and became leaders in the fields of sociology, psychology, anthropology, and political science, helping to organize research and instruction to fit the social, political, and economic needs of the emerging social order.

The general aim of reform (and the task to which scholarly research was put) involved the realization of the conditions for an integrated, efficient, and stable social order without altering the basic economic institutions and the class structure linked to them. If all classes shared a political culture, democratic capitalism could be preserved from political instability. Influential reformers and adherents of organic theory including Dewey, William James, E. A. Ross, Teddy Roosevelt, Walter Lippmann, and Lewis Terman, considered many key traditional ideas and institutions to be out of touch with contemporary realities. They focused on competitive individualism, the labor theory of property and classes, and laissez-faire economics. These same reformers argued that in the absence of an effective socialization institution in the new urban industrial order, the state, through the local schools, had to intervene in the social process and guide its minions. The goal was stable, peaceful social relations based on the existing social division of labor. In the final analysis, schools became the key institution for socializing the individual to the emerging corporate industrial order. The movement to alter the ideological and institutional structures of society had a large-scale impact affecting policies nearly everywhere.

Progressive educational reforms operated on two levels. On the level of culture as shared information, Progressives aimed at inculcating a common culture that would bind together the various classes. On the level of the educational process, they sought effective training of the individual as a producer. The reforms instituted to these ends included testing, tracking, curriculum differentiation (i.e., vocational education vs. courses for the "gifted"), Americanization, and segregation. As they spread and took root, the mass migration from Mexico began its long historical course, and the immigrant community confronted not only the new large-scale economic enterprises, but also the reforms they had spawned.

The Socioeconomic Character of the Mexican Community

The economic integration of the Southwest into the national economy during the second half of the nineteenth century laid the foundations for its development in the twentieth. This process began as the capitalist political and economic system replaced the Mexican feudal system. The emergence of an incipient national democratic capitalism and the penetration of U.S. corporate enterprises into Mexico coincided with agricultural and extractive growth in the American Southwest. The increasing tempo of economic development in the agricultural economy of the Southwest—a labor intensive enterprise at the time—created a labor vacuum filled by a number of nationalities and native workers. Immigration from Mexico became a crucial factor in the economy of the Southwest in the early 1900s and has continued to be so. Between 1910 and 1930, 661,538 Mexicans legally crossed the border, and it has been estimated that during the 1920s, at least 3 percent of the population of Mexico emigrated to the United States. The vast majority of the immigrants included small families (husband, wife, and unmarried children) whose able-bodied members sold their labor to corporate farmers, mining, commerce and industry, and transportation for construction and maintenance jobs.[7]

The sharp rise in Mexican residents during this period far outstripped the increase in the white American population. In the five southwestern states, the Mexican community grew from some 159,000 in 1910, to 1,283,000 by 1930, while the total non-Mexican population grew from 8,605,000 to 13,397,000 during that same period. In terms of percentages, Mexicans comprised 4.2 percent of the population in these five states in 1910, and nearly 10 percent by 1930. In one generation Mexicans had become much more visible and, in a rapidly changing environment, much more identifiable.[8]

The flow of Mexican immigrants into rural and urban areas where their labor was in demand, created a strained and unequal relationship between the Mexican communities and the more privileged sectors of the society. Poverty, segregation, and employment in low-skilled occupations, characterized the experiences of the Mexican community during the era of school segregation. A 1928 study in California showed that 35.7 percent of the first- and second-generation Mexicans were primarily employed as agricultural laborers, most often in the form of migrant family labor; 31.4 percent were employed in manufacturing, 12.2 percent in transportation (other than railroad) and trade, and 10 percent on the railroads.[9]

Mexican workers replaced Greek, Italian, Japanese, and Korean workers on the Southwest railroads between 1909 and 1929. For example, in 1909 Greek workers numbering 7,653, comprised nearly 22 percent of the total work force on nine western railroads. By 1929 only one tenth as many Greeks (767) were employed by these same nine railroads. In 1909, 5,972 Mexicans were employed on the same lines, comprising 17.1 percent of the force. In 1929 Mexican workers numbered 22,824 and constituted 59.5 percent of that force. In the same two decades, the Italian percentage fell from 17 to 3.5 percent, whereas the combined Japanese and Korean percentage fell from 11.2 to 1.0 percent.[10]

According to one study of agricultural workers in the Southwest, three fourths of the fruit and vegetable workers and half of the cotton workers were Mexican in 1922.[11] Seven years later three quarters of the 400,000 migratory cotton workers in Texas were Mexican. Because of a longstanding reliance upon foreigners for cheap labor, the southwestern labor force was largely segmented according to nationality. Because of concentration of Mexican labor in particular industries and their relegation to a limited range of unskilled and semiskilled occupations, Mexican labor became synonymous with unskilled, cheap manual labor. Differentials in living and wage standards between the United States and Mexico allowed employers to lower wage levels for Mexican labor, taking advantage of the lower expectations and often desperate situation of the immigrant. According to Victor Clark, a "Mexican wage" existed in agriculture as early as 1908. West Texas farmers, for example, paid Mexican workers $1.00 to $1.25 daily and native Anglo labor $1.75 to $2.00. Twenty years later Paul S. Taylor found that Dimmit County farmers paid Mexican workers $1.50 to $2.00 daily, while American workers received $2.50.[12] Such differences in wage rates also appeared in mining, railroads, and industry.

The rapid rise in immigration and the concentration of immigrants about their places of work created a "belt" of Mexican settlement approximately 150 miles wide extending from San Francisco south along the Pacific Coast, then inland along the Mexican border through Arizona, New Mexico, and Texas to the Gulf of Mexico. The cotton growers of the Rio Grande Valley, the Imperial and San Joaquin Valley farmers of California, the Salt River Valley enterprises of Arizona, and the great citrus and truck ranches of southern California, actively recruited a large force of Mexican families to work the fields. Mexican immigration was, moreover, not restricted to rural areas. Large numbers settled in or near cities as early as 1920. Indeed, 51 percent of the Mexican population was urban by 1930 (compared with 56 percent for the total population). In Mexico only 31 percent of the population was urban in 1930.[13]

Contemporary studies have documented the extreme precariousness and poverty of life in the barrios in the twenties, thirties, and forties. Dirt streets, makeshift shacks, dirt floors, and single-room habitations for entire families were common conditions in the hundreds of barrios in both the rural and urban centers of America. A higher incidence of disease and mortality prevailed in these communities than in the dominant community. The urban and rural *colonias,* labeled "spik-towns" and "Little Mexicos" by outsiders, existed neatly tucked away, often across a natural division such as a river or gulley or across the railroad tracks. Of course, the dominant society found this useful mainly for locating a necessary force of workers, even though its members classified Mexicans as "problems," "misfits," "welfare burdens," "carriers of disease," and "social deviants."[14]

Another salient feature of the Mexican population was its youthfulness. In 1930 the median age for Mexicans was twenty, in contrast to a median for the rest of the population of twenty-six.[15] Large numbers of preschool and school-aged Mexican children posed administrative and teaching problems for public educators. Fifteen percent of the Mexican population was of preschool age and 35 percent of school age;[16] for the total U.S. population, the corresponding figures were 9.3 and 30 percent. Forty-eight percent of all Mexicans were of working age, as compared with 56 percent for the total population. As compulsory education extended to all residents, disproportional numbers of the poorest sector in the society found themselves forced into the educational enterprise.

Mexicans became integrated into a dynamic economic process that conditioned their lives as capitalization in railroads, mining, agriculture, and industry created the basis for the incorporation of Mexicans into the nation. Almost without exception they became part of the working class—albeit a limited labor sector within that class. The status of Mexicans within the larger economic class structure without question influenced the educational experience of the Mexican community. The education of Mexicans reflected two emphases: political socialization shaped by the dominant economic forces at play, and training for horizontal movement on the hierarchical socioeconomic scale. Thus, public education of the Mexican community via segregation, tended to reproduce its class character from one generation to the next.

Framework for Segregation

As early as 1892, Mexican children were being denied entrance into "American" schools in Corpus Christi (Texas). Taylor found that "practically coincident with the entry of Mexican children to the city schools, a separate school was provided for them."[17] By the late 1890s, enrollment in the Corpus Christi Mexican school stood at 110, and thirty years later the same school enrolled 1,320.

While Mexicans integrated into the economy and as their numbers increased, school boards established a de jure segregationist policy that was to last until midcentury. A typical scenario across the Southwest was recorded in the Ontario, California, Board of Education minutes for 11 April 1921. "Mr. Hill made the recommendation that the board select two new school sites; one in the southeastern part of the town for a Mexican school; the other near the Central School. ..."[18] His motion was seconded and passed unanimously. By 1920 most communities with sizable Mexican populations segregated Mexican children as a matter of course. In Texas, school districts often segregated Anglo, black, and Mexican children in a tripartite system.[19] Although Texas law mandated the segregation of only black children, Texas custom prevailed throughout as district officials assigned each black and Mexican minority to its own school. Thus, as the pattern of Mexican residential segregation into *colonias* developed, school segregation followed. Educational theory quickly assimilated the practice, and thus academics legitimized, strengthened, and otherwise assisted in the extension of the segregation of Mexican schoolchildren.

Rather than being shaped by local or regional pressures, as some scholars have suggested,[20] the education of Mexican children has always been an integral part of national educational theory and practice. Officials practiced segregation, for example, on a national scale in addition to widespread use of progressive educational techniques such as testing, tracking, curriculum differentiation, and Americanization. Moreover, U.S. foreign policy in the decade of the 1940s played a key role in an anti-segregation campaign orchestrated from Washington that affected social attitudes as well as the desegregation court decisions of the 1950s. The segregation of Mexican children attempted to extend an existing duality demarcating the colored minorities, including Mexicans from the Anglo communities. Thus, segregation reflected and recreated the social divisions within the larger society formed by residential segregation, labor and wage rate differentials, political inequality, socioeconomic disparities, and racial oppression. Public school segregation involved an extension of a prior condition to the socialization process—the psychological and socioeconomic reproduction of a social relationship dividing a dominant from a subordinate community. Education for the Mexican community therefore meant change as well as the preservation of their subordination. It brought the community into contact with new knowledge and skills, but at the same time prevented it from changing its economic and political relationship to the dominant society.

In the mid-1930s one study found that 85 percent of surveyed districts in the Southwest were segregated in one form or another, some through high school, others only through the fifth grade.[21] In some areas, such as in the south Rio Grande Valley of Texas, strict segregation existed through most of the grades. In others, as in some of the smaller districts of California, no such uniform pattern prevailed. Nevertheless, de jure segregation of Mexican children remained common throughout the Southwest until the late forties and early fifties when various court orders declared such segregation a violation of the Constitution's equal protection clause. According to educators favoring segregation, its general purpose was to "Americanize" the child in a controlled linguistic and cultural environment, and its specific purpose was to train Mexicans for occupations considered open to, and appropriate for, them.[22] Nevertheless, the "acculturated" Mexican child (one who had assumed the dominant society's language, dress, manners, and the like) experienced segregation as well. Although proponents justified segregation on grounds of language and culture, the essential factor involved the economic function of the Mexican community as cheap labor.[23] Popular as well as academic opinion held that Mexicans posed an "educational problem," a consequence of an alleged intellectual, social, economical, cultural, moral, and physical inferiority.[24] Whether U.S.-born or naturalized, many members of the dominant society commonly looked upon them as aliens or cultural outcasts whose principal function was to sell their productive human capacities, that is, their labor, in the lowest-paid occupations. Consequently, the American community perceived equal educational opportunities for Mexicans as a burden and of little value for the Mexican community. Segregation became, therefore, the ideal policy when legislators and other authorities enacted and enforced compulsory education laws. These laws created an inferior and separate education that reflected and reproduced the socioeconomic relations in the surrounding community and region.[25]

Inadequate resources, poor equipment, and unfit building construction made Mexican schools vastly inferior to Anglo schools. In addition, school districts generally paid teachers at Mexican schools less than teachers at Anglo schools, and many times a promotion for a teacher at a Mexican school meant moving to the Anglo school. Quite often, however, teachers in Mexican schools were either beginners or had been "banished" as incompetent. One investigator, a high school teacher in Sugarland, Texas, wrote that teachers placed in a Mexican school were resentful and that "most of the teachers in the Mexican schools hope to be transferred to the school for the other whites as soon as vacancies may occur."[26] They often realized their wishes because the frequent moving of teachers from Mexican to Anglo schools seems to have been the rule. Consequently, instruction was often left "in charge of teachers who are not specially prepared by training or experience for the particular work of teaching the Spanish-speaking pupils."[27] Pauline R. Kibbe noted that in 1943 in one six-room Mexican school in West Texas, which enrolled 357 pupils, the head teacher "changed three times," and that in several classes a new teacher arrived "every three weeks." One wonders what degree of Americanization could take place in such a setting. Officials in urban areas elaborated better-organized programs of segregation.

For the most part, instruction periods for Mexican schools in agricultural areas coincided with farm-labor demands. Thus, school officials shortened or modified semesters depending on the dominant agricultural products of the region in which the schools were located. Moreover, children of migrant farm workers usually had little or no access to public schooling.

If, however, Mexicans attended school, whether in a segregated school, in a specific Mexican room within a nonrestricted school, or in a mixed school, the transition from Spanish to English was expected to take place in the first and second grades. Consequently, in many school districts the bulk of the children enrolled in the first two grades, with a rapid decline in enrollment by the sixth and seventh. The policy requiring Mexican children to repeat the first and second grades, combined with the practice, in many districts, of modifying the academic year to allow for child labor, tended to retard school progress. In addition, the unwritten tradition of tracking Mexican children into vocational and slow learner classes became institutionalized almost everywhere. By their sixteenth birthdays, many Mexican children had barely reached junior high, and the dropout problem, which subsequently became notorious, began to manifest itself. Since the schools strongly advocated manual vocations, and since most Mexican families lived in poverty, many expected the majority of Mexican children to leave their segregated schools before high school in order to enter the labor force.

The legal justification for segregating Mexican children generally rested upon educational, not racial grounds. Meyer Weinberg notes that, in a 1930 unofficial opinion, California State Attorney General U. S. Webb declared segregation justifiable on the basis that Mexicans were Indians and therefore subject to the state law allowing their segregation.[28] Webb's interpretation strained credulity as well as the law. Of course, it did not apply to *all* Mexicans in fact, but law and facts do not always converge. A 1935 revision of the California education code attempted to close Webb's loophole by legalizing the segregation of "Indians" (excepting descendants of U.S. Indians, who, after 1924, were citizens of the United States). Certainly, one could have interpreted the revised code in such a way as to justify the segregation of Mexicans given that they descended from Indians.[29] However, it seems that the code seldom if ever applied to the segregation of the Mexican community. It made no direct mention, however, of the Mexicans even though this group comprised the most commonly segregated community in the state. Therefore, where segregation existed, it did so mainly on the basis of educational argument. In the research of Dr. George I. Sanchez—professor of education at the University of Texas, Austin—and Virgil E. Strickland on segregation in Texas, a survey of ten school districts found that the "language handicap is the official reason [to justify segregation] found in the school board minutes."[30] However, most arguments went beyond language; a San Bernardino, California, teacher stated that segregation was the outcome of the deliberations of the Anglo community and "based largely on the theory that the Mexican is a menace to the health and morals of the rest of the community."[31] These opinions attached "a stigma to [the Mexicans'] very being," prompting one investigator of the segregation of Mexican children to write that Americans take for granted that, among other things, "Mexicans are dirty, lawless, disease spreaders, stupid, and lazy."[32] Not surprisingly, given the strength of such public and official opinions, the practice of an official though illegal segregation eventually anchored educational policy with regard to the Mexican community.

Not all opinions justifying segregation demonstrated such a vicious attitude toward the Mexican community. A number of prominent researchers and academics viewed segregation as the preferred method of meeting the educational needs of the Mexican community. They often considered this practice an educational asset for the Mexican community. Yet even here, these shallow arguments masked the same prejudices that motivated the overt racists. The Arizona State Department of Education, for example, concluded that segregation "gives opportunity for the inauguration of a special program to meet the bilingual group interests."[33] A superintendent of a southern California district alleged that experience had demonstrated the pedagogically sound nature of segregation by showing "that Mexican children advance more rapidly when grouped by themselves," and therefore profited "most by the instruction offered in such classes."[34]

Although 10 percent of the students in one South Texas Mexican school were tracked into the educationally mentally retarded group, one of its teachers argued that "the Mexican child is not discriminated against," and that "in the majority of cases, the [class] room is the child's best home. ..."[35] In describing the impact on Mexican children, another teacher wrote of "a most impressive" change in them. "Their faces radiated joy, they had thrown off the repression that held them down when they were in the schools with the other children. ... There was no one to laugh at any peculiarity they might possess, and they were free."[36]

These two arguments justifying segregation often intertwined. For example, the superintendent of the Garden Grove, California, elementary school district stated on the witness stand in the *Mendez* v. *Westminster* desegregation case, that integration would make Mexican children "feel inferior because of their clothing they have to wear."[37] This same superintendent had also written on the education of Mexican children in which he justified segregation with an opposite approach.

Because of (1) social differences between the two races; (2) much higher percentage of contagious disease (among Mexican children); (3) much higher percentage of undesirable behavior characteristics; (4) much slower progress in school, and (5) much lower moral standards, it would seem best that ... Mexican children be segregated. ...[38]

Most districts that practiced segregation maintained a "Mexican" school, which admitted only Mexican children. Some districts, such as the Los Angeles City School District, segregated via districting boundaries (rather than a simple identification of nationality), because, according to one teacher, "One of the first demands from a community in which there is a large Mexican population is for a separate school."[39] In Los Angeles, the district did not refer to these separate institutions as "Mexican schools," as in many districts, but as "neighborhood schools" and sometimes as "foreign schools." One Los Angeles school administrator wrote that neighborhood (read "Mexican") schools existed as such "because the district gerrymandered schools [so] that they can be nothing but foreign schools and remain foreign schools."[40] The consequences of either policy were the same, although the Los Angeles system may have appeared to be a de facto system of segregation.

According to arguments raised by educators, one of the main aspects of the Mexican school was that it allowed a curriculum tailored to the needs of the student, thereby preparing him to transfer to an American elementary or junior high school. In the American school, educators expected Anglos and Americanized Mexicans to eventually compete in an integrated setting. Actually, that rarely happened. Mexicans seldom, if ever, Americanized to the extent that they no longer remained bilinguals. In fact, most retained their Mexican cultural heritage. Segregation seldom accomplished its objectives, then, and as Mexican children moved into integrated junior high, school officials tracked them into slow learner groups. This practice, wrote one teacher about a southern California school district, "appears to be a disadvantage to many of the Mexican boys and girls. With few exceptions these students are placed, as a result of the testing program, in the slower-moving classes. ..."[41]

However, since many, if not most, students began dropping out at this point, such integration usually affected only a minority. Thus, a different type of segregation followed Mexican children when they graduated from their Mexican school to what was, for all practical purposes, an Anglo school that opened its doors to Mexican enrollment. In the late twenties at one Los Angeles junior high, Mexican children comprised sixty out of eighty entering lower-track students; the percentage of Mexican children in lower tracks at four other schools varied from 33 to 55 percent.[42] By the midforties the situation remained as such, prompting the superintendent of the Los Angeles County schools to comment that when the Mexican child entered the junior high, "he again finds himself segregated" into ability groups, and consequently, a "vicious cycle" of segregation was unbroken even in an "integrated" setting.[43]

A most significant aspect of the segregated program was that it not only applied to the education of children; it also included the adults of the community, especially women. In fact, in most districts where the segregation of schoolchildren appeared, a segregated adult education program generally accompanied it. In one southern California district, educators offered language instruction for both men and women. However, for women, these courses addressed "the care of infants, cleanliness, house sanitation, and economical house management, including sewing, cooking, and thrift"; for men these programs offered "courses in thrift, in gardening, and ... principles of the American government."[44] Both adult and children's programs had similar objectives for substantially identical reasons, and through the same general method—the segregated school.

Segregated schools functioned not only as the center of the socialization of the Mexican child, but also as laboratories for research into the "Mexican educational problem." In the early 1920s, the California State Department of Education assigned Grace C. Stanley, formerly of the Los Angeles School District, to undertake and supervise "an experiment in the education of the foreign child." Ten schools were selected throughout southern California "as centers for experimentation, with the "Mexican school" in Cucamonga as the principal station for experimentation, and it was from this project that teaching "methods were recommended throughout the State,"[45] including schools with "foreign" populations other than Mexican. Many districts established special departments entrusted with the design of the curriculum for the education of Mexican children. In the Southwest, various names identified such departments: the Department of Immigrant Education, the Department of Americanization, or simply the Department of Mexican Education. In one district in southern California, the superintendent, Merton Hill (who was soon to become the director of admissions for the University of California), ordered the Department of Mexican Education "to make a scientific study of the Mexican ... the temperament of the race ... those qualities and abilities that are recognized as peculiar to the Mexican people. ..."[46] Furthermore, the "peculiar attitudes of these good-natured and kindly people" should be "developed along the best possible lines," and their "capacities to perform different types of service should be set forth [so] that their employers may utilize them to the best interests."[47] Such studies merely reinforced existing theories and practices subordinating the Mexican community in nearly every phase of their lives to the larger society.

Such schooling resulted in an education that recapitulated the migration of Mexicans to the United States as a supply of flexible and cheap labor. Thus, segregation grew out of policy decisions corresponding to the economic interests of the Anglo community; it became a means of domination and control, the antithesis of equality and freedom; and it was intrinsically racist both in that it was based on racial social theories, and in that it led to educational practices that reinforced a pattern of social inequality based on nationality and race.

Politics of Desegregation

The Mexican community never accepted segregation. Indeed, records for the twenties and thirties demonstrate the fact that community organizations and representations voiced their opposition and struggled against segregation.[48] However, the big wave of protest occurred during and shortly after the Second World War, about the same time that anti-Mexican hysteria was sweeping Los Angeles and other urban centers. Ironically, the Mexican community resorted to the legal system to gain its democratic rights despite the violent attacks against Mexicans, the sympathetic defense of these attacks by police and courts, and the historical bulwark in defense of segregation by the courts.

The most significant court case affecting the de jure segregation of Mexican children in the Southwest was the *Mendez* v. *Westminster* decision of 1947 in California. The 1930 *Lemon Grove* case, also in California, the nation's first successful desegregation court decision, had had only local repercussions, and the Salvatierra, Texas, case of the same year, which enunciated the doctrine that Mexicans could not be legally segregated (as were blacks) on the basis of race, had simply underscored the widespread opinion that the only basis for separate schooling for Mexicans was educational (language, culture, etc.) and, in any case, it was struck down by the Delgado, Texas, decision of 1947. The plaintiffs in the *Mendez* case could not have known that their struggle would lead to an historic legal decision reaching far beyond their small community. It was the first federal court decision and the first use of the Fourteenth Amendment to overturn the widespread segregation of a minority group. That social scientists came forward to offer "expert" testimony in a court trial added to the case's significance. The anthropologist Ralph Beals, for example, successfully argued that segregation retards rather than helps the assimilation process. Robert Carter, one of the frontline attorneys for the NAACP (National Association for the Advancement of Colored People), was impressed by the utilization of social science knowledge to criticize segregation. Carter suggested to his friend Thurgood Marshall that the "social science approach would be the only way to overturn segregation in the United States."[49] Later, attorneys for the NAACP employed with success this particular strategy in the 1954 Supreme Court decision, *Brown* v. *Board of Education*. Carter, who later became a district court judge in New York, also felt that the *amicus curiae* that he and Marshall filed in the appellate court in support of the district court's *Mendez* decision was a "dry run for the future." Indeed, the attorney for the Mendez plaintiffs, David Marcus, provided Marshall with all of the briefs and notes compiled during the case. It is probably true, therefore, that Mendez was the first stage in the process of overturning the *Plessy* v. *Ferguson* doctrine of "separate but equal."

The *Mendez* case can be ranked as one of the key legal cases in U.S. history. Thus, one contemporary legal analyst wrote that the *Mendez* decision "must be ranked among the vanguard of those making a frontal attack upon the equal but separate canon of interpretation of the equal protection clause."[50]

The immediate effects of the Mendez case in the Southwest were widespread, and Mexican parents and civil rights organizations such as the LULAC and the GI Forum in Arizona, Colorado, New Mexico, and Texas, entered the campaign against school segregation shortly thereafter. Eventually, de jure segregation in schools ended throughout the Southwest,[51] but not before an educational policy reinforcing socioeconomic inequality severely victimized generations of Mexican children.

Notes

1   Robert F. Drinan, "The Administration and Civil Rights: The First Thousand Days," *America*, 24 September 1983.

2   James Weinstein, *The Corporate Ideal in the Liberal State* (Boston: Beacon, 1968), xiv.

3   Clarence Karier, *Shaping the American Educational State, 1900 to the Present* (New York: Free Press, 1975), pp. 8, 9.

4   Gilbert G. Gonzalez, *Progressive Education: A Marxist Interpretation* (Minneapolis, Minn.: Marxist Educational Press, 1982). See also Meyer Weinberg, *A Chance to Learn: A History of Race and Education in the United States* (Cambridge: Cambridge University Press, 1979); and James Weinstein, *The Corporate Ideal in the Liberal State, 1900–1918* (Boston: Beacon, 1968).

5   See Gonzalez, *Progressive Education*. See also "Public Education and Its Function within the Chicano Communities, 1910–1930" (Ph.D. diss., University of California, Los Angeles, 1974).

6   See Karier, *Shaping the American Educational State*, p. 5. "A preponderance of evidence seems to indicate that the major social philosophy of many of the corporate and educational leaders (during the Progressive reform era) was largely pragmatic, reflecting a good deal of John Dewey's instrumentalism." See also Gonzalez, *Progressive Education*.

7   Leo Grebler, Joan W. Moore, and Ralph C. Guzman, *The Mexican American People* (New York: Free Press, 1970), p. 64.

8   Annie S. Reynolds, *The Education of Spanish-Speaking Children in Five Southwestern States*, United States Department of the Interior Office of Education Bulletin no. 11 (Washington, D.C.: U.S. Government Printing Office), p. 7.

9   Jose Hernandez Alvarez, "A Demographic Profile of the Mexican Immigration to the United States, 1910–1950," *Journal of Inter-American Studies* 8 (July 1966): 488.

10 "Increase of Mexican Labor in Certain Industries in the United States," *Monthly Labor Review* 37 (July 1933): 82.

11 Mario Barrera, *Race and Class in the Southwest* (Notre Dame, Ind.: University of Notre Dame Press, 1979), p. 77.

12   Ibid., p. 78.

13   Fuller Roden, "Occupation of the Mexican Born Population of Texas, New Mexico, and Arizona,"
      American Statistical Association Journal 23 (March 1928): 145.

14   Examples of racial stereotyping abound in the literature of the period. For example,

      Their conversation shows an apathy and a lack of expectation that anyone will understand
      them. They worship and imitate authority. A certain group loyalty exists but is not coherent. In
      fact, they desire nothing so much as to be let alone to indulge in a liberty that often becomes
      license after they take their first drink. ... The chief amusements of the young men are smoking,
      drinking and sex. ... The above is just a hint of the real problem of a Mexican town.

      Jay Newton Holliday, "A Study of Non-Attendance in Miguel Hidalgo School of Brawley,
      California" (Master's thesis, University of Southern California, 1935)

      Other works containing similar views are Merton E. Hill, *The Development of an Americanization
      Program* (Ontario, Calif.: Board of Trustees of the Chaffey Union High School and the Chaffey
      Junior College, 1928; Kimball Young, *Mental Differences in Certain Immigrant Groups,* University
      of Oregon Publication 1, no. 11 (1922); and Edward Everett Davis, *A Report on Illiteracy in Texas,*
      University of Texas Bulletin no. 2328 (July 1923).

15   T. Wilson Longmore and Homer L. Hitt, "A Demographic Analysis of First and Second Generation
      Mexican Population," *Southwestern Social Science Quarterly* 24 (September 1943): 145.

16   Ibid.

17   Paul S. Taylor, *An American-Mexican Frontier, Nueces County, Texas* (Chapel Hill: The University
      of North Carolina Press, 1934), p. 192.

18   As quoted in Mary M. Peters, "The Segregation of Mexican American Children in the Elementary
      Schools of California. Its Legal and Administrative Aspects" (Master's thesis, University of
      California, Los Angeles, 1948), p. 37.

19   Guadalupe San Miguel, Jr., "From a Dual to a Tri-Partite School System," *Integrated Education*
      17, nos. 5–6 (1980).

20   Studies that focus upon regional factors include Ward Leis, "The Status of Education for Mexican
      Children in Four Border States" (Master's thesis, University of Southern California, 1934),
      pp. 23–24; and Charles Wollenberg, *California Historical Quarterly* 53, no. 4 (1979); also, Thomas
      P. Carter and Roberto D. Segura, *Mexican Americans in the Schools: A Decade of Change* (New York:
      College Entrance Board, 1979); and Irving G. Hendrick, *The Education of Non-Whites in California,
      1849–1970* (San Francisco, Calif.: R & E Research Associates, Inc., 1977).

21   Gonzalez, "System of Public Education and its Function within the Chicano Communities,"
      (Ph.D. diss., University of California, Los Angeles, 1974).

22   See Hill, *Development of an Americanization Program;* also Helen Walker, "The Conflict of Cultures
      in First Generation Mexicans in Santa Ana, California" (Master's thesis, University of Southern
      California, 1928).

23   See Charles Wollenberg, "Mendez vs. Westminster: Race, Nationality and Segregation in California Schools"; also, Gonzalez, "Racism, Education and the Mexican Community in Los Angeles, 1920–1930," *Societas* 4, no. 1 (1974).

24   Charles Clifford Carpenter, "A Study of Segregation versus Non-Segregation of Mexican Children" (Master's thesis, University of Southern California, 1935), p. 152.

25   Gonzalez, "System of Public Education." Virgil E. Strickland and George Sanchez summarized a survey of ten school systems, and found, in part, that the "physical facilities, equipment and instructional materials in the schools for Spanish-name children were found to be generally inferior and inadequate as compared to those existing in the Anglo schools." As quoted in Strickland and Sanchez, "Spanish-Name Spells Discrimination," *The Nation's Schools* (January 1948): 23.

26   Katherine Hollier Meguire, "Educating the Mexican Child in the Elementary School" (Master's thesis, University of Southern California, 1938), p. 64.

27   Pauline R. Kibbe, *Latin Americans in Texas* (Albuquerque: University of New Mexico Press, 1946), pp. 98–99.

28   Meyer Weinberg, *A Chance to Learn. A History of Race and Education in the United States* (Cambridge: Cambridge University Press, 1977), p. 166.

29   California Education Code Sections 8003 and 8004 provided the basis for "separate schools for Indian children, excepting children who are wards of the United States Government and children of all other Indians who are descendants of the original American Indians of the United States, and for children of Chinese, Japanese or Mongolian parentage," and "when separate schools were established ... the Indian children or children of Chinese, Japanese or Mongolian parentage shall not be admitted to any other school." As quoted in Charles Wollenberg, "Mendez vs. Westminster." Ibid., p. 318.

30   Strickland and Sanchez, "Spanish-Name Spells Discrimination," p. 22.

31   Grace C. Stanley, "Special Schools for Mexicans," *The Survey* 45 (15 September 1920): 714.

32   Carpenter, "Segregation versus Non-Segregation," p. 1.

33   Arizona State Department of Education. *Course of Study for Elementary Schools of Arizona*, Bulletin no. 13 (1939), p. 26.

34   Hill, "Development of an Americanization Program," p. 107.

35   Gladine Bowers, "Mexican Education in East Donna," *Texas Outlook* 15, no. 3 (1931): 30.

36   Stanley, "Special Schools for Mexicans," p. 715.

37   "Defense Opens in Desegregation Case," *Fullerton Daily News*, 11 July 1945.

38   "Dismissal of Segregation Charges Denied," *Orange Daily News*, 11 July 1945.

39   Stanley, "Special Schools for Mexicans," p. 714.

40   Emma Raybold, "Brotherization," *Los Angeles School Journal* 8, no. 9 (2 November 1925): 19.

41   Marguerite W. Hill, "A Proposed Guidance Program for Mexican Youth in the Junior High School" (Master's thesis, Claremont College, 1945), p. 65.

42   Florence Gordon Mason, "A Case Study of Thirty Adolescent Mexican Girls and Their Social Conflicts and Adjustments Within the School" (Master's thesis, University of Southern California, 1929), p. 6; also, Laura Lucille Lyon, "Investigation of the Program for the Adjustment of Mexican Girls to the High Schools of the San Fernando Valley" (Master's thesis, University of Southern California, 1933), pp. 34–37.

43   C. C. Trillingham and Marie M. Hughes, "A Good Neighbor Policy for Los Angeles County," *California Journal of Secondary Education* 18, no. 6 (October 1943): 343.

44   Hill, "Development of an Americanization Program," p. 106.

45   State of California. *Thirty-First Biennial Report of the Superintendent of Public Instruction* (Sacramento: California State Printing Office, 1924), p. 52.

46   Ibid.

47   Ibid.

48   See Francisco Balderrama, *In Defense of La Raza: The Los Angeles Mexican Consulate and the Mexican Community, 1929 to 1936* (Tucson: University of Arizona Press, 1982), pp. 55–72.

49   Stan Oftelie, "Murder Trial Obscured 1946 O.C. Integration Landmark," *Santa Ana Register*, 22 August 1976.

50   Lester H. Phillips, "Segregation in Education: A California Case Study," *Phylon*, no. 4 (1949): 407.

51   Jorge C. Rangel and Carlos M. Alcala in "Project Report: De Jure Segregation of Chicanos in Texas Schools," *Harvard Civil Rights-Civil Liberties Review* 7 (March 1972): 315, and Oscar Uribe, in "The Impact of 25 Years of School Desegregation on Hispanic Students," *Agenda: A Journal of Hispanic Issues* 10, no. 5 (September-October 1980): 18, pointed out that de facto segregation in the Southwest remained widespread and today is on the increase.

Our Children Are Americans

Mendez v. Westminster and Mexican American Rights

Philippa Strum

GONZALO MÉNDEZ AND HIS WIFE FELÍCITAS Méndez were running a café in the small southern California city of Santa Ana when World War II began. The two had met as farm workers in nearby Westminster, in the heart of citrus-growing country. The café was thriving but Gonzalo had long dreamed of running a farm of his own. When the Munemitsus, the Japanese American owners of a farm in Westminster, were sent to a relocation camp and worried about what would happen to the farm during their absence, the Méndezes leased it until the Munemitsus could return. That is why the Méndezes moved back to Westminster, where in 1943 they tried to enroll their three children—Sylvia Méndez, Gonzalo Méndez Jr., and Jerome Méndez—in school.[1]

Their neighborhood school was Westminster Main, an imposing, well-equipped building surrounded by manicured trees and shrubs.[2] The children were turned away at the schoolhouse door when they were taken to register, however, and told they would have to go to Hoover, the small poorly equipped "Mexican" school a few blocks away.[3] Their last name was Mexican; their skin was dark; Westminster Main didn't want them.[4] Two years later the Méndezes would lead a group of Mexican American parents into federal court, challenging the segregation of their children, and legal history would be made. The case would become the first occasion on which a federal court declared that, in education, "separate but equal" was not equal at all.[5]

Mexican Americans and Segregated Education: The Context for the *Mendez* Case

Mexicans like Gonzalo Méndez had immigrated to the United States in large numbers during the first decades of the twentieth century.[6] Pushed out of Mexico by the political and economic turmoil of its revolution, they were attracted as well by the burgeoning agricultural industry in the Southwest.[7] Railroads had expanded into the American West in the decades after the end of the American Civil War. Simultaneously, advances in irrigation enabled western growers to produce large quantities of fruits and vegetables, which could

Philippa Strum, "Our Children Are Americans: *Mendez v. Westminster* and Mexican American Rights," *The Pursuit of Racial and Ethnic Equality in American Public Schools: Mendez, Brown, and Beyond*, ed. Kristi L. Bowman, pp. 9–30. Copyright © 2015 by Michigan State University Press. Reprinted with permission.

be transported in the newly invented refrigerator cars on the railroads that now criss-crossed the United States.[8] The result was a much-increased need for cheap labor among both the growers and the railroads.[9]

Official census figures indicated that 661,538 Mexicans entered the United States between 1910 and 1930. Scholars, however, estimate that more than one million came during those years, many of them illegally.[10] By the mid-1920s, Mexican workers constituted the bulk of farm laborers throughout the citrus groves of southern California, the area where the Méndezes would bring their case to court, and accounted for three-quarters of all California farmworkers.[11] By 1930 Mexicans picked more than 80% of the Southwest's crops.[12]

Many of the immigrants settled in poorer neighborhoods—*colonias*—next to citrus groves or vegetable fields, on the outskirts of cities such as Santa Ana, California.[13] Santa Ana is the county seat of Orange County, where the *Mendez* story takes place. They found themselves in neighborhoods that for the most part lacked sewers, gas for cooking and heating, paved streets, or sidewalks. Many families built their own two-room wooden houses. There was little furniture and no refrigerators; heat came from wood-burning kitchen stoves. Clothes were made on pedal-powered sewing machines and cleaned in washtubs. With dirt streets, a lack of flush toilets, and inadequate plumbing and heating, it was difficult to maintain good sanitation. Tuberculosis was a constant threat and affected the Mexican American community at a rate three to five times that of the Anglo community. A survey undertaken in the late 1920s found that the average Mexican couple had buried two children, and many had buried three or more. Wages earned in the citrus groves were substandard, far below the national average, and unemployment was common.[14]

The laborers' children were sent to "Mexican" schools. A nineteenth-century California law specifically gave school districts the authority to create separate schools for "Indian children, excepting children of Indians who are wards of the United States government and children of all other Indians who are descendants of the original American Indians of the United States, and for children of Chinese, Japanese or Mongolian parentage."[15] The law was enacted before the large-scale Mexican immigration and did not mention Mexicans, but local school authorities interpreted it as a state endorsement of segregated education and acted accordingly when the number of Mexican and Mexican American children increased. Once that happened, school boards began creating "Mexican" schools. By the mid-1920s, there were 15 such schools in Orange County, all but one located in the citrus-growing areas that would be involved in *Mendez v. Westminster*.[16] By 1927 Mexican and Mexican American children—64,427 of them—constituted nearly 10% of all children enrolled in California's public schools, and the 2,869 who were enrolled in Orange County made up 17% of that county's public school population.[17] According to one survey, by 1931 more than 80% of all California school districts with a significant number of Mexican (non-American citizen) and Mexican

American students were segregated, usually through the careful drawing of school-zone boundaries by school boards that had been pressured by Anglo residents.[18]

The students in the "Mexican" schools were taught a curriculum quite different from the one offered to Anglo children. The boys studied gardening, bootmaking, blacksmithing, and carpentry to prepare them for the low-paying trades that school authorities assumed would be the only ones such boys could or should follow. The girls studied sewing and homemaking. Their studies took place in substandard buildings, with books and equipment cast off by the Anglo schools.[19] Many of the Mexican schools opened at 7:30 in the morning and ended the day at 12:30, so the children could go to work in the citrus or walnut groves.[20] Teachers and principals were paid markedly less than those in Anglo schools.[21] The unsurprising result was that many students had to repeat grades and gradually dropped out of school altogether. Isabel Martínez's graduation from Fullerton High School in 1931 was so unusual—she was the first Mexican American ever to graduate—that it was written up in the local newspaper.[22]

The rationale for the segregation was twofold. One justification was the children's presumed lack of English. There was, however, no systematic testing of their language skills. As was the case with the Méndez children, students were simply assigned to the Mexican schools on the basis of their last names or their skin color.[23] The second justification was biological determinism. Mexicans had only 58.1% of Anglo students' ability to pursue academic courses, the superintendent of schools in Ontario, California, asserted. "As the Mexicans show considerable aptitude for hand work of any kind, courses should be developed that will aid them in becoming skilled workers with their hands," he continued. "Girls should be trained to become domestic servants, and to do various kinds of hand work for which they can be paid adequately after they leave school."[24] He was not alone. California educator Grace Stanley asserted, in an influential 1920 article entitled "Special School for Mexicans," that Mexican children were happiest in segregated schools where they could thrive with other unfortunates just like themselves. She added that Mexican children had "different mental characteristics" than Anglo children, "showed a stronger sense of rhythm," and "are primarily interested in action and emotion but grow listless under purely mental effort."[25] Other scholars opined solemnly that Mexican children's IQs were far below those of Anglo students.[26]

The Litigation
A Case Takes Shape

Parents of children in the *colonias* knew that their children's only hope for escape from poverty lay in education. "Our children, all of our children, brown, black, and white, must have the opportunity to be whatever they want to be, and education gives them that opportunity," Felícitas Méndez would say.[27] Many *colonia* parents in Orange County and other parts of

California tried to get their children into "Anglo" schools. The *Mendez* trial would demonstrate the refusal of school authorities to acquiesce.[28] Gonzalo Méndez, for example, went to Westminster Main the day after his children were turned away and spoke to the principal, but his children were still not permitted to register. The following day he went to the Westminster school board, where he was equally unsuccessful. Eventually he went to the Orange County school board, again to no avail.[29]

These failures made the Méndezes no less determined to end what they saw as a flagrant injustice. One of their workers told them about attorney David Marcus, a son of Jewish immigrants who had himself experienced anti-Semitism and ran a practice devoted in part to civil liberties cases.[30] Marcus had recently won a case in nearby San Bernardino admitting Mexican Americans to the city's only public park and swimming pool.[31] He suggested that Méndez's case would be stronger if it could be shown that not only Westminster but other school districts in Orange County as well segregated Mexican American students.[32] Was there evidence of that?

Méndez and Marcus began roaming the county, interviewing parents and pulling evidence together. They quickly uncovered the endemic nature of the segregation, as well as the fact that other parents had also protested without success. Some had been told that their children had to be kept out of the Anglo schools because they were dirty; others, that their children knew no English.[33] Some *colonia* families were fearful of having anything to do with the lawsuit Méndez and Marcus were planning; others, however, were excited. The high wartime price of agricultural products meant that the Méndezes could provide much of the money for Marcus's fee and for expenses. Litigation was costly, however, and once four families in the three additional school districts of El Modena, Garden Grove, and Santa Ana agreed to join the suit, volunteers went door to door, collecting a dollar at a time.[34]

While the two men were putting the case together, the Méndezes followed the law by enrolling their children in Westminster's Mexican school. Sylvia Mendez remembered having to eat lunch sitting on the ground outside, because the school had no cafeteria. The school abutted a cow pasture with an electrified wire fence, and that worried her father. Worse, as far as Sylvia was concerned, were the flies that, attracted by the food, settled on the children and their lunches.[35]

Once the plaintiffs were on hand, Marcus had to decide whether to take the *Mendez* case into state court or federal court. Because the California education law permitted the segregation of Indian and Asian students but did not mention Mexican Americans, Marcus could have argued in state court that the Orange County educators were violating state law by adding to it a group of people without authority. That approach, however, assuming it was successful, would have left the door open for California legislators to rewrite the law to include Mexicans. Marcus and the plaintiff families had another reason for bringing the case in federal court. Their concern was not the violation of California law; it was segregation itself. Marcus had won the San Bernardino park case on the basis of the Equal Protection clause of the U.S. Constitution's Fourteenth Amendment.[36] The Méndezes and the other plaintiffs believed that segregated schools violated both their rights, as American citizens, to obtain for their children the best education offered by the government, and their children's rights to have access to that education. "We always tell our children they are Americans," Felícitas Méndez would tell the trial court, "and I feel I am American myself, and so is my husband, and we thought that they shouldn't be segregated like that, they shouldn't be treated the way they are."[37] Marcus planned to bring the case as a class action. If *Mendez* succeeded, the segregation of Mexican American children might conceivably be outlawed throughout California and the nation. Initially, a ruling in the Méndezes' favor would of course apply only to the four Orange County districts. If the districts appealed that decision, however, and if the losing side in the appeals court decided to take the case further, it could wind up in the U.S. Supreme Court.

The problem was *Plessy v. Ferguson*,[38] the 1896 case in which the Supreme Court declared that separate but equal facilities were constitutional, and the subsequent Supreme Court cases that specifically endorsed race-segregated education.[39] The Supreme Court and lower federal courts seemed so unlikely to revisit *Plessy* that in the mid-1940s, when Marcus was planning strategy, the NAACP considered the time not yet ripe to challenge *Plessy*.[40] Marcus decided to take another tack: He would claim that the Mendez case was not about race at all.

The Case Begins: Pre-trial Hearing

The petition Marcus filed on March 2, 1945 with the District Court for the Southern District of California bore the names of five families in four Orange County school districts and was brought against the districts, their superintendents, and their school boards. It identified the families and their children as American citizens "of Mexican or Latin descent."[41] The question at issue, Marcus would insist throughout the litigation, was not whether the four Orange County school districts segregated students on the basis of race. There was no *racial* segregation, he would tell the court, because Mexicans were members of the white race. The Fourteenth Amendment's Equal Protection clause was being violated by school districts keeping white children from being educated with other white children purely on the basis of ethnicity.[42]

Marcus could make the whiteness claim because the U.S. government classified Mexicans as white. In 1930, after having implicitly assumed for some years that Mexican Americans were white, the U.S. Census Bureau created a new category of "Mexican." The Mexican government was outraged and in 1940, with the Roosevelt administration worried about international relations at a time of impending war, the bureau eliminated the category for Mexicans who were not "definitely Indian or of other nonwhite race."[43] It might be noted that nothing could be better proof of the artificiality of racial categories than the fact that with a few strokes of a pen, Mexicans were white in 1929, nonwhite in 1930, and white again in 1940.

The case was assigned to Judge Paul J. McCormick. As he became the first federal court judge to challenge the separate but equal doctrine, it is worth examining precisely who he was.

McCormick was born in New York City in 1879 and moved to California in 1887. He was initially in private practice, remaining there until he was appointed a deputy district attorney in 1905. Five years later, Governor James N. Gillette named him to fill a position on the California Superior Court in Los Angeles. McCormick was subsequently elected to the court and then reelected, ultimately serving for 13 years and adjudicating civil, criminal, and probate cases. President Calvin Coolidge appointed him to the U.S. District Court for the Southern District of California in Los Angeles in 1924, and he remained on that court on active service until 1951.[44]

McCormick's decisions prior to 1945 reflected a strong moral streak and his solid Catholic faith. In 1923, he was so distressed by what he saw as his duty to pronounce the death sentence on a man convicted of killing a policeman that he consulted his fellow judges beforehand and told the press, "If you had an atheist on the bench he would hang them all. But a man with any religion must feel the awful, tremendous responsibility of such a task."[45] In 1942, with World War II raging, the judge sentenced a conscientious objector to a year in the county jail. "How are we going to insure free exercise of religion," McCormick asked rhetorically from the bench during the sentencing, "if we don't fight for it?"[46] Some years earlier he had written to the RKO movie production company, deploring films that did not contribute to the "social and moral welfare" and recommending the making of more movies such as *Little Women*.[47]

Judge McCormick's Los Angeles courtroom was the scene of relatively mundane citizenship hearings and swearing-in ceremonies but also the swearing-in of actors such as George Sanders and Charles Boyer.[48] In 1939, he dismissed a case in which Charlie Chaplin was accused of plagiarism for his movie *Modern Times*.[49] His docket included a full range of civil and criminal cases and—as in the case of the conscientious objector—his comments from the bench and to the press reflected his beliefs. When he sentenced a Chinese narcotics addict to three years in a federal penitentiary, he said, "It is unfortunate that we have no system of hospitalization for these cases. They are really medical instead of legal problems," thereby indicating that the judge was somewhat ahead of his time. Nonetheless, he demonstrated that in other respects he was very much a man of the moment when he added, "It is particularly vicious to sell narcotics to a white man. Trade in opium between orientals is not as dangerous as this practice."[50] He was firm with people accused of violating Prohibition laws and, as a member of President Herbert Hoover's National Commission on Law Enforcement and Observance, advocated the continuance of Prohibition. He viewed its "outstanding good" as the "abolition of the legalized open saloon." At the same time, McCormick lambasted what he called the "governmental lawlessness" involved in some Prohibition efforts, especially the tendency of law enforcement officers to search homes without a warrant.[51]

Judge McCormick's service on Hoover's commission brought him national attention. So did the part he played in the notorious Teapot Dome scandal, voiding the Pan American Petroleum and Transport Company's contract to the oil in the Elk Hills reserve. His ruling was affirmed by the Ninth Circuit Court of Appeals and by the U.S. Supreme Court.[52]

The jurist who would hear the *Mendez* case, then, was a stern moralist, someone whose feelings about racial differences were mixed at best, a man of stature in his community and in judicial circles generally, and a firm believer in the Constitution. None of that, however, gave any clue as to how he would decide in *Mendez*, and McCormick was in fact not at all certain that the case belonged in his court. He knew that the Constitution gave the federal government no power over education policy, which was implicitly left to the states. The school districts argued that segregated education was legal—the Supreme Court had said so—and all that was at issue was the question of whether the segregation of Mexican American students was warranted. That was a matter of educational policy and so did not belong in federal court. McCormick decided to let the case progress nonetheless while he withheld judgment about his court's jurisdiction.[53]

Marcus, by contrast, was insistent that the court had jurisdiction. His clients had been deprived of their civil rights and the privileges and immunities of American citizens that were guaranteed to each of them by the Constitution and laws of the United States, he asserted. In carrying out a "common plan, design and purpose" to keep the children from specific schools solely because of their "Mexican or Latin descent or extraction," the districts had caused the plaintiffs and their children "great and irreparable damage." He asked the court to declare the practice to be unconstitutional and to issue an injunction prohibiting it.[54]

The lawyer arguing for Orange County was George F. Holden, the Santa Ana County deputy counsel.[55] Holden was a former litigator in private practice, Orange County district attorney, and president of the Orange County bar association. Forty-eight years old in 1945, Holden had behind him years of experience in public office and in litigation as he prepared to face the 41-year-old Marcus.[56] Holden acknowledged that the children in the case were constitutionally entitled to equal treatment, and maintained that they were getting it. The families "of Mexican or Latin descent" in the district spoke Spanish at home, so that their children were "unfamiliar with and unable to speak the English language" when they began school. The districts therefore found it desirable and efficient to educate them separately, the separation being "for the best interests of said pupils of Mexican descent and for the best interests of the English speaking pupils." The Mexican American students were kept in segregated schools "until they acquired some efficiency in the English language." They were taught by teachers with the same qualifications and salary as the teachers in the other schools, and given "all of the facilities and all the instruction" available in them—statements that were patently untrue. The bottom line was that they were being taught separately, but equally, for sound educational reasons, and that they were never separated "solely" because of their ethnicity.[57] He inadvertently implied, however, that the real problem the children faced was that they had been born to Mexican American parents. As he said during the pre-trial hearing,

> Sure, they can speak some English, you know. They have to be able to understand a certain amount of English before they can go from one grade to another, but they cannot grasp it. Where they have lived in the Spanish language, with Spanish customs, and they talk it at home, and as soon as they are out of school they go back to their homes and commence talking. So again, thinking in Spanish, they cannot compete with the other students and advance in the same grade at the same age.[58]

The Trial

The trial began on July 5, 1945. Holden's star witness was James L. Kent, the superintendent of the Garden Grove School District, who agreed absolutely that Mexican American students did not belong in schools with "white" children. In 1941, Kent had written a master's thesis arguing that Mexican Americans were "an alien race that should be segregated socially" and that, happily, segregation had been accomplished in southern California "by designating certain sections where they might live and restricting these sections to them"—in other words, by keeping them out of "white" neighborhoods. "Upon investigation of the mental ability and moral characteristics of the average Mexican school child it is evident that this [housing segregation] is a condition which is advantageous to both the white and Mexican child," he wrote. "Segregation also into separate schools seems to be the ideal situation for both parties concerned."[59] "Mexican" students—whom he repeatedly differentiated from "American" students—were of "a less sturdy stock than the white race" and suffered from health problems as a result of eating nothing but "tortillas, a greasy mixture, or enchiladas and beans."[60] The children suffered from a "racial language handicap," and differences in IQs between the two "races" made it clear that "a separate curriculum ... based upon their abilities ... is advisable."[61]

Kent told the court that when Mexican American children first enrolled in school, "We usually find them retarded," meaning unable to work at grade level. Admittedly, some children came to the school speaking English. Of those, "the large percentage of them can speak the English language, or they can understand it, but that does not necessarily mean that they can progress in school ... by our tests we find they are a year retarded in comparison with the white children. ... Your Mexican child is advanced, that is, he matures physically faster than your white child, and he is able to do more in games. Therefore, he goes more on physical prowess than he does on mental ability."[62] Richard F. Harris, the Westminster superintendent of schools, added that Mexican American children could not keep up with others because they had not been introduced at home to Mother Goose rhymes and "stories of our American heroes, stories of our American frontier, rhymes, rhythms."[63] A "child of Mexican-speaking families ... has no conception" of such stories and so had to be educated separately.[64]

Marcus countered the county's case by putting both parents and students on the stand. Parents from each of the four districts testified about their repeated attempts to get their children into the "white" schools, and recounted the denigrating language that school officials used in denying their requests. The parents were frequently told, as noted, that all Mexican American children were dirty and spoke no English, which the officials somehow knew even though the children were given no language tests.[65] Two students testified, demonstrating that they did indeed speak proper English.[66]

Then Marcus anticipated the approach that would be used by the NAACP in *Brown v. Board of Education*. He called two educators to the stand as expert witnesses. Ralph L. Beals was a professor and chairman of the Department of Anthropology at the University of California–Los Angeles. He had done research in Mexico for the National Research Council and the Smithsonian Institution as well as for his university, and he had written roughly 30 books and articles.[67] Marie H. Hughes had been a school principal and curriculum director in New Mexico for 19 years and, in addition, had worked in Los Angeles County for the past five. She had specialized in research about Mexican American children for 20 years.[68] Both testified that separating children with limited English from more fluent children was a poor way to enhance the first group's language proficiency. More importantly, they both argued that the psychological effects of segregation interfered with the segregated students' ability to learn. "Judging by some studies that have been made under my direction," Dr. Beals told the court, "a feeling of antagonism is built up in children, when they are segregated in this fashion. They actually become hostile to the whole culture of the surrounding majority group, as a result of the segregation, which appears to be, to them at least, discrimination. ... The disadvantage of segregation, it would seem to me, would come primarily from the reinforcing of stereotypes of inferiority-superiority, which exists in the population as a whole."[69] Marie Hughes added,

> Segregation, by its very nature, is a reminder constantly of inferiority, of not being wanted, of not being a part of the community. ... I would say that any

separation of children which prevents free communication among them, on an equal basis, that is, a peer basis, would be bad because of the very fact that segregation tends to give an aura of inferiority. In order to have the people of the United States understand one another, it is necessary for them to live together, as it were, and the public school is the one mechanism where all the children of all the people go.[70]

The Decision

Judge McCormick handed down his decision on February 18, 1946, and it was a resounding victory for the plaintiffs. It was more than that, however; it was also a seminal moment in American law. McCormick found the school districts' segregation illegitimate as a matter of both California law and federal constitutional law. A California statute required school districts to admit all children over age six, whether or not their parents were American citizens, and to maintain elementary schools "'with equal rights and privileges as far as possible.'"[71] That, Judge McCormick declared, applied to all children "regardless of their ancestry or extraction" (with the notable exception of Indian and Asian children) and meant that segregation of "pupils of Mexican ancestry" was prohibited. "The common segregation and practices of the school authorities in the defendant school districts in Orange County," however, "pertain solely to children of Mexican ancestry and parentage. They are singled out as a class for segregation." Such segregation violated the state's own laws.[72]

California wanted students to be integrated, according to Judge McCormick's reading of its laws. He found it "noteworthy that the educational advantages of their commingling with other pupils is regarded as being so important to the school system of the State" that education was mandatory for both citizens and noncitizens. California law reflected "a clear purpose to avoid and forbid distinctions among pupils based upon race or ancestry."[73] Further, the Supreme Court had declared in *Hirabayashi v. United States*[74] three years earlier that distinctions made on the basis of race were "by their very nature odious to a free people whose institutions are founded upon the doctrine of equality" and "utterly inconsistent with American traditions and ideals."[75]

Judge McCormick concluded his discussion of "the utter irreconcilability of the segregation practices" with California law and went on to suggest a new interpretation of the federal equal protection clause. "'The equal protection of the laws' pertaining to the public school system in California," he wrote, "is not provided by furnishing in separate schools the same technical facilities, text books and courses of instruction to children of Mexican ancestry that are available to the other public school children regardless of their ancestry."[76] Then came the judge's formulation, so radical for its day: "A paramount requisite in the American system of public education is social equality. It must be open to all children by unified school association regardless of lineage."[77] That, simply stated, was a declaration that "separate but equal" was not equal. The boldness of the language must have made the parties to the litigation catch their breaths. McCormick was implicitly denying the legitimacy of an entire body of equal protection law, and doing so in language that would soon have civil rights organizations all over the country rushing into the case.

The only permissible grounds for the Orange County segregation, McCormick continued, were the children's language difficulties. "But even such situations do not justify the general and continuous segregation in separate schools of the children of Mexican ancestry from the rest of the elementary school population as has been shown to be the practice in the defendant school districts." Instead, there must be "credible examination" of each child, "regardless of his ethnic traits or ancestry."[78] No such examination existed here. "In some instances," McCormick continued with indignation, placement was based on "the Latinized or Mexican name of the child," even though "such methods of evaluating language knowledge are illusory and are not conducive to the inculcation and enjoyment of civil rights which are of primary importance in the public school system of education in the United States."[79] That sentence effectively asserted that civil rights and knowledge about them were key goals of American public education. So was avoidance of artificial distinctions among the students, McCormick said, drawing on the testimony of the experts:

> The evidence clearly shows that Spanish-speaking children are retarded in learning English by lack of exposure to its use because of segregation, and that commingling of the entire student body instills and develops a common cultural attitude among the school children which is imperative for the perpetuation of American institutions and ideals. It is also established by the record that the methods of segregation prevalent in the defendant school districts foster antagonisms in the children and suggest inferiority among them where none exists.[80]

What Judge McCormick did was sufficiently revolutionary to deserve emphasis here. He not only restated the Supreme Court's suggestion in *Hirabayashi* that discrimination based on ancestry was usually suspect; he applied that doctrine in declaring a state's actions to be illegal. He held that Mexican Americans as a group could not legitimately be discriminated against—a holding that would not be echoed by the U.S. Supreme Court until it heard a case involving a Mexican American in 1954.[81] He declared that school segregation impeded learning instead of enhancing it. He insisted, as the NAACP would argue in *Brown v. Board of Education*, that segregated schools fostered unwarranted feelings of inferiority in the students who were segregated. Most importantly, of course, he declared that "separate but equal" education was a violation of the Fourteenth Amendment. There, again, this district court judge anticipated the Supreme Court by almost a decade.

The Appeal

The NAACP had known nothing about the *Mendez* case. Once McCormick's decision was handed down, however, the case received nationwide publicity. The school districts promptly announced that they would appeal the verdict, and NAACP Assistant Special Counsel Robert Carter, Thurgood Marshall's second-in-command, knew that he wanted to be involved. Marshall was in the Virgin Islands, recuperating from an illness, so Carter was effectively in charge. The school districts had announced that they would appeal the decision and Carter immediately understood that if the case reached the Supreme Court, it could be the one to attack segregated education on its face. It might even, he thought, signal the beginning of the end for "separate but equal."[82]

Carter had come to believe that sociological evidence, depicting the psychological and pedagogical effects of school segregation, could be a useful weapon in the litigation arsenal. Other lawyers who worked with the NAACP were less sanguine. The social sciences, they said, weren't pure science, and so their findings were too weak to use in cases. Carter nonetheless thought that the *Mendez* case was too good an opportunity to pass up, and he began drafting a brief that he would later call the NAACP's trial brief for *Brown v. Board*.[83] The NAACP entered the case as an *amicus*.

So did the American Jewish Congress, the Japanese American Citizens League, the American Civil Liberties Union, and the Los Angeles chapter of the National Lawyers Guild.[84] The NAACP brief took educational segregation head on. Although Marcus continued to insist that *Mendez* was about ethnicity, not race, the NAACP brief focused on race. There was nothing, Carter wrote, to keep a federal court from declaring that segregation in a public school system was unconstitutional. *Plessy* dealt only with railroad cars, not with education, and a line of cases since indicated that the Court was moving toward a holding that "classifications and distinctions on the basis of race [are] contrary to our fundamental law." The conclusion: "It is clear, therefore, that segregation in our public schools must be invalidated as violative of the Constitution and laws of the United States."[85]

The brief of the American Jewish Congress (AJC) lambasted segregation in general and, in language that echoed that of the experts who had testified at trial, segregation in education in particular. "The value and the desirability of an educational institution is particularly dependent on intangible elements," the AJC asserted. "The physical characteristics of the benches and desks of a school shrink into utter insignificance when compared with the social and psychological environment which the school offers to its children." That "social and psychological environment" could be devastating. Children who were "deemed superior are often, in manifesting their innocent pride, more cruel than normal adults usually are. On the other side, children who feel that they are treated as inferior are more bitterly humiliated by the social stigma that strikes them than adults can be."[86] They are likely to suffer the "deepest and most lasting social and psychological evil results." Segregation based on assumptions of inferiority "perpetuate[s] racial prejudice and contributes to the degradation and humiliation of the minority children."[87]

The state of California also weighed in, and it quickly became apparent that segregation of Mexican American students did not have the state's support. In November 1946, Robert W. Kenny, Governor Earl Warren's attorney general, entered the case as an *amicus*. He argued that any segregation in California schools was unconstitutional, and Warren and the state legislature began the process of implementing that idea.[88] In January 1947, with the blessing of Governor Warren, four members of the California Assembly introduced a bill to end segregated education in the state.[89] It passed on April 10 which, as it turned out, was only four days before the *Mendez* decision was handed down by a unanimous Court of Appeals on April 14.[90]

Writing for the court, Judge Albert Lee Stephens rejected the county's argument that the Supreme Court's segregation decisions were controlling. His reason was quite different from McCormick's, however. Those decisions, Stephens wrote, were written in cases where the state legislature had mandated segregation. That was not the situation here. "Nowhere in any California law is there a suggestion that any segregation can be made of children within one of the great races." Mexican Americans were neither American Indians nor Asians, and those were the only categories of children whom California law permitted to be segregated. Stephens was willing to concede that California could enact a law permitting the segregation of Mexican Americans but it had not done so, and so the school boards had deprived the plaintiff children of liberty and property without due process of law and the equal protection of the laws.[91]

Stephens specifically declined to get into a discussion of whether racial segregation was constitutional.[92] The country's legal elite, however—at least the part of it outside the South—soon indicated that it was willing to go further than he. Northern and Western law reviews such as the *Yale Law Journal*, the *Michigan Law Review*, the *Columbia Law Review*, and the *Southern California Law Review* saw Judge McCormick's decision as the handwriting on the wall and called for the end of segregated schools.[93]

The school districts involved in the case gave up after the appeals court decision was handed down and integrated their schools, so the case did not make its way to the U.S. Supreme Court. The case nonetheless had ramifications beyond those districts. A few months after Judge McCormick handed down his decision, David Marcus filed suit on behalf of segregated African American and Mexican American school children in Riverside County. The school district promptly ended segregation.[94] At the same time, Orange County's Ontario School Board decided to integrate its formerly all-Anglo Grove School. Anglo parents managed to collect 1,400 signatures on a petition asking the board to rescind its action. The board held firm, however, and once the Anglo parents saw that protest was of no use, they agreed to cooperate. In September of that year the Grove School had 177 Mexican American and 155 non-Mexican-American students.[95] In 1948 scholar Mary Peters surveyed 100 nonurban school districts in southern and central California; 78% of the districts that responded replied that they had segregated Mexican American students; only 18% said that they still did so.[96]

And the Supreme Court did eventually weigh in on the subject that was at the heart of the *Mendez* case. Eight years after Judge McCormick handed down his ruling, Chief Justice Earl Warren wrote for the unanimous court in *Hernandez v. Texas*, the first case argued before that court by Latino attorneys. The decision specifically recognized Mexican Americans as a class entitled to the protection of the Fourteenth Amendment.[97] Mexican American rights had finally been endorsed by the nation's highest court.

Conclusion

The *Mendez* case probably would not have succeeded had it been brought ten years earlier. World War II had a notable effect both on American thinking about racism and on the roughly 350,000 Mexican American soldiers who had fought in the war and returned to begin demanding the same kind of justice at home they believed they had been fighting for abroad.[98] Gilbert Gonzalez has noted that "the California courts heard the *Mendez* case in a period of policy shift toward 'intercultural understanding,'" in which prejudice and discrimination had come to be seen as "negative social forces."[99] There is an ongoing relationship between law and society, and societal attitudes had to change before a judge would write that segregation, with its implication of inferiority, was unjust, or law reviews would publish articles calling for the overturn of *Plessy v. Ferguson*. Law, in turn, affects societal dynamics. *Mendez* clearly heartened the Mexican American community and its activists, encouraging the spate of litigation and pressure on school boards that gradually ended segregation policies in many districts.

Despite its significance, few scholars outside of California knew about the *Mendez* case until the twenty-first century. It was not featured in most constitutional law casebooks; it went unmentioned in the majority of biographies of Earl Warren. One reason may be that most twentieth-century constitutional scholars focused almost entirely on Supreme Court decisions and ignored the work of the lower federal courts. Another possibility is that the orthodox narrative of civil rights in the United States portrayed the African American movement for legal equality as seminal, with other minority groups supposedly piggybacking on the successes of that movement. Little attention was paid to the pre-1950s activism of Mexican American and other Latino/Hispanic communities, although such activism was not at all uncommon.[100]

Mendez is no longer ignored. That is in part due to the efforts of Sylvia Mendez, who has tirelessly taken information about the case to schoolchildren and other audiences around the nation, and in part because of Sandra Robbie's Emmy-winning documentary, *Mendez vs. Westminster: For All the Children/Para Todos los Niños*. It is also because of the emergence of a solid cadre of Chicano and other scholars eager to give Mexican American activism in general and *Mendez v. Westminster* in particular their proper place in United States history.[101] In 2007, the U.S. Postal Service issued a stamp in honor of the case; in 2010, President Barack Obama presented Sylvia Mendez with the Medal of Freedom for her work in publicizing the case; and in 2012, the courthouse in which *Mendez* was tried was declared to be a National Historic Landmark.[102]

Mendez, a seminal moment in American law, deserves all the attention. It also exemplifies the truism that rights are attainable in the American political system—sometimes not early enough, sometimes in no more than small increments, yet attainable all the same—but only if they are fought for. The Méndezes and David Marcus accepted the challenge and, in the process, helped change the definition of equality under the law.

Notes

1   GILBERT G. GONZALEZ, CHICANO EDUCATION IN THE ERA OF SEGREGATION, 149 (The Balch Institute Press 1990); The Honorable Frederick P. Aguirre, Mendez v. Westminster School District: *How It Affected* Brown v. Board of Education, 4 JOURNAL OF HISPANIC HIGHER EDUCATION 321, 323 (2005); Jennifer McCormick & César J. Ayala, *Felícita "La Prieta" Méndez (1916–1998) and the End of Latino School Segregation in California*, 19 CENTRO JOURNAL 13, 23–24 (2007).

2   A photograph of the Westminster Main school is available at http://www.nps.gov/history/nr/travel/American_Latino_Heritage/Los_Angeles_US_Court_House_and_Post_Office.html.

3   A photograph of Hoover is available at http://www.winifredconkling.com/images/hoover.jpg.

4   Molly Nance, *The Landmark Decision that Faded into Historical Obscurity*, 24 DIVERSE: ISSUES IN HIGHER EDUCATION 28 (2007); McCormick, *Felícita "La Prieta" Méndez*, 24.

5   Transcript of Record, 461–62, Mendez v. Westminster [as in original] School District of Orange County, 64 F. Supp. 544 (S.D. Cal. 1946) (file folders 4292-M, box #740, Civil Cases 4285–4292, RG 221, Records of the District Court of the United States for the Southern District of California,

Central Division, National Archives and Records Administration (Pacific Region), Laguna Niguel, California) [hereinafter Trial Transcript] available at http://mendezetalvwestminster.com/court. html. The transcript refers to the lead plaintiff as "Mendez," without an accent mark, so the case is referred to that way throughout this article.

6   Felícitas Méndez was born in Puerto Rico and thus was an American citizen. By the time of the case, Gonzalo Méndez was a naturalized American citizen.

7   Aguirre, Mendez v. Westminster School District, 322; JUAN GÓMEZ-QUIÑONES, ROOTS OF CHICANO POLITICS, 1600–1940, 303 (University of New Mexico Press 1994).

8   DAVID GUTIÉRREZ, WALLS AND MIRRORS: MEXICAN-AMERICANS, MEXICAN IMMIGRANTS, AND THE POLITICS OF ETHNICITY, 41 (University of California Press 1995); GEORGE J. SÁNCHEZ, BECOMING MEXICAN AMERICAN: ETHNICITY, CULTURE, AND IDENTITY IN CHICANO LOS ANGELES, 1900–1945, 19 (Oxford University Press 1993).

9   GUTIÉRREZ, WALLS AND MIRRORS, 41; GILBERT G. GONZÁLEZ, LABOR AND COMMUNITY: MEXICAN CITRUS WORKER VILLAGES IN A SOUTHERN CALIFORNIA COUNTY, 1900–1950, 19–20 (University of Illinois Press 1994); SÁNCHEZ, BECOMING MEXICAN AMERICAN, 19.

10   Vicki L. Ruiz, *Tapestries of Resistance: Episodes of School Segregation and Desegregation in the Western United States*, in PETER F. LAU, ED., FROM GRASSROOTS TO THE SUPREME COURT: EXPLORATION OF *BROWN V. BOARD OF EDUCATION* AND AMERICAN DEMOCRACY, 56 (Duke University Press 2004); Vicki L. Ruiz, *South by Southwest: Mexican Americans and Segregated Schooling, 1900–1950*, ORGANIZATION OF AMERICAN HISTORIANS MAGAZINE OF HISTORY, 23 (Winter 2001); CHARLES M. WOLLENBERG, ALL DELIBERATE SPEED: SEGREGATION AND EXCLUSION IN CALIFORNIA SCHOOLS, 1955–1975, 109 (University of California Press 1976); GUTIÉRREZ, WALLS AND MIRRORS, 40; SÁNCHEZ, BECOMING MEXICAN AMERICAN, 18; CAMILLE GUERIN-GONZALEZ, MEXICAN WORKERS AND AMERICAN DREAMS: IMMIGRATION, REPATRIATION, AND CALIFORNIA FARM LABOR, 1900–1939 (Rutgers University Press 1994).

11   GUTIÉRREZ, WALLS AND MIRRORS, 45; GONZÁLEZ, LABOR AND COMMUNITY, 7; see also JUAN GÓMEZ-QUIÑONES, MEXICAN AMERICAN LABOR, 1790–1990 (University of New Mexico Press 1994).

12   GONZÁLEZ, LABOR AND COMMUNITY, 7; see also GÓMEZ-QUIÑONES, MEXICAN AMERICAN LABOR.

13   GONZÁLEZ, LABOR AND COMMUNITY, 62.

14   Guerin-Gonzalez, *Mexican Workers*, GUERIN-GONZALEZ, MEXICAN WORKERS 120–21; GONZÁLEZ, LABOR AND COMMUNITY, 32, 59–69; Ruiz, *South by Southwest*, 23.

15   Act of March 12, 1885, California Statutes, Chapter 117, §§ 1–2, Laws and Resolutions passed by the legislature of 1883–84 at its extra session, 99–100; California Education Code § 1662 (Deering 1886); California Education Code §§ 8003–04 (1945).

16   Gilbert G. Gonzalez, *Segregation of Mexican Children in a Southern California City: The Legacy of Expansionism and the American Southwest*, 16 THE WESTERN HISTORICAL QUARTERLY 55, 57 (1985).

17   WOLLENBERG, ALL DELIBERATE SPEED, 110–11; Christopher J. Arriola, *Knocking on the Schoolhouse Door*: Mendez v. Westminster, *Equal Protection, Public Education, and Mexican Americans in the 1940s*, 8 LA RAZA LAW JOURNAL 166, 170 (1995); GONZALEZ, CHICANO EDUCATION, 137–38; Charles Wollenberg, Mendez v. Westminster: *Race, Nationality and Segregation in California Schools*, 53 CALIFORNIA HISTORICAL QUARTERLY 319 (1974).

18   NICOLÁS C. VACA, THE PRESUMED ALLIANCE: THE UNSPOKEN CONFLICT BETWEEN LATINOS AND BLACKS AND WHAT IT MEANS FOR AMERICA, 63 (HarperCollins 2003); GONZÁLEZ, LABOR AND COMMUNITY, 99–100; IRVING G. HENDRICK, THE EDUCATION OF NON-WHITES IN CALIFORNIA, 1849–1970, 91–92 (R & E Research Associates 1977).

19   GONZALEZ, CHICANO EDUCATION, 138, 142; GONZÁLEZ, LABOR AND COMMUNITY, 102.

20   Arriola, *Knocking*, 181; GONZALEZ, CHICANO EDUCATION, 146–47.

21   GONZALEZ, CHICANO EDUCATION, 142, 182.

22   GONZÁLEZ, LABOR AND COMMUNITY, 109–11.

23   Pre-Trial Transcript at 21–22, 43–44, Mendez, 64 F. Supp. 544, [hereinafter Pre-trial Transcript] available at http://mendezetalvwestminster.com/pdf/Pre_Trial_Transcript.pdf.

24   Merton Earle Hill, *The Development of an Americanization Program*, 189, 195, passim (Graduate Division of the University of California, doctoral dissertation for Doctor of Education, 1928).

25   Grace Stanley, *Special School for Mexicans*, THE SURVEY, 714 (September 15, 1920).

26   B. F. Haught, *The Language Difficulty of Spanish-American Children*, 15 JOURNAL OF APPLIED PSYCHOLOGY 92 (February 1931) (quoted in GONZALEZ, CHICANO EDUCATION, 72); William H. Sheldon, *The Intelligence of Mexican Children*, SCHOOL AND SOCIETY (February 2, 1924) (cited in WOLLENBERG, ALL DELIBERATE SPEED, 115); Thomas Garth, *The Intelligence of Mexican School Children*, SCHOOL AND SOCIETY (June 28, 1928) (cited in WOLLENBERG, ALL DELIBERATE SPEED, 115).

27   Felícitas Méndez, quoted in English translation from Spanish in VICKI L. RUIZ, FROM OUT OF THE SHADOWS: MEXICAN WOMEN IN TWENTIETH CENTURY AMERICA (Oxford University Press 1998) (cited in McCormick & Ayala, *Felícita "La Prieta" Méndez*, 27).

28   Gonzalez, *Segregation of Mexican Children*, 68–70. These are all quotes from the October 1943 minutes of the Santa Ana Board of Education.

29   Trial Transcript, 79–80, 90–92, 102–103.

30   Author's telephone interviews with Maria Dolores Lane (David Marcus' daughter), January 9, 2008; Stephen DeLapp (grandson), January 6, 2009; Anne K. McIntyre (granddaughter), January 8, 2008; author's email interview with Melissa Marcus (granddaughter), December 10, 2008.

31   Lopez v. Seccombe, 71 F. Supp. 769 (S.D. Cal. 1944).

32   Aguirre, Mendez v. Westminster, 321, 324.

33   Trial Transcript, 64–67, 130, 152, 442, 477.

34   Author's telephone interview with Alex Maldonado, January 22, 2009; GONZALEZ, CHICANO EDUCATION, 152.

35   Author's interview with Sylvia Mendez, February 27, 2009. The Mendez family no longer uses the accent mark in "Mendez."

36   U.S. Constitution, Amendment XIV, Section 1 ("No state shall … deny to any person within its jurisdiction the equal protection of the laws").

37   Trial Transcript, 469.

38   Plessy v. Ferguson, 163 U.S. 537 (1896).

39   Cumming v. Board of Education, 175 U.S. 528 (1899); Berea College v. Commonwealth of Kentucky, 211 U.S. 45 (1908); Gong Lum v. Rice, 275 U.S. 78 (1927).

40   Memo from Thurgood Marshall to Roy Wilkins, November 27, 1945, Library of Congress, National Association for the Advancement of Colored People Records, 1842–1999, Part 2 (hereafter NAACP records), Box 136 Folder 11; Thurgood Marshall to Carl Murphy, President, *The Afro-American Newspapers*, December 20, 1946, and Thurgood Marshall speech, Association of Colleges and Secondary Schools for Negroes, Nashville, Tennessee, December 6, 1945, NAACP records, Part 2, Box 136, Folder 3.

41   Petition, 2, 6–7, Mendez v. Westminster School District of Orange County, Civil Action No. 4292 (S.D. Cal. March 1, 1946), available at http://mendezetalvwestminster.com/pdf/Petition.pdf.

42   Trial Transcript, 44, 109.

43   U.S. Department of Commerce, Bureau of the Census, *Abridged Instructions to Enumerators*, 7 (1940) ("Mexicans are to be returned as *white*, unless definitely of Indian or other nonwhite race."), available at http://1940census.archives.gov/downloads/instructions-to-enumerators.pdf. See also U.S. Department of Commerce, Bureau of the Census, *200 Years of US Census Taking: Population and Housing Questions, 1790–1990*, 60 (1989).

44   *Coolidge Picks M'Cormick*, LOS ANGELES TIMES, A5 (February 8, 1924); *Judge's Colleagues Did Not Forget the Day*, LOS ANGELES TIMES, A5 (April 24, 1948); *Fellow Judges Praise Service of McCormick*, LOS ANGELES TIMES, B2 (July 29, 1951).

45   Alma Whitaker, *Death Penalty Brings Emotion*, LOS ANGELES TIMES, A1 (April 8, 1923).

46   *Objector Given Year in Jail*, LOS ANGELES TIMES, A1 (November 10, 1942).

47   *Galaxy of Stars Due at Loew's*, LOS ANGELES TIMES, A9 (January 8, 1934).

48   *Laughton and Elsa File U.S. Citizen Applications*, LOS ANGELES TIMES, A1 (April 23, 1949); *Actor Charles Boyer Becomes U. S. Citizen*, ATLANTA CONSTITUTION, 6 (February 14, 1942).

49   *Chaplin Wins Decision in Plagiarism Suit*, LOS ANGELES TIMES, 3 (November 19, 1939).

50 *Addict Given Sympathy: Judge McCormick Expresses Regret for Lack of Any Hospitalization System for Narcotic Slaves*, LOS ANGELES TIMES, 12 (February 27, 1930).

51 *Commissioners Who Made Exhaustive Prohibition Study*, LOS ANGELES TIMES, 4 (January 21, 1931); *Crime Viewed by M'Cormick: Wickersham Commissioner Returns Home*, LOS ANGELES TIMES, A1 (July 6, 1931).

52 United States v. Pan American Petroleum and Transport Company, 6 F.2d 43 (S.D. Cal. 1925); *Confirms Revoking of Doheny Leases*, NEW YORK TIMES, 6 (July 12, 1925).

53 Pre-trial Transcript, 28, 107.

54 Trial Transcript, 2, 7–8.

55 The defense team was formally headed by Joel E. Ogle, the Santa Ana County Counsel. He effectively turned the case over to Holden, however, and played only a minimal role in it.

56 Email to author from Daniel W. Holden, Mar. 14, 2009; email to author from Chris Jepsen, Assistant Archivist, Orange County Archives, March 10, 2009; email to author from Jack Golden, Senior Assistant County Counsel, Orange County, March 9, 2009; *Mexican Students To Be Unchanged*, ORANGE DAILY NEWS, 1 (September 13, 1946).

57 Pre-trial Transcript, 5.

58 Ibid., 46–47.

59 James L. Kent, *Segregation of Mexican School Children in Southern California*, 3 (University of Oregon, Ed.M. thesis, June 1941).

60 Ibid., 23.

61 Ibid., 67.

62 Trial Transcript, 101, 139.

63 Ibid., 376.

64 Ibid., 377. See also PHILIPPA STRUM, *MENDEZ V. WESTMINSTER*: SCHOOL DESEGREGATION AND MEXICAN-AMERICAN RIGHTS, 82–90 (University Press of Kansas 2010).

65 Trial Transcript, 64–67, 130, 152, 442, 477.

66 Trial Transcript, 258–70. See also STRUM, *MENDEZ V. WESTMINSTER*, 79–80, 90–92, 102–103.

67 Trial Transcript, 660–61. See also Walter Goldschmidt, Ralph H. Turner, & Robert B. Edgerton, *Ralph Leon Beals, Anthropology and Sociology: Los Angeles*, http://texts.cdlib.org/view?docId=hb-767nb3z6&doc.view=frames&chunk.id=div00006&toc.depth=1&toc.id=

68 Trial Transcript, 687–89.

69 Ibid., 676.

70 Ibid., 691, 699.

71 Mendez, 64 F. Supp. 548 (quoting California Education Code § 8002).

72 Ibid.

73 Ibid.

74   Hirabayashi v. United States, 320 U.S. 81 (1943).

75   Mendez, 64 F. Supp. 548 (quoting Hirabayashi, 320 U.S. 81, 100, 110).

76   Ibid., 549.

77   Ibid.

78   Ibid., 549, 550.

79   Ibid., 550.

80   Ibid., 549.

81   Hernandez v. Texas, 347 U.S. 475 (1954).

82   Author's interview with Robert L. Carter, October 17, 2008; Robert L. Carter to Claude G. Metzler, December 26, 1946, and Robert L. Carter, Memo to NAACP's Public Relations Department, April 24, 1947, NAACP records, Part 2, Box 136, Folder 3; ROBERT L. CARTER, A MATTER OF LAW: A MEMOIR OF STRUGGLE IN THE CAUSE OF CIVIL RIGHTS, 65–66 (The New Press 2005); RICHARD KLUGER, SIMPLE JUSTICE: THE HISTORY OF *BROWN V. BOARD OF EDUCATION* AND BLACK AMERICA'S STRUGGLE FOR EQUALITY, 400 (Knopf 1975); MARK V. TUSHNET, THE NAACP'S LEGAL STRAGEGY AGAINST SEGREGATED EDUCATION, 1925–1950, 120 (University of North Carolina Press 1987).

83   Author's interview, Robert L. Carter; CARTER, A MATTER OF LAW, 65–66; KLUGER, SIMPLE JUSTICE, 400.

84   The briefs in *Westminster School District v. Mendez* are in Case Files, Ninth Circuit Court of Appeals, Record Group 276, Box 4464, National Archives-Pacific Sierra Region, San Bruno, CA.

85   Brief for the National Association for the Advancement of Colored People as *Amicus Curiae*, 7, 29, Westminster School District of Orange County v. Mendez, 161 F.2d 774 (9th Cir. 1947) (No. 11310).

86   Brief for the American Jewish Congress as *Amicus Curiae*, 13, Westminster, 161 F.2d 774.

87   Ibid., 14.

88   Brief of the Attorney General of the State of California as *Amicus Curiae*, Westminster, 161 F.2d 774; ED CRAY, CHIEF JUSTICE: A BIOGRAPHY OF EARL WARREN, 167 (Simon & Schuster 1997).

89   1947 California Statute chapter 737, September 10, 1947; WOLLENBERG, ALL DELIBERATE SPEED, 132. Governor Warren signed the bill on June 14.

90   Westminster, 161 F.2d 774. No transcript appears to have been kept of the oral argument.

91   Westminster, 161 F.2d 789–81.

92   Ibid., 780.

93   Note, *Segregation in Public Schools—A Violation of "Equal Protection of the Laws*," 56 YALE LAW JOURNAL 1059 (1947); Neal Seegert, Comment, 46 MICHIGAN LAW REVIEW 639 (March 1948); Note, *Is Racial Segregation Consistent with Equal Protection of the Laws? Plessy v. Ferguson Reexamined*, 49 COLUMBIA LAW REVIEW 629 (May 1949); Harry L. Gershon, Comment,

Restrictive Covenants and Equal Protection, 21 SOUTHERN CALIFORNIA LAW REVIEW 358 (1947–1948).

94 Lawrence E. Davies, *Segregation of Mexican American Students Stirs Court Fight*, NEW YORK TIMES MAGAZINE, 6 (December 22, 1946).

95 Wollenberg, Mendez v. Westminster, 329.

96 Mary M. Peters, *The Segregation of Mexican American Children in the Elementary Schools of California— Its Legal and Administrative Aspects* (UCLA, M.A. in Education thesis, July 1948).

97 Hernandez, 347 U.S. 477–78, 480.

98 The 350,000 number is in the National WWII Museum, "Latino Americans in WWII At a Glance," http://www.nationalww2museum.org/learn/education/for-students/ww2-history/at-a-glance/latino-americans-in-ww2.html.

99 Gonzalez, *Segregation of Mexican American Children*, 75.

100 Petition for Writ of Mandate No. 66625, Alvarez v. Lemon Grove School District (Superior Court of the State of California, County of San Diego 1931); Salvatierra v. Del Rio Independent School District, 33 S.W.2d 790 (Tex. Civ. App. 1930) (certiorari denied, 284 U.S. 580 (1931)); Lopez v. Seccombe, 71 F. Supp. 769 (S.D. Cal. 1944); Delgado v. Bastrop Independent School District, Civ. No. 388 (W.D. Tex. June 15, 1948); Gonzalez v. Sheely, 96 F. Supp. 1004 (D. Ariz. 1951). GONZÁLEZ, LABOR AND COMMUNITY; GÓMEZ-QUIÑONES, MEXICAN AMERICAN LABOR; RUIZ, FROM OUT OF THE SHADOWS; RICHARD GRISWOLD DEL CASTILLO, ED., WORLD WAR II AND MEXICAN AMERICAN CIVIL RIGHTS (University of Texas Press 2008); MARIO T. GARCIA, MEXICAN AMERICANS: LEADERSHIP, IDEOLOGY, & IDENTITY, 1930–1960 (Yale University Press 1989); Enrique M. López, *Community Resistance to Injustice and Inequality: Ontario, California, 1937–1947*, 17 AZTLAN No. 2, 1–29 (1988).

101 Vicki L. Ruiz, *We Always Tell Our Children They are Americans:* Mendez v. Westminster *and the California Road to* Brown v. Board of Education, 200 THE COLLEGE BOARD REVIEW (Fall 2003) (another version is in 6 THE BROWN QUARTERLY (Fall 2004); Thomas A. Saenz, Mendez *and the Legacy of* Brown: *A Latino Civil Rights Lawyer's Assessment*, 2004 BERKELEY WOMEN'S LAW JOURNAL 395 (2004); Richard Valencia, *The Mexican American Struggle for Equal Educational Opportunity in* Mendez v. Westminster: *Helping to Pave the Way for* Brown v. The Board of Education, 107 TEACHERS COLLEGE RECORD (March 2005); Guadalupe San Miguel, Jr., *The Impact of* Brown *on Mexican American Desegregation Litigation, 1950s to 1980s*, 4 JOURNAL OF LATINOS AND EDUCATION 221 (2005). STRUM, *MENDEZ V. WESTMINSTER*; RICHARD R. VALENCIA, CHICANO STUDENTS AND THE COURTS: THE MEXICAN AMERICAN LEGAL STRUGGLE FOR EDUCATIONAL EQUALITY (New York University Press 2008); JOSÉ F. MORENO, ED., THE ELUSIVE QUEST FOR EQUALITY: 150 YEARS OF CHICANO/CHICANA EDUCATION (Harvard Educational Review 1999); RUBEN DONATO, THE OTHER STRUGGLE FOR EQUAL SCHOOLS (SUNY Press 1997); HERSHEL T. MANUEL, THE EDUCATION OF MEXICAN AND

SPANISH-SPEAKING CHILDREN IN TEXAS (The Fund for Research in the Social Sciences 1930); GUADALUPE SAN MIGUEL, JR., "LET ALL OF THEM TAKE HEED": MEXICAN AMERICANS AND THE CAMPAIGN FOR EDUCATIONAL EQUALITY IN TEXAS, 1910–1981 (University of Texas Press 1987).

102 https://about.usps.com/postal-bulletin/2007/html/pb22213/info.4.13.html; http://www.whitehouse.gov/photos-and-video/video/2011/02/16/2010-presidential-medal-freedom-recipient-sylvia-mendez; http://www.nps.gov/history/nr/travel/American_Latino_Heritage/Los_Angeles_US_Court_House_and_Post_Office.html.

DISCUSSION QUESTIONS

1. What is the significance of *Mendez v. Westminster*?

2. How did the curriculum between Mexican and Anglo-American schools differ? Why was it different?

3. What was the risk of taking the *Mendez* case into state court rather than federal court?

4. What was the basis of Marcus's argument in the *Mendez* case?

5. What were the ramifications of the *Mendez* case beyond the school districts involved in the case?

6. Why did few scholars outside of California know about the *Mendez* case until the 21st century? What do you think this says about how Mexican American history is valued or prioritized in US history?

Chapter 6

Borderlands and 21st-Century Mexican Americans

Editor's Introduction

This chapter covers two topics: borderlands and 21st-century Mexican Americans. At first glance, the two readings in this chapter appear to have very little in common. However, the issues they confront are loosely interconnected. One reading focuses on the borderlands and the other focuses on immigration reform and its impact on mixed-status families, dreamers, and "daca-mented" youth.

The borderlands add an additional barrier for undocumented persons and mixed-status families. They live in a restrictive 100-mile border zone where Border Patrol agents operate with additional authority, including managing immigration checkpoints. This traps undocumented people in the periphery of the United States unless they are willing to take the additional risks of clandestinely crossing yet another boundary. It also restricts educational opportunities for undocumented youth who are living within this borderlands zone. For example, prior to Deferred Action for Childhood Arrivals (DACA), this meant that undocumented children could not leave the Rio Grande Valley for college even if they had been accepted. That left them with minimal higher education options.

"Space and Place in the Borderlands," by Suzanne Simon, also discusses the environmental challenges that exist in the Rio Grande Valley (among other border zones) and how these challenges have had detrimental health consequences for the residents of the valley. As "Legislative Inaction and Executive Action: Mixed Status Families, the Dreamer Movement, and DACA," by scholars Marjorie S. Zatz and Nancy Rodriguez, reveals, mixed-status families, in which the parents are undocumented and children are documented or are DACA recipients, often will not take advantage of the health and social services available to children for fear of the parents' citizenship status becoming exposed. This is particularly dangerous considering the environmental toxicity described in the first reading.

Thus, while it may not seem that these readings have much in common, I urge the reader to think critically about how the borderlands and its environment impact undocumented, dacamented, and mixed-status families.

"Space and Place in the Borderlands," is an excerpt from the 2014 book *Sustaining the Borderlands in the Age of NAFTA: Development, Politics, and Participation on the US-Mexico Border*. It provides an overview of borderlands history with an emphasis on the Lower Rio Grande region. The reading then analyzes how the region has been impacted by the globalizing and spatializing forces of transnational capital. The author provides a detailed explanation of the environmental consequences of the *maquila* industry and how its effects are unequally distributed between the United States and Mexico.

This reading is useful for its historical context on the borderlands and its examination of the contemporary issues plaguing the region. The author's aim is to demonstrate the importance of the border "as a territorial marker designating sovereign limits and possibilities, to the production and reproduction of the borderlands as a culturally, economically, and environmentally marginal region." She wants readers to understand that despite its location on the periphery of the nation, for both the United States and Mexico, the borderlands is a critical region that informs transnational relationships.

The second reading, "Legislative Inaction and Executive Action: Mixed Status Families, the Dreamer Movement, and DACA," by Marjorie S. Zatz and Nancy Rodriguez, is an excerpt from their book *Dreams and Nightmares: Immigration Policy, Youth, and Families*, published in 2015. This reading discusses the "policy process and political mobilizations leading up to DACA, preliminary data on who has benefited from the program and who has been left behind, and, for those receiving deferred action," the reading examines the transition from being undocumented to being "dacamented".

This reading is captivating because the authors draw upon oral testimonies and embed the firsthand accounts throughout their writing. This strategy adds a layer of humanity that is sometimes missing in writing on immigration legislation. The reading is helpful in understanding how people—both documented and undocumented—are impacted by US immigration policies and attitudes. Zatz and Rodriguez want readers to understand the everyday experiences of undocumented youth and the children of undocumented parents and shed light on the "Dreamer" social movement that is finally pushing these teenagers and young adults to claim the rights and privileges of membership in the country they call home.

These readings combine to demonstrate how people influence change in politics, immigration, the environmental, and society. They further illustrate the power of the borderlands region and how happenings there have a reach far beyond its geographic position.

Space and Place in the Borderlands

Suzanne Simon

T HE BORDER BETWEEN MEXICO AND THE United States has often been referred to as the longest boundary in the world to separate the so-called first and third worlds (cf. Alvarez 1995, 451). Gloria Anzaldúa's famous description of the border as an "open wound" where the "Third World grates up against the first and bleeds" (1987, 3) has often been summoned to drive home this empirically well-documented point. Anzaldúa's prescient words have, in recent years, been transformed from (rough) metaphor to visceral reality as border cities like Ciudad Juarez (Cd. Juarez), Reynosa, Nuevo Laredo, Matamoros, and others have been transformed into bloody battlegrounds for drug cartel turf wars. Since the relative success of US anti-drug efforts in closing off Caribbean and waterborne trafficking routes in the late 1980s (Andreas 1998) and the unfortunate drug violence that has engulfed parts of Mexico since the launching of former President Felipe Calderón's Drug War in 2006 (Castañeda 2010; Cockcroft 2010; Grayson 2010), the line has come to serve a different function. Now it helps to corral violence within Mexican border cities, as demonstrated by the especially horrific violence in Cd. Juarez since 2008 (Campbell 2011) or the massacre of seventy-two aspiring migrants just outside Matamoros in the spring of 2010.

As a productive limit to state sovereignty and territoriality (Heyman 1999), the US-Mexico border has supported the clustering of off-shore assembly plants, with all their attendant conditions, on the southern side of the US-Mexico border. As a territorial limit, the border is productive because it has historically accommodated and reinforced postmodern production regimes of flexible production and accumulation (Harvey 1989). The territorial limits of modern nation-states are essential components of the globalized capitalism that took root from the early 1970s onward. They are not incidental to, but constitutive of, contemporary global capitalist production regimes. The borders of modern nation-states—and the discordant environmental, labor, and human rights protection regimes they preserve—make present-day flexible and transnational production processes both possible and highly productive. The Mexican side of the US-Mexico border is one of the most obvious and instructive examples of this global phenomenon.

This chapter provides a sketch of borderlands history, with a focus on the lower Rio Bravo/ Rio Grande region. As ethnographic setting, the border region is decidedly liminal and has been so since the first western advancing Anglo-Saxon populations encountered the northward moving Spanish conquistadores, and as each ran amuck over the indigenous populations that had previously inhabited American and Mexican territories (Truett 1999; Stern 1998; Worcester 1988). The first section briefly sketches out general borderlands history, with particular focus on the dynamics of the Lower Rio Grande/Rio Bravo region. It does not pretend to do justice to the extraordinarily rich historical literature devoted to this topic. The second portion is devoted to the border's more recent history, in which the region has been produced and reproduced by the globalizing and spatializing forces of transnational capital. Neoliberalism and the *maquila* industry stand out as particularly important non-local forces that have produced both border populations and the conditions in which they live, even as these global forces intertwine and interact with local forces. Both have come together to produce the borderlands as a marginal zone vis-à-vis its respective nation-states (cf. Das and Poole 2004).

The US-Mexico Borderlands

The term borderlands was first used by historian Herbert Bolton in his 1921 book, *The Spanish Borderlands* (cited in Truett 1999). For Bolton, the American West was but one of two equally important moving frontiers shaping the region, and it was the meeting of these two frontiers that produced the borderlands as cultural contact zone (cf. Stern 1998; Worcester 1988). Bolton was a student of the famed frontier theorist, Frederick Jackson Turner, but he also turned Turner's thesis on its head. Unlike Turner, who had theorized the American West through a largely Anglo-Saxon conquest lens (arguing that the act of taming the West built American democratic character), Bolton drew attention to the fact that the conquered regions had previously been Spanish territory, even as he also neglected the histories of the Native American populations (Truett 1999). For him and his followers, there were multi-ple frontiers (cf. Weber 1988, xii) rather than a single one ordained by Manifest Destiny. "Bolton argued that the borderlands found their greatest significance not within a one way narrative of European-American colonization, but rather as the 'meeting place and fusing place of two streams of European civilization, one coming from the south, the other from the north'" (Truett 1999, 164). This border only became fixed as a permanent territorial marker with the end of the Mexican-American War in 1848 and the signing of the Treaty of Guadalupe Hidalgo.

Stern has also described the early borderlands as a "diffuse zone of acculturation" and a "complex zone of cultural, social, economic, genetic, military, political, religious and linguistic interaction between many different groups of people" (Stern 1998, 157) that made the colonial Spanish and Mexican frontier experience unlike the US frontier expe-rience. Whereas the West functioned as both escape valve and opportunity for American pioneers, the Spanish colonial frontier was essentially an extension of colonial society. It was, therefore, a place for marginalized or the underclass: "In the Spanish Borderlands they were escaped black slaves, mestizos, and mulattos chaffing at discrimination, runaway mission Indians, Spanish presidial deserters, itinerant miners and peddlers, and assorted malcontents—horse and cattle thieves, murderers, and renegades" (Stern 1998, 158).

Many authors have described the pre-Mexican-American War period as a comparatively harmonious one in which the challenges of settler life took precedence over national politics or loyalties. There was relative interethnic harmony that mirrored the fact that all shared a common geographic space and faced similar challenges (Richardson 1999; Truett 1999). After the Texas declaration of Independence in 1836 and the Mexican-American War of 1846–1848, the region became rife with everyday violence; cattle rustling, lynching of Mexican-Americans by Anglo settlers, and raids from one side of the border to the next became the norm (Richardson 1999, 5–8). This was due partly to the ways in which the newly founded US-Mexico border mapped novel national and ethnic identities onto existing populations, and it provides an early example of how nonlocal factors have often had dire consequences for the locale of the border region. When the US-Mexico war ended, many ethnic Mexicans who had originally settled South Texas or the Rio Grande area became second-class citizens overnight vis-à-vis their Anglo neighbors. Although cross-border familial or community networks persisted then, as they do now, "the borderlands became more divided than ever, as land and life split into different worlds" (Truett 1999, 169).

Low-grade violence escalated to a new level with the onset of the Mexican Revolution in 1910 (Meed 1992; cf. Johnson 2004, 275), the use of the border for arms smuggling, United States meddling in Mexican internal politics, and cross-border skirmishes. For those of Mexican origin, the collective sense of threat was perhaps most vividly captured by the Ballad of Gregorio Cortez, and eloquently described by famed border anthropologist and folklorist Américo Paredes in *"With His Pistol in His Hand": A Border Ballad and Its Hero* (1958). This *corrido* chronicled the shooting of an American, South Texas sheriff by a Mexican farmer and the subsequent vicious hunt for Cortez by the Texas Rangers and posses. Tellingly, the initial shooting resulted from a simple miscommunication, but quickly spiraled into a heated manhunt fueled by the ethnic hatred, suspicion, and paranoia that shaped the region at the time. As Saldivar notes in his commentary on Paredes' august work, *corridos* are meant to demonstrate collective, rather than individual sensibilities. The experience of being hunted like an animal, assumed guilty without trial, and the terrors of vigilante justice were meant "to stand not as an individual but as an epic-like construction of the South Texas societies that interpellated him. As is well known, Cortez's fate, for Paredes, cannot be distinguished from communal fate" (Saldivar 1997, 40). Cortez's fate was a crystallization of the ethnic tensions that saturated the border region in the early twentieth century and which, to different degrees and through different mechanisms, continue in the contemporary era.

Lower Rio Grande History

The Lower Rio Grande Valley region sits in an alluvial plain extending outward from the river. In times past, the river would sometimes overflow its banks, naturally irrigating the flood plains that surrounded it. Also in times past, the Lower Rio Grande was lined with extensive Sabal palms, leading to its naming by Spanish explorers as the *Rio de Palmas*. The palms once extended from a fairly lush area of vegetation at the mouth of the river far up its length. However, "the centuries of clearing for farms and communities have today reduced the Sabal palms known by Cabeza de Vaca to one last stand in a small Audubon preserve outside Brownsville, and a withering drought had this summer [2002] left most of the wetlands as dry as chalk" (Reid 2004, xix). Spanish explorer, Cabeza de Vaca, found his way across the Gulf of Mexico and to the River of Palms after being shipwrecked. There he was adopted into a Native American tribe believed by many to have been Coahuiltecan.

During the early years of conquest and settlement, the Lower Rio Grande Valley remained somewhat below the Spanish Crown's radar (Zavaleta 1986). The French and English were able to settle the area heavily. The relative quiet of the early settlements came to an abrupt end after Mexico's independence in 1822, which led the decolonized state to establish area outposts. At the time, the small, relatively bucolic, and dispersed river communities were converted into a strategic military outpost and given the name Matamoros (Zavaleta 1986, 131–132, 135).

The region changed dramatically after the Texas Declaration of Independence in 1836 and the Mexican-American War of 1846–1848. Although originally located within the cultural contact zone of the Spanish Borderlands, the area was now located on the southern boundary of the United States and the northern border of Mexico. The Rio Bravo/Grande was made a permanent territorial marker between the two emergent nation-states. Although the Matamoros-Brownsville area had not moved, the region suddenly became peripheral. Later author and border native José David Saldivar described the necessary respatialization of the "native" in order to understand his or her own identity: "I tried, like Paredes, to spatialize on the map before me how this 'periphery' was once the 'center' of the imperial Spanish border province of Nuevo Santander, colonized in 1749 by José de Escandon to hold the line against English, French, and Anglo-American encroachment" (Saldivar 1997, 18).

Following the Mexican-American war, Texas and the Lower Rio Grande Valley regions became sites of continually escalating violence, due at least partially to the ways in which the redrawing of national territorial boundaries affected local social and property relations. Since the mid-eighteenth century, cattle ranching had been central to the region's economy, which also "lay at the heart of South Texas's social structure" (Johnson 2004, 276). Cattle-rustling, stealing, banditry, and the lynching of Mexicans and Mexican-Americans became more commonplace, and "Mexican-Americans living in South Texas lost much of their property to Anglo ranchers through theft, extortion, and trickery" (Richardson 1999, 7). One lifelong resident of the Lower Rio Grande Valley reported the terror of that period this way:

> If they saw you walking down the street, and one told you to come, you went. They would take a man to the outskirts of town and tell him to start running. They would shoot him in the back as he ran and report to the man in charge that they just shot another bandit. People were really afraid of them. They could do whatever they wanted, and no one ever questioned them. I still don't trust them. (quoted in Richardson 1999, 8)

In short, if the borderlands were originally imagined as a lawless region because of the allegedly unsavory characters that inhabited the lands, in the aftermath of the Mexican-American War, it became a liminal space of violence and lawlessness in which suspicion and terror increasingly reigned. Elites encouraged views of the borderlands as a marginal, uncivilized space by calling "upon images of savagery to legitimate efforts to control nature and society, the border, or la *frontera*" (Truett 1999, 167), allowing them to argue for the need to develop and so tame the region: "Many Mexican and Anglo-American power-holders claimed that smugglers and so-called 'bandits' and 'cowboys' stood in the way of 'civilized' development, and they advocated their removal from the region" (ibid.).

At the turn of the twentieth century, the South Texas border region also changed dramatically because the economy ceased to be organized predominantly around cattle-ranching and became organized around agriculture. The combination of Northern Tamaulipas and South Texas cotton farming, irrigation, agriculture, and the building of railroads all came together to make the area attractive for in-migration (Arreola 2002, 44–53). The value of farm property increased 500 percent between the years 1900 and 1920, forcing many landowners to sell their properties when they could not keep up with property taxes (Johnson 2004, 276). Later construction of the Falcon and Amistad Dams provided irrigation to otherwise arid lands and helped support the cotton boom that swept Northern Tamaulipas (and other northern Mexico regions) in the mid-twentieth century (Walsh 2008). Although in 1850 the Rio Bravo was reported to have been as "wide as the Hudson at Troy," in the current era, dams for irrigation have largely destroyed the river and caused innumerable border water skirmishes (Walsh 2004), while simultaneously drying up the area's many picturesque *resacas* (Ruiz 2000, 196).

Little remains of the original dense forest that once covered the banks of the "Great River." Most of what remains exists within protected areas and, if it is in unprotected areas, it is under continuous threat by both the development objectives of towns on both sides of the border, as well as the security measures of the border patrol agents, such as those in Brownsville where "agents of the patrol who are intent on stopping the flow of illegal migrants bulldoze virgin lands for roads, erect fences, and nightly light up the banks for the Rio Grande, thus jeopardizing the ecosystem" (Ruiz 2000, 197).

In both earlier periods and the contemporary one, the border zone has also been a region of intense connectivity, especially as it is experienced at the immediate local level among cross-border populations (Herzog 1990; Heyman 1991; Kearney and Knopp 1991; Ortiz 2001, 1999; Zavaleta 1986). Much of this connectivity emerges from local cross-border networks, such as family and social ties, civic groups and activities, and a range of economic linkages that run the gamut from the expansive macro-level connections (e.g., the *maquila* industry, drug cartels) to everyday shopping performed on both sides.[1] One can add to that list the cross-border environmental advocacy that has grown steadily in the post-NAFTA era. Local cross-border economies are also mutually interdependent. In the contemporary era, economies on the US side of the border suffer when Mexican workers fail to shop on the US side or, alternatively, *maquila* employment decreases due to contractions in the US economy, as happened in the wake of 9/11.[2]

From Space to Place: The BIP and Maquilization of the Border Zone

Even since the US-Mexico border emerged as territorial limit at the end of the US-Mexico War, it has registered extraordinary breadth and depth due to the cultural differences, natural environment, and regional specificities that configure its length. Border cities did not emerge whole cloth from the *maquila* boom. Rather, each has its own colonial and post-colonial history, rural-urban dynamics, and cultural or regional influences not reducible to the border. As Alvarez (1995) and other border theorists have observed, there are multiple cultures within the border zone that break down not only along class and ethnic lines, but which are also heavily circumscribed geographically throughout the border's 2,000-mile length. Given the combination of contingency and consistency that has historically characterized the region, it is virtually impossible to capture a succinct border culture. Alvarez describes the latter term as a misnomer and a false starting point for analysis, due to the way in which it "either glosses over or essentializes traits and behavior" or "pigeonhole[s] this geographic region into a Wisslerian culture area type" (Alvarez 1995, 450).

Nevertheless, the sense of place in the border region has, in some ways, been overwhelmed by the spatializing forces of globalized, *maquila* production. Ruiz gives eloquence to the historical and site-specific sense of place that has steadily been eclipsed by the geographic and spatial monotony of *maquila*-based development: "Today, life on the Mexican side of the borderlands only rarely conjures up that of the 1920s. For those of us who knew the old, the dissimilarity is striking. Since the 1960s, the arrival of assembly plants, an adjunct of the global economy, has radically altered the contours of Mexican border society" (2000, 61).

The structural similarities that emerged with the mid-1960s and early 1970s *maquilization* of the border zone give external observers the impression of a seamless and distinct border culture that exists throughout its length but which, in fact, is a function of this relatively recent imposition of spatializing forces on local places and peoples. Many of the structural similarities that repeat themselves throughout the length of the border zone can be traced more or less directly to two separate, but intertwined, phenomena: first, the creation of the Border Industrialization Program (BIP) in 1965 and the lesser known Programa Nacional Fronterizo (PRONAF) in 1961; and, second, global outsourcing trends that took root from the early 1970s onward.

The ostensible primary purpose of the BIP was to provide employment to former Bracero workers (suddenly unemployed with an end to that program) and to attempt to stem the tide of illegal immigration to the United States through the creation of an economic fence (Rivera-Batiz 1986, 263). With the closing of the Bracero program, many guest workers and their families became stranded on the Mexican side of the border with few resources. Many Bracero workers had relocated their families to cities and towns on the immediate Mexican side of the border so that they could be close by when the workers crossed back into Mexico. "Indeed, the BIP was established in the aftermath of the Bracero program (that ended in 1965) and its main purpose was to absorb the former Braceros into the Mexican labor force so as to prevent their illegal immigration to the United States" (Rivera-Batiz 1986, 263; cf. Baerresen 1971; Fernandez-Kelly 1983, 209–210; Seligson and Williams 1981).

The program aimed to attract foreign investment to the area with the promise of cheap labor and an absence of import and export tariffs on imported raw materials and exported goods (taxes were and are applied only to the "value added" in the production process; Heyman 1991, 41). An additional attraction for investors was the non- or poorly-unionized character of the *maquiladora* labor force (Kopinak 1995, 30; Rivera-Batiz 1986, 263). The BIP allowed the construction of *maquila* factories and free trade zones by foreign-owned corporations, mostly from the United States, but also from Asian countries as well, particularly in the western portion of the border (Quintero Ramírez 1997). The off-shore assembly plant industry grew exponentially from the time of its founding: In 1967, there were fifty-seven *maquilas* in border cities; by 1976 there were 552, and in 1981 there were more than 600—over 90 percent of which were in the border zone (Seligson and Williams 1981, 1). The growth of assembly plants also produced enormous growth in the rates of employment associated within them; from 1969 until 1985 the number of employees jumped from an initial 15,000 to more than 240,000 (Rivera-Batiz 1986, 264).

Although *maquilas* were originally developed to cure anticipated Bracero unemployment problems, the exponential population growth throughout the region that started with the BIP era indicates that the industry simultaneously encouraged ongoing migration to the border zone, even if, as Seligson and Williams argue, the BIP was merely one of several factors exerting a "pull" during that period (Seligson and Williams 1981, esp. pp. 59, 71–74). While NAFTA was supposed to decrease migration, Cornelius and others maintain that migration has increased in the post-NAFTA period, with *maquiladoras* and border cities still functioning as "powerful magnets" (Cornelius 2002, 295) and migrating populations providing a reliable labor pool. The only Mexican resource that makes a direct contribution to the *maquila* production process is labor (Delgado Wise 2007), as Heyman's succinct description of the border assembly process also suggests: "In the maquiladoras, parts and items are put together by Mexican workers, by hand or with machinery that is usually fairly simple. (...) The purpose of the maquiladora is to obtain inexpensive effort at the labor-intensive steps of manufacturing" (Heyman 1991, 41).

An additional contradiction between the stated mission of the BIP and its consequent results is that the labor force has historically been predominantly female. Rather than target unemployed men, *maquilas* virtually immediately targeted women, and young women in particular (Fernandez-Kelly 1983; Kopinak 1995, 31) in a manner consistent with the outsourcing trends of multinationals seeking "docile" and young female labor (Mies 1986; Nash and Fernandez-Kelly 1983; Ong 1987). Young women were particularly favored in the largely Asian-dominated electronics or microchip industries of the western border region (which also had weak "ghost" unions, as noted in Quintero Ramírez 1997) for their small fingers and excellent eyesight (cf. Ong 1987), but they have historically represented the majority of the *maquila* labor force, even as more men began to be brought in during the 1980s and 1990s (Richardson 1999, 98). In the *maquila* industry's preference for young, female labor, it exhibited patterns consistent with manufacturing outsourcing practices beginning in the 1960s and 1970s, based on an "ideology that justifies the employment of women (preferably young women) in low-paying assembly operations by referring to presumed biological and emotional differences between the sexes" (Fernandez-Kelly 1983, 181).

In their early preference for female labor, the *maquilas* were simply regional manifestations of globalization outsourcing trends. As a legal, national and territorial marker, the

US-Mexico border performed the function of providing a safe haven for predominantly US or multinational corporations searching for cheap labor (Fatemi 1990) or a "pollution haven" (Leonard 1988; Reed 1998, 3) for the production of commodities ranging from microchips to automobiles. Global economic dynamics that have produced the northern Mexico frontier are remarkably consistent with other core-periphery outsourcing trends that emerged at that time. However, the Mexican side of the US-Mexico border provided an exceptionally generous stretch of territory "in the margins of the state" (Das and Poole 2004) in which the negative externalities of intentionally under-regulated and overpro-duced production wastes could be housed [...]. It is precisely such less stringent pollution controls with which developing economies sometimes barter, laying waste to vast swaths of land and peoples, so that "nations with the lowest environmental standards and the least resource-conserving policies will acquire a comparative cost advantage over those with high standards and conservation-oriented policies" (Harris 2000, 119).

Within this broader border context, the more recent four-decade history of Matamoros has been both similar to and different from that of other border cities. The Matamoros-Brownsville area has historically been connected by the Mexican and Mexican-American populations that predominate in both cities, the fact that South Texas originally belonged to Mexico, and the extensive legal and illegal networks that bind the two (Arreola 2002; Kearney and Knopp 1991; Richardson 1999; Zavaleta 1986). The experience of Matamoros has been similar to that of other border cities like Nuevo Laredo, Cd. Juarez, Nogales, and Tijuana in the sense that city industry is now dominated by the *maquila* sector and the majority of the city's occupants are poor migrants from other regions of Mexico. As Richardson notes, "Campesinos have been pushed off their *ejidos* (communal farms) by a combination of government edicts, overpopulation, and drought. Massive migrations bring them to the cities and to the border. For example, Reynosa and Matamoros, the border cities facing McAllen and Brownsville, have grown by 600% since 1950" (Richardson 1999, 98). The Matamoros-Reynosa area saw a 74 percent population increase between 1970 and 1990 (Russell 1994, 254).

Matamoros' population explosion and geographic expansion has followed a pattern common to other border cities. In-migrating and squatting populations settle in *colonias* in the city's peripheries, gradually becoming incorporated into the city's neighborhoods. The city is heavily contaminated with organic and chemical wastes due to the lack of sanitary and public health infrastructure. Like most border cities, the populations of both Matamoros and Brownsville evidence higher than average rates of respiratory disorders, hepatitis, tuberculosis, and other air- or water-borne diseases traceable alternately to air, water, or ground water contaminants. Unlike other border cities, however, the Matamoros-Brownsville region gained a certain amount of notoriety because of a neural tube defect

(NTD) cluster that occurred in the area in the early 1990s, resulting in a numerous cases of anencephaly and spina bifida. [...]

Social scientists have been studying the *maquiladora* phenomenon in relation to development, globalization, labor, gender, migration, environment, public health, and a host of other related issues for decades now (e.g., Brenner et al. 2000; Carrillo 1986; Denman 1992, 1991; Peña 1997; Fernandez-Kelly 1983; Heyman 1994, 1991; Nash and Fernandez-Kelly 1983; Quintero Ramírez 1997; Moure-Eraso et al. 1997, 1994). Originally demonized as sweatshops or satanic mills, the literature on *maquiladoras* has become more sophisticated with time. It now incorporates studies of *maquilas* in relation to both national and global economies and the effect of the industries on border environment and ecology, as well as the differences in individual or regional *maquila* practices (Quintero Ramírez 1997).

Mexican Environmental Law and the Border as Pollution Haven

The *maquila* industry and the hardships of life in border cities garnered significant public attention during the course of the NAFTA debates of the early 1990s. For both Mexican and US labor and environmental constituencies, the US-Mexico borderlands came to function as a symbol of the hazards of globalization and free trade worldwide, with many maintaining that all of Mexico would be transformed into a free trade zone under NAFTA conditions. During this period, certain iconic images came to function as "establishing shots of the border" (Fox 1999, 41–67), including images of chain link fences, the river (Rio Grande), waste water canals or *aguas negros*, or "stock shots of the 'poor but dignified people'" (Fox 1999, 61). These images came to symbolize the border at the same time that NAFTA and free trade suddenly became common household terms in the United States.

Unlike its prescience with regard to labor law (in which Mexico anticipated US labor protections by decades), Mexico did not begin to develop environmental regulations until the 1970s (Janetti-Díaz et al. 1994; Mumme 1992; Mumme, Bath, and Assetto 1988; Najera 1999). Historically, there has been strong private and indigenous interest in the protection of the natural environment in Mexico (Simonian 1995), but the federal government lagged far behind. Mexican environmental laws were modeled to a degree on US environmental laws (Carlos Vasquez 1993, 363), as were its environmental institutions. In 1971, the Ley Federal para Prevenir y Controlar la Contaminación Ambiental (Federal Law for the Prevention and Control of Environmental Pollution), the country's first comprehensive environmental law, was passed. In 1982, the Mexican Congress initiated the Ley Federal de Protección del Ambiente, which was directed specifically to the conservation and preservation of the natural environment. Also, the Ley General del Equilibrio Ecologico y la Protección al Ambiente (LGEEPA) was passed in 1988, which addressed the exploitation of natural resources through mining and forestry, as well as the protection of waters and issues related to occupational and environmental health. The current primary environmental agency is the Secretaría de Medio Ambiente y Recursos Naturales, (SEMARNAT).

Several reasons have been put forth for the well-known and historic lack of enforcement of environmental law in Mexico that provided the rationale for the environmental side accord. The first reason typically cited pertains to the oft-noted tendency of "global south" nations to function as pollution havens for globalized first world manufacturing activities (Leonard 1988; Stebbins 1992), even as NAFTA was intended to obviate this tendency through a salutary first world imitation effect (Garcia-Johnson 2000). As Leonard notes, "Although not fundamentally responsible for Mexico's rising position as an exporter of manufactured goods, the relative dearth of effective environmental and health controls has enhanced Mexico's attractiveness to some US firms participating in the *maquiladora* program, in the mineral processing sector, and in certain types of chemical manufacturing" (Leonard 1988, 154). Mexico's situation has been similar to that of other so-called developing nations in that the need to attract foreign capital has discouraged effective enforcement of environmental policies (Mumme, Bath, and Assetto 1988). Second, the PRI's decades-long one-party rule and authoritarianism proved a hindrance to environmental policy making, especially when the exploitation of natural resources was tied to aggressive Import Substitution Industrialization (ISI) policies (ibid.). Third, Mexican environmental laws were historically framed in language that was largely symbolic and rhetorical. As Mumme notes with respect to the 1971 Federal Law for the Prevention and Control of Environmental Pollution, the basic law was so "general in content and wanting in force that it remained little more than a symbolic document" (Mumme 1992, 126). The government's approach to environmental regulation reflected a general preference for regulatory methods based on award, incentives, and abatement, rather than punishment (Mumme, Bath, and Assetto 1988, 18–19).

With regard to the border environment, both the Mexican and US governments have historically demonstrated some level of concern. Largely ineffectual efforts have periodically been hashed out in an effort to cooperate and manage the border environmental problems. The first binational effort at border management produced the 1889 International Boundary Commission, which eventually led to the creation in 1944 of the Water Utilization Treaty and the creation of the International Boundary and Water Commission (IBWC), a treaty and organization still in effect today (Barry 1994, 31; Mikulas 1999, 3). Following a lapse of almost forty years, the next international accord signed into place was the 1983 La Paz Agreement between the United States and Mexico, otherwise known as the Agreement for the Cooperation for the Protection and Improvement of the Environment of the Border Area. The La Paz Agreement specifically addressed border pollution problems with fairly explicit acknowledgement of the fact that border pollution was largely attributable to *maquila* forces (Ellis 1996, 640–641). The agreement also addressed the problems of toxic waste dumping throughout the region that had become publicly acknowledged by the early 1980s (Barry 1994, 47–68; Simon 1997, 205–235).

The 1992 Border Plan was an attempt to remedy La Paz's ineffectiveness, meanwhile simultaneously increasing the tracking and repatriation of *maquila* wastes to the United States and ending the practice of illegal dumping (Reed 1998). The Border Plan purported to encourage the monitoring and collection of information concerning border pollution, increase enforcement of actually existing laws, introduce new initiatives for pollution reduction, and increase cross-border environmental cooperation. In particular, it aimed to increase cooperation between the EPA and the Secretaría de Desarrollo Urbano y Ecologia (SEDUE; SEMARNAT's name at the time), as well as public participation in monitoring and information gathering. As Ellis points out, the Border Plan failed due to lack of funding and enforcement provisions (Ellis 1996, 649–653). NAFTA's environmental side accord was intended to replace all of these previous bi-national accords and successfully address the environmental pollution problems that had failed to be remedied by previous accords (Eaton 1996, 741–743).

Environmental Destruction in the Borderlands

The border's two thousand mile stretch begins on the Pacific Coast between Tijuana and San Diego, then continues across the sometimes treacherous and often soaring Arizona and New Mexico deserts, climbing high into the Sierra Madre and Big Bend corridors, finally plunging into the long flatlands of the lower Rio Grande Valley to meet the Gulf of Mexico. While the frequently barren landscape might not meet the tastes of certain middle class American preservationists who have historically preferred green and moist landscapes as symbols of pristine, untouched nature (Cronon 1996), the border's rugged barrenness holds a special appeal for those with more Spartan tastes. The desert and arid, scrappy, scrubby environments are a part of Nature too, as much as soaring mountains and plunging waterfalls. The entire border region remains home to rich bio-diversity of plant and animal life, including such rare and protected animals as the jacuarundi, oncelot and javalina. At least two books, *Two Eagles/Dos Aguilas: The Natural World of the United States, Mexico Borderlands* (Steinhart 1994) and *Mountain Islands and Desert Seas: A Natural History of the US-Mexican Borderlands* (Gehlbach 1993) are devoted explicitly to describing the enormous and richly textured natural landscape of the borderlands region. Gehlbach, in particular, provides a virtually encyclopedic account of the flora and fauna that inhabit the region, as well as the ongoing desertification that threatens both human and non-human inhabitants. Both authors emphasize the role that man-made destruction has played in transforming border ecology. Gehlbach, for example, devotes an entire chapter to the discussion of DDT and its presence in jackrabbits, whiptail lizards, Merriam Kangaroo rats, "silky and desert pocket mice" (ibid., 44), and people. He notes that bat populations—which reproduce at a much lower rate than rodents—are particularly susceptible to DDT toxicity and claims that "bat populations are declining in the Borderlands, and I believe it legitimate to suspect pesticide poisoning along with natural factors" (ibid., 47). He goes on to note that the "once spectacular evening flight of eight million Brazilian free-tailed bats from Carlsbad Caverns, New Mexico, has all but ceased" (ibid.).

Much of the environmental destruction of the Lower Rio Grande Valley region began with the introduction of cattle and accelerated with the early twentieth century shift from ranching to agriculture. For many decades, the region of northern Tamaulipas ranging through southern Texas has been dominated by industrialized agriculture with all that implies: dams, irrigation, pesticides, and fertilizers. In southern Texas farmers have historically grown peaches, lettuce, melons, and any variety of fresh produce; in northern Tamaulipas, the agricultural preference has been for cotton, sorghum, and wheat.

Nevertheless, environmental destruction of the borderlands took a sharp and distinctive turn with the introduction of the *maquila* industry. Since that time, the border region has become massively, and perhaps irreparably, contaminated with chemical and organic wastes. The contamination is so rampant that the authors of one study have suggested that "there is a Bhopal taking place in the border zone; it is merely taking place over months and years, rather than seconds and minutes" (Brenner et al. 2000, 280; cf. Peña 1997, 279). Saldivar has provided a firsthand account of this transformation in the Lower Rio Grande Valley. It merits quoting at length:

> In my childhood in Cameron County in South Texas, I saw the Texas-Mexico borderlands turn into an ecological wasteland, with more than ninety-three maquiladoras pouring out toxic waste and endangering life chances and life experiences on both sides of the border. As a result of these unregulated factories (of General Motors, Quimica Fluor, PEMEX, among others), there have been in the last decade what the border journalist Ana Arana calls "a disturbingly high number of anencephalic births" (a rare disorder that leaves infants without a complete brain) in the Rio Grande Valley. (Saldivar 1997, 19)

In both the pre- and post-NAFTA era, numerous toxicological, public health, and environmental studies have been done, demonstrating beyond dispute the high levels of toxic chemicals that saturate the border environment. In 1990, the June 26 *El Paso Herald Post* reported that the American Medical Association referred to the US-Mexico border as "a virtual cesspool and breeding ground for infectious disease" (quoted in Moure-Eraso et al. 1994, 315). Border cities in which *maquilas* thrive are particularly toxic, but many of the wastes are carried downstream via the Rio Grande and other estuaries. These same water-ways, soils, and ground waters are often contaminated with the pesticide and fertilizer run-off from agriculture as well, even as they are used for irrigation. Extremely high levels of mercury, nickel, lead, chromium, arsenic, DDT, phthalate, zinc, copper, xylene, toluene, benzene, ammonia, battery acids, among other chemicals, have been found (Brenner et al. 2000, 278–279; Moure-Eraso et al. 1994, 1997). A 1991 report of the National Toxic Campaign Fund, "Border Trouble: Rivers in Peril," (Lewis, Kaltofen, and Ormsby 1991) tested three dif-ferent sites along the Rio Grande and found multiple toxins at between twenty and 215,000 times the levels permissible under US laws (Simon 1997, 211). Additionally, there have been ongoing problems with gas leaks, explosions, fires, and other dangerous incidents in the Lower Rio Grande Valley (Moure-Eraso et al. 1994).

In addition to chemical contamination, there is the organic waste problem. The presence of dangerously high levels of organic wastes in the border environment is directly related to the fact that most border cities experienced exponential population growth within a few short years. Not only do border cities burden local ecologies and water resources, but explosive growth has systematically outpaced the capacity of city planners and municipal resources to keep pace with the construction of sufficient infrastructure for the appropriate management of human wastes. Most poor *colonias* have limited plumbing, if any. Ditches typ-ically drain *aguas negras* (sewage) from indoor plumbing, dumping the wastes into human dug canals, estuaries, and larger rivers, such as the Rio Bravo. In the Matamoros area, these wastes travel directly to the Laguna Madre and Gulf of Mexico. The following sketch is typ-ical, and more than just a "stock shot":

> Two of Matamoros' *colonias* (or squatters' camps), where *maquiladora* workers live, are next to open drainage ditches. Residents of one *colonia* obtain water from shallow wells (less than 20 feet deep) made by improvised hand-drilling methods, within approximately 100 feet of the drainage ditches of FINSA, an industrial park. The canal collecting the effluent of one *maquiladora* plant in the park has such a high level of volatile organics in the drainage ditch that the stream itself would be classified in the United States as hazardous waste. (Moure-Eraso et al. 1994, 316)

Aguas negras, one of the "main vehicle[s] for disease transmission" (Barry 1994, 30), are clearly a public health threat, but one that is numbingly familiar in Mexican border cities. Barry puts it bluntly: "As border cities expand, so do the massive quantities of sewage. In the absence of industrial waste treatment facilities, mixed in with fecal matter are the chemical wastes from industrial manufacturers, mostly *maquiladoras*" (ibid., 30). The handling and management of waste-waters has been one of the most challenging issues for border cities, as noted as late (or early) as 1992 in Cd. Juarez: "Sixty percent of Cd. Juarez is served by sewage lines, but there are no sewage treatment facilities in this city. Sewage mains discard into ditches, and the unlined ditches carry the sewage out of the city to agricultural fields, where this wastewater is used for crop irrigation" (Cech and Essman 1992, 1056–1057).

Stebbins has put a political economy slant (similar to the approach of critical medical anthropology) on the problems of hazardous and toxic waste dumping in so-called third world countries by industrialized nations. He argues that systematic toxic waste transfers play a causal role in exacerbating health risks for underdeveloped nations' populations. Debt-ridden nations find it difficult to resist monetary incentives to accept hazardous wastes. Stebbins describes this first world/third world relation as a form of "garbage imperialism": "Because of environmental regulations, landfill closings, and citizen opposition to local waste disposal facilities, industrialized countries are increasingly disposing of their dangerous waste by shipping it to the third world, where people are often poorly informed about the threats that such wastes pose to human health and the environment" (Stebbins 1992, 82).

This form of garbage imperialism has been a persistent feature of *maquila* dumping on the Mexican side of the US-Mexico border since the creation of this marginalized sector. It is a well-documented fact that *maquilas* have historically dumped into surrounding rivers, ground waters, surrounding desert, or municipal dumps (Reed 1998; Simon 1997), sowing wanton destruction for future generations to clean up. One of the most important accomplishments of environmental organizing in the immediate pre- and post-NAFTA days was the achievement of an agreement similar to the 1992 Border Plan whereby all hazardous by-products generated by *maquilas* during the production process were to be repatriated to the United States. Monitoring and accounting of repatriated wastes was performed by the US Environmental Protection Agency (EPA) until October of 2003, when the EPA hazmat tracking system was dissolved due to lack of funding.[3]

Space, Place and Back Again

Given the border region's tumultuous and conflicted history, it is impossible to overstate the importance of the border, as a territorial marker designating sovereign limits and possibilities, to the production and reproduction of the borderlands as a culturally, economically, and environmentally marginal region. As Philip Abrams argued many years ago, the state is not a monolithic affair, but an assemblage of sometimes disaggregated practices (Abrams 1988). The demarcation and policing of territorial limits is a hallmark practice of modern nation-states, alongside control over legitimate uses of force, taxation, citizenship requirements, birth and death registries, and so forth. Buchanan has remarked on the importance of spatializing non-local actors, including the state and globalized capitalism, to the production and reproduction of the place of the border region:

> If 'place' is constructed in and through social processes, differentiation between places becomes as much an artifact of uneven capitalist development as the differences between classes. [...] There is an important distinction between the notion of a border as the legal and spatial delimitation of the State, as a boundary or defining line, and the border as a geographic and cultural zone or space, the borderlands. Instead of having a stable identity, economy or geography, the border region is defined and redefined in different contexts. (Buchanan 2001, 286)

Ortiz has similarly argued that the interests of non-local actors, such as the state, business, and immigration laws continually cross-cut local border interests and capacities (1999, 2001). At the same time, local actors are hardly united because class, ethnic, national, and nationalistic interests cross-cut border lives. As he puts it in reference to Cd. Juarez-El Paso: "In the overlapping of the 'no man's land' space and the living places of local residents, most border dwellers conduct, or try to conduct, their everyday lives beyond, along, or in spite of the dislocating impacts and overriding presence of the non-local" (Ortiz 2001, 105). He goes on to note that, "what distinguishes the border situation is the pervasiveness of non-local actors and agendas" (ibid., 105), a point this chapter has also attempted to demonstrate.

The NAFTA side accords were ultimately a pragmatic, neoliberal response to a recurring quandary: How can seemingly underdeveloped nations enforce their national environmental and labor laws in a manner similar to their developed counterparts, but without the corresponding resources of developed nations? At the same time that the accords fell back on neoliberal truisms, they also articulated a future vision in which citizens and activists would cooperate in the immediate cross-border environment and participate in transparent and problem-solving public debates. The success of this novel vision, however, hinged on the anticipated success of neoliberal economic development policies. New wealth and resources created by NAFTA-inspired free trade was supposed to trickle down to the downtrodden and poor of the Mexican side of the border. This newfound wealth was then supposed to be channeled into enhanced oversight and enforcement by national regulatory agencies, ostensibly raising labor and environmental law enforcement to a level that would satisfy the treaty's critics, flush corruption from the Mexican political system, and ultimately bring Mexican political culture up to (imaginary) US standards. The environmental side accord, in particular, ignored the fractious history and place-based social identities of border populations, preferring instead to cast border residents as a homogenous population henceforth charged with an environmental stewardship model incubated by the accord itself.

Regardless of the aspirations of both accords, the fact remains that the Mexican side of the US-Mexico border was profligately saturated with environmental and workplace wastes before and after the signing of NAFTA. The saturation of the border region with wastes in proportions that would be considered unthinkable elsewhere is both product and function of the border region's characterization as a marginal, frontier zone. The assiduous and painstaking investigation of these wastes by Matamoros border actors will be explored in the next chapter.

Bibliography

Abrams, Philip. 1988. "Notes on the Difficulty of Studying the State." *The Journal of Historical Sociology* 1(1): 58–89

Alvarez, Robert. 1995. "The Mexican-US Border: The Making of an Anthropology of Borderlands." *Annual Review of Anthropology* 24: 447–470.

Andreas, Peter. 1998. "The Political Economy of Narco-Corruption in Mexico." *Current History* 97 (618) 160–165.

Anzaldúa, Gloria. 1987. *Borderlands: The New Mestiza = La Frontera*. San Francisco: Aunt Lute Books.

Arreola, Daniel D. 2002. *Tejano South Texas: A Mexican American Cultural Province*. Austin: University of Texas Press.

Baerresen, Donald. 1971. *The Border Industrialization Program of Mexico*. Washing-ton, D.C.: Heath Lexington Books.

Barry, Tom. 1994. *The Challenge of Cross-Border Environmentalism: The US-Mexico Case*. Albuquerque, NM: Resource Center Press.

Brenner, Joel, Jennifer Ross, Janie Simmons, and Sarah Zaidi. 2000. "Neoliberal Trade and Investment and the Health of Maquiladora Workers on the US-Mexico Border." In *Dying for Growth: Global Inequality and the Health of the Poor*, edited by Jim Yong Kim, Joyce Millen, Alec Irwin, and John Gershman, 261–292. Monroe, ME: Common Courage Press.

Buchanan, Ruth. 2001. "Border Crossings: NAFTA, Regulatory Restructuring, and the Politics of Place." In *The Legal Geographies Reader*, edited by Nicholas Blomley, David Delaney, and Richard T. Ford, 285–297. Malden, MA: Blackwell Publishers.

Campbell, Howard. 2011. "No End in Sight: Violence in Ciudad Juarez." *NACLA Report on the Americas* 44 3: 19–22.

Carlos Vasquez, Xavier. 1993. "The North American Free Trade Agreement and Environmental Racism." *Harvard International Law Journal* 34 (2): 357–379.

Castañeda, Jorge. 2010. What's Spanish for Quagmire? *Foreign Policy*, no. 177 (January/February), 76–81.

Cech, Irina and Amelia Essman. 1992. "Water Sanitation Practices on the Texas-Mexico Border: Implications for Physicians on Both Sides." *Southern Medical Journal* 85 (11): 1053–1064.

Cockcroft, James. 2010. "Mexico: 'Failed States, New Wars, Resistance.'" *Monthly Review* 62 (6): 28–41.

Cornelius, Wayne. 2002. "Impact of NAFTA on Mexico-to-US Migration." In *NAFTA in the New Millennium*, edited by E Edward J. Chambers and Peter H. Smith, 287–304. San Diego: Center for US-Mexican Studies.

Cronon, William. 1996. "The Trouble with Wilderness; or Getting Back to the Wrong Nature." In *Uncommon Ground: Rethinking the Human Place in Nature*, edited by William Cronon. New York: W. W. Norton.

Das, Veena, and Deborah Poole. 2004. "State and Its Margins: Comparative Ethnographies" In *Anthropology in the Margins of the State*, edited by in Veena Das and Deborah Poole, 3–33. Santa Fe: School for American Research Press.

Delgado Wise, Raúl, and James M. Cypher. 2007. "The Strategic Role of Mexican Labor under NAFTA: Critical Perspectives on Current Economic Integration." *The Annals of the American Academy of Political and Social Science* 610 (1): 120–142. March.

Denman, Catalina. 1998. "Salud y Maquila: Acotaciones del Campo de Investigación en Vista de las Contribuciones Recientes." *Revista Relaciones*, 19 (74).

———. 1992. "Productos Toxicos y Potencialmente Peligrosos en la Industria Fronteriza." In *Ecologia, Recursos Naturalies y Medio Ambiente en Sonora*, edited by Jose Luis Moreno. Hermosillo, Sonora: Gobierno del Estado de Sonora, Secretaría de Infraestructura Urbana y Ecologica y el Colegio de Sonora.

Eaton, David. 1996. "NAFTA and the Environment: A Proposal for Free Trade in Hazardous Waste Between the United States and Mexico." *St. Mary's Law Journal* 27: 715.

Ellis, Elizabeth. 1996. "Bordering on Disaster: A New Attempt to Control the Trans-boundary Effects of Maquiladora Pollution." *Valparaiso Law Review* 30: 621.

Fatemi, Khosrow, (editor). 1990. *The Maquiladora Industry: Economic Solution or Problem?* New York: Praeger Press.

Fernandez-Kelly, Maria Patricia. 1983. *For We Are Sold, I and My People: Women and Industry in Mexico's Frontier*. Albany: State University of New York Press.

Fox, Claire. 1999. *The Fence and the River: Culture and Politics on the US-Mexico Border*. Minneapolis: University of Minnesota Press.

García-Johnson, Ronie. 2000. *Exporting Environmentalism: U.S. Multinational Chemical Corporations in Brazil and Mexico.* Cambridge, MA: MIT Press.

Gehlbach, Frederick. 1993. *Mountain Islands and Desert Seas: A Natural History of the US-Mexican Borderlands.* College Station: University of Texas Press.

Grayson, George. 2010. *Mexico: Narco Violence and a Failed State?* New Brunswick, NJ: Transactions Press.

Gutierrez Najera, Raquel. 1999. "The Scope and Limits of Mexican Environmental Law." *Borderlines* 7 (10): 1–5.

Harris, Jonathan. 2000. "Free Trade or Sustainable Trade? An Ecological Economics Perspective." In *Rethinking Sustainability,* edited by Jonathan Harris, 117–140. Ann Arbor: University of Michigan Press.

Harvey, David. 1989. *The Condition of Postmodernity.* Cambridge, MA: Blackwell Press.

Herzog, Lawrence. 1990. *Where North Meets South: Cities, Spaces, and Politics on the US-Mexico Border.* Austin, TX: Center for Mexican American Studies.

Heyman, Josiah. 1991. *Life and Labor on the Border: Working People of Northeastern Sonora, Mexico, 1886–1986.* Tucson: University of Arizona Press.

———. 1994. "The Mexico-United States Border in Anthropology: A Critique and Reformulation." *Journal of Political Ecology* 1: 43–65.

———, ed. 1999. *States and Illegal Practices.* Oxford: Berg Press.

Janetti-Díaz, María Emilia, Jose Mario Hernandez-Quezada, and Chadwick Benjamin DeWaard. 1995. "National Environmental Policy and Programs in Mexico." In *Environmental Policies in the Third World,* edited by O.P. Dwivedi and Dhirendra Vajpeyi, 175–203. Westport: Greenwood Press.

Kearney, Milo, and Anthony Knopp. 1991. *Boom and Bust: The Historical Cycles of Matamoros and Brownsville.* Austin: Eakin Press.

Kopinak, Kathryn. 1995. "Gender as a Vehicle for the Subordination of Women Maquiladora Workers in Mexico." *Latin American Perspectives* 22 (1): 30–48.

Leonard, H. Jeffrey. 1998. *Pollution and the Struggle for the World Product: Multinational Corporations, Environment, and International Comparative Advantage.* Cambridge: Cambridge University Press.

Lewis, Sanford, Marck Kaltofen and Gregory Ormsby. 1991. "Border Trouble: Rivers in Peril: A Report on Waste Pollution due to Industrial Development in Northern Mexico." Boston: National Toxics Campaign Fund.

Meed, Douglas. 1992. *Bloody Border: Riots, Battles and Adventures Along the Turbulent US-Mexico Borderlands.* Tuczon: Westernlore Press.

Mies, Maria. 1986. *Patriarchy and Accumulation on a World Scale: Women in the International Division of Labor.* London: Zed Books.

Mikulas, Nicole. 1999. "Comment: An Innovative Twist on Free Trade and International Environmental Treaty Enforcements: Checking in on NAFTA's Seven-Year Supervision of US-Mexico Border Pollution Problems." *Tulane Environmental Law Journal* 12: 497.

Moure-Eraso, Rafael, Meg Wilcox, Laura Punnett, Leslie MacDonald, and Charles Levenstein. 1997. "Back to the Future: Sweatshop Conditions on the Mexico-US Border. II. Occupational Health Impact of Maquiladora Industrial Activity." *American Journal of Industrial Medicine* 31 (5): 587–599.

Moure-Eraso, Rafael, Meg Wilcox, Laura Punnett, Leslie Copeland, and Charles Levenstein. 1994. "Back to the Future: Sweatshop Conditions on the Mexico-US Border. I. Community Health Impact of Maquiladora Industrial Activity." *American Journal of Industrial Medicine* 20: 311–324.

Mumme, Stephen. 1992. "Systems Maintenance and Environmental Reform in Mexico: Salinas's Preemptive Strategy." *Latin American Perspectives* 72 (19) 1: 123–143.

Mumme, Stephen, Richard Bath, and Valerie J. Assetto. 1988. "Political Development and Environmental Policy in Mexico." *Latin American Research Review* 23 (1): 7–34.

Nash, June, and Patricia Fernandez-Kelly. 1983. *Women, Men, and the International Division of Labor.* New York: SUNY Press.

Ong, Aihwa. 1987. *Spirits of Resistance and Capitalist Discipline: Factory Women in Malaysia.* Albany: State University of New York Press.

Ortiz, Victor. 1999. "Only Time Can Tell if Geography is Still Destiny: Time, Space, and NAFTA in a US-Mexican Border City." *Human Organization* 58 (2): 173–181.

———. 2001. "The Unbearable Ambiguity of the Border." *Social Justice: A Journal of Crime, Conflict, and World Order* 28 (2): 96–112.

Paredes, Américo. 1958. *With His Pistol in His Hand: A Border Ballad and Its Hero.* Austin: University of Texas Press.

Peña, Devon Gerardo. 1997. *The Terror of the Machine: Technology, Work, Gender, and Ecology on the US-Mexico Border.* Austin: Center for Mexican American Studies, University of Texas at Austin Press.

Quintero-Ramírez, Cirila. 1997. *Restructuración Sindical en la Frontera Norte: El Caso de la Industria Maquiladora.* Tijuana: El Colegio de la Frontera Norte.

Reed, Cyrus. 1998. "Hazardous Waste Management on the Border: Problems with Practices and Oversight Continue." *Borderlines* 6 (5): 1–5.

Reid, Jan. 2004. "Prologue." In *Rio Grande,* edited by Jan Reid, xiv-xxiii. Austin: University of Texas Press.

Richardson, Chad. 1999. *Batos, Bolillos, Pochos, and Pelados: Class and Culture on the South Texas Border.* Austin: University of Texas Press.

Rivera-Batiz, Francisco L. 1986. "Can Border Industries be a Substitute for Immigration?" *The American Economic Review* 76 (2), Papers and Proceedings of the Ninety-Eighth Annual Meeting of the American Economic Association: 263–268.

Ruiz, Ramón Eduardo. 2000. *On the Rim of Mexico: Encounters of the Rich and Poor.* Boulder: Westview Press.

Russell, Philip. 1994. *Mexico Under Salinas.* Austin: Mexico Resources Center.

Saldivar, José David. 1997. *Border Matters: Remapping American Cultural Studies.* Berkeley: University of California Press.

Seligson, Mitchell, and Edward Williams. 1981. *Maquiladoras and Migration: Workers in the Mexico-United States Border Industrialization Program.* Austin: University of Texas Press.

Simon, Joel. 1997. *Endangered Mexico: An Environment on the Edge.* San Francisco: Sierra Club Books.

Simonian, Lane. 1995. *Defending the Land of the Jaguar: A History of Conservation in Mexico.* Austin: University of Texas Press.

Stebbins, Kenyon Rainier. 1992. "Garbage Imperialism: Health Implications of Dumping Hazardous Waste in Third World Countries." *Medical Anthropology* 15: 81–102.

Steinhart, Peter. 1994. *Two Eagles/Dos Aguilas: The Natural World of the United States-Mexico Borderlands.* Berkeley: University of California Press.

Stern, Peter. 1998. "Marginals and Acculturation in Frontier Society." In *New Views of Borderlands History,* edited by Robert Jackson, 157–188. Albuquerque: University of New Mexico Press.

Truett, Samuel. 1997. Neighbors by Nature: Rethinking Region, Nation, and Environmental History in the US-Mexico Borderlands. *Environmental History* 2 (2): 160–178.

Walsh, Casey. 2004. "'Aguas Broncas': The Regional Political Ecology of Water Conflict in the Mexico-U.S. Borderlands." *Journal of Political Ecology* 11: 43–58.

———. 2008. *Building the Borderlands: A Transnational History of Irrigated Cotton on the Mexico-Texas Border.* College Station: Texas A&M University Press.

Worcester, Donald. 1988. "The Significance of the Spanish Borderlands to the United States." In *New Spain's Far Northern Frontier: Essays on Spain in the American West, 1540–1821,* edited by David Weber, 1–16. Dallas: First Southern Methodist University Press.

Zavaleta, Antonio. 1986. "The Twin Cities: An Historical Synthesis of the Socio-Economic Interdependence of the Brownsville-Matamoros Border Community." In *Studies in Brownsville History,* edited by Milo Kearney, 125–171. Brownsville: Pan American University Press.

Notes

1   More specifically, Mexican businesses can often be dependent on the tourist economy, meanwhile both poor and more well-to-do Mexicans might shop on the US side for nontourist items. Poor people often go to the grocery or dollar stores on the US side that, ironically, often provide goods at cheaper prices than in Mexico. The better-off seem to be attracted to the upscale shopping malls in the US towns.

2   Ginger Thompson, "Fallout of US Recession Drifts South into Mexico," *New York Times*, December 26, 2001, *www.nytimes.com/2001/12/26/business/worldbusiness*. Daniel Wood, "Border Factories Hit Hard By Recession, Winds of Trade: Maquiladores, A Symbol of Growing US-Mexican Economic Ties, See Fortunes Plunge for the First Time," *Christian Science Monitor*, January 23, 2002, *www.csmonitor.com/2002/0123/p02s02-woam.html*.

3   Joe Cantlupe, "EPA Ends Database Tracking Hazardous Waste from Mexico, *San Diego Union Tribune*, October 26, 2003.

Legislative Inaction and Executive Action

Mixed Status Families, the Dreamer Movement, and DACA

Marjorie S. Zatz and Nancy Rodriguez

Learning you are undocumented *"is the beginning of this process of the other, of otherness, and not having the same level of security as the people around you."*

—Lorella Praeli, advocacy and policy director,
United We Dream (interview, May 14, 2014)

It is like *"awakening to a nightmare."*

—Roberto Gonzales and Leo Chavez (2012)

DACA *is life changing.*

—Doris Meissner, former commissioner of the
Immigration and Naturalization Service
(Interview with Doris Meissner, December 6, 2012)

F ROM THE PERSPECTIVE OF THE IMMIGRANT community and their advocates, Deferred Action for Childhood Arrivals (DACA) has been the high point of the administration of President Barack Obama. DACA responds to a clear need for safety from the threat of deportation and for work authorization for the 1.76 million young people who are potentially eligible. It was put into place quickly, and it lays out a fair and equitable policy with consistent procedures for eligible youth and young adults to apply to have their status "dacamented."

DACA provides recipients a temporary reprieve from the threat of deportation, but it is a far cry from comprehensive immigration reform. Like other forms of prosecutorial discretion, decisions are made on a case-by-case basis consistent with stated guidelines. Under DACA, the guidelines have been formalized into an orderly, efficient, and relatively transparent review process that occurs in a context outside of law enforcement. DACA also confers work authorization and paved the way for some states to permit dacamented youth to obtain driver's licenses and to pay in-state college tuition. Even more important, we suggest, DACA

Marjorie S. Zatz and Nancy Rodriguez, "Legislative Inaction and Executive Action: Mixed Status Families, the Dreamer Movement, and DACA," *Dreams and Nightmares: Immigration Policy, Youth, and Families*, pp. 49–76, 169, 173–193. Copyright © 2015 by University of California Press. Reprinted with permission.

provides a model for broader systemic change designed to mitigate harm to youth that is squarely within the purview of the executive office.

We focus in this [reading] on the policy process and political mobilizations leading up to DACA, preliminary data on who has benefited from the program and who has been left behind, and, for those receiving deferred action, we examine the transition from being undocumented to being "dacamented."

First, though, we address why DACA was so necessary. Drawing on our own interview data as well as findings of other researchers, we examine the challenges confronting families whose members have a mixture of legal statuses, their experiences of integration and marginalization in the United States, and the impact of a parent's undocumented status on child development, early education, and health outcomes.

We then consider the experiences of members of the "1.5 generation" as they enter adolescence and early adulthood. These youth, who came to the United States as young children, cannot easily be categorized as either first or second generation. They are themselves immigrants, and thus first generation, but they grew up attending US schools, speaking English, and knowing only the United States as home, like second-generation youth. In the past decade, these youth have boldly come out of the shadows to claim their place within American society. They have renamed themselves Dreamers, reminding themselves and others not only of the DREAM (Development, Relief, and Education for Alien Minors) Act, which would legally cement their status in the United States, but also of their dreams, their untapped potential, and the many contributions they can make to US society.

We conclude with an assessment of the reauthorization of DACA and efforts to expand the eligibility criteria to include those who would have been eligible for legalization under Senate Bill S.744 had it passed the House of Representatives in 2013. This discussion brings us back to our starting point: In the absence of legislative action, what structural mechanisms are available to mitigate harm to youth and families, and what structural mechanisms exacerbate harm?

Growing Up in Mixed Status Families

In 2010, 5.5 million children of undocumented parents resided in the United States. Eighty-two percent of them, or about 4.5 million youth, were born in the United States and are US citizens. The remaining one million children are themselves undocumented. Nearly half of these undocumented youth—about 400,000—have one or more siblings who were born in the United States. And if we count up everyone living in these "mixed status" families, the total reaches nine million (Taylor et al. 2011).

Strained Family Dynamics

When family members hold different legal statuses, tensions are inevitable. Parents who came to the United States to provide a better life for their children may be afraid to apply for the very social services that would benefit their children. Siblings see that a brother or sister has opportunities denied to them solely because of when and where they were born. These distinctions lead to complicated, and often strained, family dynamics and to what Cecilia Menjívar (2006) has called "liminal legality," a sense of being caught in between statuses (see also Menjívar and Abrego 2009; Menjívar and Kanstroom 2013).

An attorney told us of a situation in which a parent disclosed to the child that he was unlawfully present in the United States in the safety of her office. She said, "They had lied to him his entire life. I mean, those situations are heart wrenching, because then the child is resentful. 'Why did you do this to me and not my other siblings? Why do I have to be the one that's penalized while everybody else gets to live a real American life?' Yeah, it's definitely a serious problem." Similarly, a child advocate described the sometimes painful dynamics in mixed status families where (pointing in one direction) "Oh, you are the US citizen kid, you are the hope of our future" and (pointing in the other direction) "You're going to be the one that needs to go to work at a minimum wage job so there is money for your brother to go to college."

Regardless of their own immigration status, fear of a parent's deportation shapes early life experiences for children of undocumented parents. As Dreamer activist Lorella Praeli told us, when we tell our "story of self," people will talk of being young and of their mothers handing them a piece of paper and saying, "This is who you call if *la migra* comes for me." She continued, "You're young, and you're supposed to feel like your mom is going to take care of you, and all of a sudden you are being told, 'I may not come back.' You don't quite understand why, but you are taught to understand that, it is the beginning of this process of the other, of otherness, and not having the same level of security as the people around you."[1] If a parent is deported, family dynamics may change again. For example, an immigration advocate we interviewed recounted a situation in which a boy's father had been picked up by Immigration and Customs Enforcement (ICE): "I mean, just going to school and coming back and knowing that your dad's been detained, or he's in Mexico now. Sometimes Mom's crying. I talked to one of the kids and his life changed completely. He says that he got older [snaps fingers] like that. Now he is in charge. His dad is out of the loop. These fears that Mom has, he can see that. ... The only income they had was his dad, and now that's gone, so now he needs to start looking for a job."

Although members of one's family and community are important sources of information and resources, their efforts to be helpful can also create pressure. For instance, undocumented young adults in romantic relationships with US citizens may be pressured to marry before they feel ready, told it is their responsibility to marry and start the clock on applying for visas for parents or other family members at risk of deportation. Likewise, if the family is undocumented and the teenager needs a car to go to work or school, someone else must buy the car, and the family must go through this intermediary to arrange car loan payments and purchase insurance. We were told of a situation in which a car was rear-ended; when the family contacted the insurance company they learned that their monthly payment was actually covering the cost of their own car and three others. This is likely not an unusual occurrence, because undocumented immigrants may not know the typical rate for car insurance in the United States, and they are vulnerable to exploitation by others within their community as well as outsiders.

Regardless of the child's legal status, children suffer when their parents are undocumented. Children must often serve as language and cultural brokers for their parents, which can alter family dynamics in multiple ways. Their parents' status affects young children's development and early educational experiences, as well as their later educational and employment opportunities and their sense of belonging and political integration. We turn next to a discussion of these consequences and how they have shaped the Dreamer political movement and policy processes.

Child Development and Early Education

Child development experts refer to the paradox of immigrant risk and immigrant promise, noting that children of immigrants tend to outperform children of native-born parents, particularly in lower-income communities. This is most apparent during adolescence, when children of immigrants who have not dropped out of school tend to perform especially well. Very little, however, is known about how parents' *unauthorized status* affects the educational, health, and social development of children and youth.

Research by Carola Suárez-Orozco, Marcelo Suárez-Orozco, Hirokazu Yoshikawa, and others is starting to fill this gap (see, for example Suárez-Orozco, Suárez-Orozco, and Todorova 2008; Suárez-Orozco et al. 2011; Yoshikawa 2011; Yoshikawa and Kholoptseva 2012). They find that young children of undocumented immigrants show significantly lower levels of language and cognitive development compared with the children of legal immigrants and native-born parents, increasing their risk of lower school performance and an array of later problems, such as dropping out of high school, blocked mobility, and economic stagnation. Thus, at least some of the positive effects of being a child of immigrants wash out when the parents are undocumented.

Hirokazu Yoshikawa's three-year study of the lives of four hundred children born in public hospitals in New York City to Mexican, Dominican, and Chinese parents finds that US-citizen children's cognitive development and language skills are harmed by ages two and three if their parents lack a pathway to citizenship. These deleterious effects surface through multiple channels. Parents who are trying to avoid contact with government authorities are often afraid to enroll their children in preschool, child care subsidies, food stamps, and other programs that improve children's development. These programs may also require information about the parents' employment, and parents who do not have work authorization may be unable or unwilling to provide this information. Yoshikawa notes one element of the paradox experienced by undocumented parents: "The very same government that could deport them also offered resources to their citizen children, in the form of public supports for families in poverty. ... But of course, children cannot walk into offices and enroll themselves in these programs. When parents are reluctant to do so, children cannot benefit. ... Far too often, that paradox leads to citizen children of the undocumented being excluded from supports from which their peers with documented or citizen parents benefit" (2011, 53).

Immigrant families, and particularly families in which the parents are unauthorized, have high rates of living in poverty. This has repercussions for children's cognitive development, language skills, and early education. For example, many immigrant parents cannot afford preschool learning materials or stimulating childcare, and they may experience food and housing insecurities (Capps and Fix 2012; Chaudry et al. 2010; Yoshikawa 2011). Parents may also owe significant debts to smugglers, further reducing family finances. Although these costs tend to be highest for Chinese immigrants, they are common to everyone who employs a smuggler. Moreover, because undocumented workers typically receive minimal pay, they often must work long hours at multiple jobs. This leaves them with little time to spend with their children, and their absence has psychological and developmental consequences.

Parents without work authorization move frequently in search of work; as a result, their children may change schools several times. School mobility, in turn, has been linked to lowered school performance (Suárez-Orozco et al. 2011). Regardless of the child's citizenship status, having parents who are unauthorized immigrants limits the youths' and parents' engagement in school. Parents are less likely to interact with teachers or be active in school when they fear deportation (Suárez-Orozco et al. 2011). They may also be leery of allowing their children to participate in field trips or afterschool sports because this requires paperwork, including health forms, that parents fear could expose their status. As immigration attorney and scholar Nina Rabin reflected on findings of her study of the effects of Arizona's SB 1070 on youth:

> The level of stress that these immigrant families are under impacts children at school, and that's a real issue for the schools to contend with. A lot

of teachers we spoke to, in the really small study that I did, talked about the fact that they saw an impact on kids' performance in school and their level of stress and anxiety as a result of all the stress about SB 1070, and what was going to happen with it. And ... with the climate being so hostile, in general, I think it places a strain on schools to encourage participation from parents ... to come to conferences or meetings, or just generally be involved with the kids' education.[2]

In contrast, another attorney who worked on immigration cases in an urban community center suggested that parents felt that schools were safe, but other institutions were not. She recounted:

> I think parents generally feel like schools are a safe zone. They can go to school. They can ask questions. They can be there. They feel a general safety. I don't think that they think there's any raids going on at schools. ... Outside of school, there's not many other venues. In fact, I've had a lot of parents who are scared to go to the hospital. A lot of parents are scared to take their kids to the hospital, they'll require somebody else to take their kids to the hospital because, if the child is documented, they're not going to the hospital because they're afraid that ICE or DHS [Department of Homeland Security] will be called to pick them up because they don't have proof of insurance for the child. Undocumented children, even more so.

Access to Health Care and Other Benefits

US-citizen children are eligible for state and federal health benefits. Their undocumented siblings, however, are not. As a result, some children within a family may receive very good health care, including regular preventative care, dental checkups, and access to mental health provisions if needed. Others in the family do not have access to this care. This means that if one child in a family has a serious medical condition, treatment is available at relatively low cost, while the same treatment is not available for the undocumented sibling because the family cannot afford the expense.

Yet often even those children entitled to benefits do not receive them because of their parents' fear of engagement with authorities. Immigration scholar David Thronson suggests, "Citizen children in mixed status families thus often take on the status of undocumented children" (2010, 247; see similarly Menjívar and Abrego 2012; Suárez-Orozco et al. 2011; Yoshikawa 2011). Immigrant and children's welfare advocates and attorneys recounted numerous such stories, noting that these fears were especially virulent during the period 2006 through 2011, when state and local governments across the country were enacting the most vehemently anti-immigrant laws.[3]

As one attorney suggested, "I think one of the issues that really bears following is the implication of all the state-level anti-immigration legislation on US-citizen kids' abilities to access benefits," noting that the climate of fear led to beliefs that medical and other social service providers would be required to report undocumented parents to authorities. Similarly, attorney Victoria López of the Arizona American Civil Liberties Union [ACLU] told us that such proposals, whether enacted into law or not, send ripples of fear throughout the community. Her agency conducted a series of information campaigns to make sure people knew

> that first of all, US-citizen children still qualified for these specific benefits, and that even if you are undocumented, you can still access emergency medical services and certain other services under federal law, and that public benefit employees should still not be asking certain questions of you even if you are undocumented and you are trying to access services that you or your child are still eligible for. ... Even the announcement of these kinds of bills, even if they don't become law, have such damaging impacts for families. ... Because if the school can ask me about my kid's immigration status, well maybe the doctor can ask me about my kid's immigration status, and maybe all these other folks that you would go to to access public services also put me in a position where I could be, where I or my family member, could be arrested and deported.[4]

This comment from a local attorney is consistent with findings across the country and reflects parents' fears of exposing themselves to the risk of deportation and their concern that use of public resources, even for their citizen children, could make them ineligible for legalization under future legislation (Menjívar 2006, 2012; Thronson 2010; Van Hook, Landale, and Hillemeier 2013).

In addition, a growing number of researchers have documented the ongoing stress caused by children's fears that their parents, and in some cases the children themselves, could be deported at any time. This manifests in depression, anxiety, and separation disorders, and other mental health problems that affect children's development and educational success (see Boehm 2012; Bra-beck and Xu 2010; Brotherton and Barrios 2011; Capps et al. 2007; Chaudry et al. 2010; Hagan, Eschbach, and Rodríguez 2008; Hagan, Rodríguez, and Castro 2011; Menjívar and Abrego 2012; Yoshikawa 2011).

Undocumented Teens and Young Adults

Throughout the K–12 years, schools provide a safe cocoon for undocumented students. In *Plyler v. Doe* (1982), the Supreme Court decreed that every child living in the United States has a right to attend public schools, regardless of his or her immigration status. The rationale for this decision was that the students were not responsible for their citizenship status because they had entered the country as young children. To deny these youth education, Justice Brennan argued, would create a lifetime of hardship and a permanent underclass, and would "not comport with fundamental conceptions of justice" (*Plyler v. Doe* 1982, 220; see also Gleeson and Gonzales 2012; Olivas 2012b; Shaina and Small 2013). As Justice Brennan recognized, the primary and secondary school years are formative to youths' later success. Shannon Glee-son and Roberto Gonzales take this a step further, arguing, "The result of the school socialization experience is to empower undocumented youth to dream big irrespective of their immigration status" (2012, 10).

By the end of high school, however, undocumented teenagers have come to realize tangible consequences of their immigration status. In most states they are unable to obtain driver's licenses. They do not have valid Social Security numbers and so cannot legally work. They are ineligible for federal financial aid for college, and in most states are not eligible for state-based aid. If they are also denied in-state tuition, the cost becomes exorbitant, making higher education, especially at four-year colleges and universities, an unattainable goal for many youth (Abrego 2011; Gonzales 2010).

Roberto Gonzales and Leo Chavez (2012) call this recognition "awakening to a nightmare." They draw upon Sarah Willen's (2007) concept of abjectivity to demonstrate how abjectivity and illegality combine to define and constrain daily life for members of the 1.5 generation. Based on interviews and surveys conducted in Orange County, California, they found that, as children, most undocumented youth "were not required to produce identification. It is only when they attempted to assert their position in the American mainstream that the importance of identification became essential. This was a defining moment, a challenge to their taken-for-granted identity and sense of belonging. This often came as a surprise to many who were unaware of their unauthorized immigration status or its significance" (2012, 262). Similarly, Abrego (2006, 2008, 2011), Coutin (2007), Gleeson and Gonzales (2012), and Menjívar and Abrego (2012) find that this awareness of not fully belonging, questioning of identity, and associated shame and stigma, typified the experiences of adolescents and young adults who came to the United States as young children. These feelings could materialize at any moment. For example, a Dream movement activist recalled going to the movies at age seventeen with a friend in her predominantly white neighborhood, only to be turned away because she did not have identification to get into the R-rated movie. In this way, everyday experiences can become defining moments, as youth "awaken to the nightmare" of what it means to be undocumented.

Following this awakening, Gonzales (2011) suggests that youth begin "learning to be illegal." With this change in their legal consciousness, youth come to recognize that they do not have all of the rights and privileges available to their friends, neighbors, and classmates. Their membership in American society is partial—what Susan Coutin (2000, 2003) calls the contradiction between one's physical and social presence in the country. These youth are not fully incorporated into American society, yet their sense of belonging is no greater anywhere else, as they grew up in the United States, speak English, attend US schools, and have always assumed that the United States was home.

Drawing on Cecilia Menjívar's (2006) work, Suárez-Orozco et al. assert that these youth are "in the untenable position of interminable liminality. These 'betwixt and between' residents of the United States attempt to perform symbolic and ritual claims of belonging without the corresponding reciprocal condition of acknowledgment" (2011, 444). Liminality theory, they suggest "becomes a particularly useful frame for understanding how their formal entry into adulthood is complicated—while, on the one hand, they are inevitably propelled into adulthood, on the other, they are denied participation in state-sanctioned rites of passage, like getting a driver's license or passport and facile entry into college or legally sanctioned passage into the work force" (2011, 454). Leisy Abrego (2011) adds that immigrants' understanding of this liminal legality, that is, their legal consciousness, is experienced differently depending upon their social position. Among the relevant factors contributing to undocumented immigrants' legal consciousness, Abrego assigns primary importance to the age at which they migrated and whether they are in the relatively protected confines of school or in the workforce. Even within the comfort of a college dormitory, the simple question, "Where are you from?," can raise anxieties and questions about what identity the undocumented college student can claim. As one respondent recounted to us, "I really struggled, I think it was the beginning of really owning what it means to be undocumented and not knowing how to deal with it."

Unauthorized teens and young adults must learn what they are not allowed to do, how to avoid drawing attention to themselves, and what to do if they are caught by immigration authorities. By paying attention to these changes in legal consciousness, we see "the effects laws have on migrants' day-to-day lives, revealing the ways in which undocumented persons experience inclusion and exclusion and how these experiences can change over time, in interactions with different persons, and across various spaces" (Gonzales 2011, 606; see also Menjívar and Kanstroom 2013). The ramifications can be huge. As Suárez-Orozco and her colleagues state, "Unauthorized young adults may find themselves tempted to secure false Social Security cards or driver's licenses in order to find work. ... Once they dip their toes in the underground waters of false driver's licenses and Social Security numbers, they are at risk of getting caught in the undertow of a vast and unforgiving ocean of complex legal currents" (2011, 455).

Unlike their peers, for whom a minor delinquent act would likely result in probation or a diversion program, the results can be disastrous if undocumented teens get into trouble with school or legal authorities. Emily Butera of the Women's Refugee Commission told us this story of a boy she met in an Office of Refugee Resettlement (ORR) facility in Arizona:

> He told me that he was picking on a girl, but I think he was trying to flirt with her in that awkward way that adolescent boys do. In the process, he took her iPhone out of her hands. School security got involved and called the police. He was living in Maricopa County and the next thing you know, he has an ICE hold on him and he's placed into the ORR system. At the time I met him, he'd been away from his family for months. I can't even remember how long it was, but it was a significant period of time. This kid spoke perfect English. He'd been here since he was one. He didn't remember Mexico. He just wanted to go back to his school and back to his mom.[5]

For these youth, many of whom did not even know they were undocumented until their teenage years, the possibility of deportation is suddenly very real. They have no claim to relief, and in the blink of an eye they could be deported to a country they don't remember, where they don't speak the language or speak it poorly, and where they don't know anyone.

Going to College While Undocumented

One of the primary paths to success in US society is a college education. Yet for undocumented students to attend college requires that they "have squeezed their way through narrow openings along the educational pipeline" (Abrego and Gonzales 2010, 147). Not surprisingly, Passel and Cohn (2009) report that 40 percent of undocumented young adults ages 18–24 have not completed high school, compared to 8 percent of the general US population. Of those who did graduate from high school, only 49 percent went on to college, compared to 71 percent of the US population. These educational outcomes bifurcate, depending upon the age when the undocumented youth came to the United States. Three-quarters (72 percent) of the youth who came to the United States before age fourteen graduated high school, compared to 54 percent of their counterparts who arrived when they were age fourteen or older. And, 61 percent of those youth who came to the United States by age fourteen are in college or have attended college, compared to 42 percent of those who were fourteen or older when they arrived (Passel and Cohn 2009). Thus, youth who arrived in the United States as younger children have educational outcomes closer to the national norm.

Prior to about 2006, some states, such as Arizona, allowed their high school graduates to pay resident tuition, regardless of their immigration status. They were not eligible for financial aid, but at many public universities, the tuition was affordable. Then, in the wave of anti-immigrant legislative fervor sweeping the country, Arizona, Alabama, Colorado, Georgia, South Carolina, and Indiana passed legislation excluding previously eligible undocumented immigrants from paying resident tuition. This largely froze undocumented students out of a college education, especially because they could not obtain federal financial aid such as loans, grants-in-aid, or work study, or state-based aid in most of the country (Flores 2010; Gonzales 2010; Suárez-Orozco et al. 2011). Georgia went as far as to ban undocumented students from enrolling in selective state colleges and universities in 2010 if the institution "has not admitted all academically qualified applicants in the two most recent years" (National Conference of State Legislatures 2014a).

The Dream Act, Daca, and Political Mobilization

Although some state and federal legislators have called for measures to curtail Fourteenth Amendment guarantees of citizenship for all those born within the United States (Preston 2011), there is also widespread sympathy for those youth who entered the country as young children and who have grown up calling the United States home. This sympathy has crystalized in the DREAM (Development, Relief, and Education for Alien Minors) Act, which would regularize the status of these young people and put them on a path to citizenship.

First introduced in April 2001 by Representative Luis Gutiérrez as H.R. 1582, the bill has been reintroduced almost annually. While it varies slightly from one iteration to another, the DREAM Act would make those youth within the ages specified (depending on the bill, this fluctuates between a minimum age of 12–15 and a maximum age of 30–35 at the time of the law's passage) eligible for conditional permanent residency status if they arrived in the United States before the age of sixteen, lived in the United States for at least five years prior to the date of the bill's enactment, graduated from a US high school or earned a GED or have been accepted to a US college or university, and have good moral character (that is, do not have a criminal record or pose a security risk, and are not inadmissible or removable on other grounds).

The DREAM Act has appeared in multiple formats. Some years, it has stood on its own; other years, it has been incorporated into comprehensive reform or attached to different bills, such as the 2007 Department of Defense authorization bill. It came very close to pass-ing into law in 2007 and 2010. As Michael Olivas recounts:

> A little luck might have helped turn the corner: had Senator Kennedy been well, had Senator Specter not backed away, had the fires not broken out in California, had Senator Dodd not taken a walk, had there not been a presidential elec-tion looming, all for want of a nail. But all legislation, not just that affecting immigration, has to face the cards in play on the table at the time of its consid-eration. The 2010 efforts were also doomed, this time by extremely partisan politics and the crowded calendar of events in the 111th Congress, especially with voting just before and just after the midterm 2010 elections. (2012b, 81)

The Dreamer Political Movement

The youth who would have been eligible for regularized status under the DREAM Act have come to be known as "Dreamers." They have largely succeeded in their efforts "to capture the imagination of the American people and redefine what it means to 'be American' "(Aber and Small 2013, 88). They have developed a strong social movement and viable political presence and have "consciously and consistently established themselves and their movement as the heirs to the struggle for equality of Civil Rights era activists, staging provocative sit-ins and nonviolent protests, marches and acts of civil disobedi-ence" (Aber and Small 2013, 89).

As occurs in every political movement, the various Dreamer organizations and their allies do not all agree on which tactics and strategies will be most effective in a specific context, or on the ideal end goals. These differences in perspectives manifest, for example, in dis-agreements as to whether and how far to align themselves with the Obama administration, whether pushing hard for executive action will derail possible legislation, and whether to publicly expose others who are undocumented.

Borrowing from the civil rights movement, Dreamers organized mass May Day marches in cities across the country in 2006, and in 2010 they enacted the Trail of Dreams—a 1,500-mile walk from Miami, Florida, to Washington, DC. They have also drawn from the experiences of the LGBT (lesbian, gay, bisexual, transgender) and Chicano movements. From the GLBT community, they learned the importance of putting a face and a human story to their expe-riences (Sharry 2013). They are coming out publicly so that neighbors, classmates, and coworkers are forced to recognize that they know many undocumented people, that they share similar values and goals, and they are not alien "others" to be ignored or condemned. Dreamers have staged events at border crossings and in schools, demonstrating the many ways in which they could, and in many cases already do, contribute to US society, and how their immigration status is a barrier to further contributions they might make. Some of the most visible examples include Jose Antonio Vargas, a Pulitzer Prize–winning journalist who came out as undocumented in 2011 in a *New York Times Magazine* story in an effort to advocate for passage of the DREAM Act, and groups of Dreamers dressed in graduation robes seeking entrée at border crossings in Arizona and Texas.

Lorella Praeli, director of advocacy and policy for the largest of the Dreamer organizations, United We Dream, told us that Dreamers learned five key lessons from earlier social movements. First, they came to recognize the importance of incremental change and small wins. Although comprehensive immigration reform is a primary goal, she said, if that does not seem likely at a given moment, then go for the narrower DREAM Act, and if that isn't possible, push for administrative relief, such as DACA. Second, they learned the power of personal narratives and oral histories. Third, as a youth-led movement, they quickly came to recognize the role that youth play in fighting for social change. Fourth, they realized that they have the agency to create change. Being young, she suggests, allows them to take risks. But they are also capable of taking charge, and they are not to be patronized or placated. And fifth, they have learned that when they come forward in public spheres as an organized group, they have the ability to confront power and demand action.[6]

Some immigrant rights advocates have at times been reluctant to push for a stand-alone DREAM Act out of concern that it would peel away the most popular element of comprehensive reform, making it even harder to enact the broader legislation they sought. When we asked Lorella Praeli how her organization chose between administrative and legislative strategies, she replied that she does not see them as exclusive strategies. Moreover, as a vibrant youth organization, she sees the movement as being in a good position to take the lead in making difficult, risky choices. As she recalled:

> In 2010 the broad immigrant rights movement was focused on pursuing a CIR [comprehensive immigration reform] strategy. They wanted to push for comprehensive immigration reform. And we said no. Halfway through the year we realized it was actually not a winning strategy. We don't have the votes for CIR. We may not even have the votes for DREAM. But why don't we try to push for something narrow, and at that point compelling. Because this was a time … in 2010, Dreamers were just really beginning a lot of the forceful coming out. And I don't think before then people really knew or understood what it meant to be undocumented. Right? And so, we made the shift. We literally shifted the movement from CIR to DREAM. And then you had the lame duck vote. So then, DREAM fails December of 2010.

She continued, explaining the shift in the organization's focus from a legislative solution, which they determined was unlikely to succeed in the short term, to administrative relief:

> And then we get together in Memphis Tennessee in March of 2011. And that is when we said ... I mean in 2010 we had begun the conversations on administrative relief strategies, but we were still learning about it, we wanted to understand it. And in 2011 we said our primary target is going to be the administration. Based on our own political analysis, we don't believe that a permanent legislative solution is possible right now. And so, what is going to get us a win to build power, to give people temporary certainty and security, to resource our community so that they have the ability to work, and to feel safe from the threat of deportation? I mean, those were the things we were considering, and to continue to build, because if you are not making incremental wins, it is very hard. People need wins. And that is when we said we are going to shift, we are not going to focus on legislation, we are going to push the administration. That was early 2011.[7]

United We Dream and its allies decided on a multipronged strategy, highlighting thirty legal cases to educate others about undocumented youth. They developed the Education Not Deportation (END) campaign, and then in 2012 rebranded this as the "Right to Dream" campaign. As the 2012 elections approached, it was clear to movement activists that the Obama administration had failed to champion immigration reform. The Dreamers had helped to energize the Latino and youth electorates in 2008, and all they had seen from the Obama administration in return were more and more deportations. President Obama needed a strong Latino vote turnout in the 2012 elections, so movement activists asked themselves, How can we leverage this moment to get what we need? Although many on the left were concerned that the Dreamers were asking for too much, and this could risk the Obama presidency and result in a win for Republican candidate Mitt Romney, Dreamers used the opportunity to demand change and successfully pushed for administrative relief. As a former government official concluded, "The only reason there is DACA is because these kids stood up and they blocked and they chained and they put it in Obama's face and there wasn't any way he could win the election without doing something. Could he have done it the first time he promised to do it? Hell yes, he could have. He could have done a ton of different things."

On June 15, 2012, President Barack Obama, Secretary of Homeland Security Janet Napolitano, and Director of US Citizenship and Immigration Services (and since December 2013, Deputy Secretary of Homeland Security) Alejandro Majorkas announced the Deferred

Action for Childhood Arrivals Program, with an effective date just two months later, on August 15, 2012.

DACA

Deferred action is not new, though prior to DACA it was best known as the mechanism that allowed late Beatle John Lennon to remain in the United States in the 1970s while Lennon and his wife, Yoko Ono, searched for Ono's daughter. Lennon had an earlier drug conviction in the United Kingdom, and this precluded his being granted residency (Olivas 2012a; see also Wadha 2010). Ironically, today a drug conviction is one of the key factors that would make an immigrant ineligible for DACA.

DACA is administered by the agency within DHS that is most supportive of immigrant integration, US Citizenship and Immigration Services (USCIS). The eligibility criteria have been well publicized, so those who are clearly not eligible do not need to risk coming out of the shadows and then being denied. DACA also has enormous symbolic value, providing a blueprint for how a legalization program might proceed under comprehensive immigration reform. For these reasons Tom Wong and his colleagues, among others, conclude, "The DACA announcement represented a victory for undocumented youth and their allies" (Wong et al. 2013, 1).

Yet as a policy analyst told us, because it is a form of prosecutorial discretion and does not have the force of law, "DACA can help, but it's the uncertainty, and PD continues that uncertainty" of whether a loved one can remain in the country indefinitely or whether the program will end and family members will once again be at risk for deportation.

Meeting the Eligibility Requirements

Approximately 1.76 million young people are potentially eligible for DACA (Batalova and Mittelstadt 2012). Of these, 72 percent, or 1.26 million, met the age requirement at the time DACA was announced, and another 28 percent were under age fifteen but could be eligible in the future. It is estimated that about 800,000 of the potential beneficiaries were enrolled in K–12 schools in 2012, another 390,000 had graduated from high school or had a GED, 80,000 had a college degree, and 140,000 were enrolled in college. The remaining 350,000 did not have a high school degree and were not enrolled in school, meaning they would need to re-enroll or complete their degrees or GEDs to qualify (Batalova and Mittelstadt 2012).

USCIS and community organizations have made substantial efforts to publicize eligibility criteria and resources. USCIS posted detailed Frequently Asked Questions on its website, and immigrant-serving community organizations and legal service providers have shared information and posted a host of resources online. The Immigration Advocates Network has collaborated with national partners to help advocates and applicants alike learn more about the program. In December 2013, they sent out emails to subscribers of relevant listservs announcing the availability of information through United We Dream's "Own the Dream" campaign website. These resources include an interactive online screening and application interview to help applicants learn about eligibility criteria and how to fill out the forms, a directory of free or low-cost nonprofit immigration legal services providers, another Frequently Asked Questions page that, when we visited it on May 12, 2014, included forty-seven questions, training materials, events, and news updates. The website also includes resources for advocates, such as guides for completing the application forms, strategies for proving that the education and residency requirements have been met, screening guides for other potential sources of relief (for example, Special Immigrant Juvenile Status), and tips for writing affidavits. The email from the Immigration Advocates Network also provided links to advocacy alerts, information regarding the availability of a driver's license in different states, and resources relevant to college attendance, including an interactive map showing which states provide some degree of tuition eligibility or financial aid for undocumented students.

Reflective of the technology-savvy generation to which DACA applicants belong, the Immigration Advocates Network, American Immigration Council, and American Immigration Lawyers Association jointly created a free "Pocket DACA" app, available for Android and Apple smartphones and tablets, to help prospective applicants learn about DACA eligibility. Social media such as Facebook and Twitter supplement traditional media to provide information and to publicize success stories designed to inspire other eligible youth to apply (Wong et al. 2013). In addition, several universities and colleges, mostly in California, have opened Dreamers Resource Centers, which provide information about financial aid, internships, and other resources as well as academic and emotional support for undocumented college students. Finally, the Mexican consulate has been proactive in providing assistance to Mexican immigrants needing birth certificates, passports, and consular identification cards to establish their place and date of birth. Mexican consular offices across the United States have expanded their hours of operation, provided public outreach, and offered assistance to DACA clinics. Like the Pocket DACA app, the Mexican Consulate has also created a free micro-consular app, "MiConsulMex," for the Android and Apple platforms.

The availability of these resources has meant that very few individuals are applying for DACA unless they are clearly eligible. This may change if applicants with less clear-cut cases start coming forward in increasing numbers. With time, however, new sources of documentation are emerging. For example, in addition to school records, rent and utility receipts, vaccination records, and records confirming participation in a religious ceremony, we have heard stories of youth who have successfully used Facebook postings with GPS locators to show that they were in the United States on a given date.

DACA Implementation: Year 1 Applicant Demographics

Initial analyses of the first year of DACA's implementation have been conducted by Batalova et al. (2013), Singer and Svejlenka (2013), and Wong et al. (2013). Their analyses differ slightly in their estimates of the immediately eligible population because the true number of unauthorized immigrants living in the United States who were between the ages of fifteen and thirty-one on June 15, 2012, arrived in the United States before June 2007, were under age sixteen at arrival, and meet DACA's other requirements is unknown.[8]

Tom Wong and his colleagues estimate that 53.1 percent of the DACA population was immediately eligible to apply, and 61 percent of that population applied by August 15, 2013, the first anniversary of USCIS accepting DACA applications. Jeanne Batalova and her colleagues at Migration Policy Institute (2013) estimate that a slightly higher percentage, 57 percent of the potential applicants, were immediately eligible, and 49 percent of those currently eligible had applied by June 30, 2013. Their findings also vary a bit as a consequence of their differing sources. To supplement publicly available USCIS data, Singer and Svejlenka (2013) and Wong et al. (2013) obtained data on applicants from Freedom of Information Act (FOIA) requests to DHS. Their FOIA requests, and thus their findings, differ slightly, primarily in the time frame covered by the request.

Although the foreign-born noncitizen population in the United States is only 48.5 percent female, women are more likely to successfully apply for DACA. Wong et al. (2013) report that 51.2 percent of their FOIA sample was female, with men 1.4 times more likely than women to have their applications denied (see, similarly, Singer and Svejlenka 2013). The data also indicate substantial variation in application rates by national origin. Applicants in Wong et al.'s FOIA sample came from 205 countries, while Singer and Svejlenka's FOIA sample includes applicants from 192 countries. Both studies, however, report that more than 90 percent of the applicants were from Mexico, Central America, and South America, with the vast majority coming from Mexico. The far higher application rates from Latin Americans than from immigrants hailing from other parts of the world are generally attributed to the very effective outreach efforts by Spanish language media and immigrant-serving organizations in Latino, and especially Mexican, immigrant communities. There is also substantial intragroup variation within the Asian population, with the Korean ethnic media being far more proactive than the Chinese media (Wong et al. 2013, 31). This could explain the high application and approval rate for South Korean applicants. Immigrants from South Korean followed Mexicans, Salvadorans, Guatemalans, and Hondurans in the number of applications, and Batalova et al. report that 33 percent of the currently eligible Korean immigrants applied for DACA in its first year. The lowest application rates are from African immigrants, with only 1 percent of the applicants in Wong et al.'s FOIA sample migrating from Africa.

The average age of initial applicants in Wong et al.'s FOIA sample was twenty years old, and Singer and Svejlenka report that more than half (54 percent) were under the age of twenty-one. Advocacy organizations recognize that they did a better job of reaching young people than those at the older end of the eligible age range. As Allison Posner, advocacy director of Catholic Legal Immigration Network Inc. (CLINIC) told us, "The advocacy community did a great job reaching out to people in high schools and colleges. However, eligible applicants who are older and out of school, especially those with young families, did not receive as much outreach and thought that DACA did not apply to them. Some thought that because they had children of their own, they were ineligible. That's not true. Organizations are now trying to do a better job at reaching out to those who are eligible but have not applied and to dispel misconceptions about the program."[9]

Older applicants are more likely to be denied than younger applicants, probably because of the greater difficulty in establishing eligibility for people who have been out of school for a while and may have moved frequently. Although three-quarters of the applicants overall are from the western and southern parts of the United States (Wong et al. 2013), applicants over the age of twenty-one tend to live in states with long-established immigrant populations, such as California, Illinois, New York, and New Jersey (Singer and Svejlenka 2013). This may reflect the greater number of immigrant-serving community organizations, including churches and legal aid providers, in traditional destination sites.

Going from Undocumented to "Dacamented"

Gonzales, Terriquez, and Ruszczyk (2014) explore the initial implementation of DACA through analysis of a national Web survey of DACA recipients, the National Undacamented Research Project. This project surveyed young adults ages 18–32 who were eligible to receive DACA during the first sixteen months of its availability. They found that just over half of the survey respondents obtained driver's licenses, 59 percent obtained new jobs, 45 percent reported increased job earnings, and 21 percent obtained health care after receiving DACA. In addition, nearly half of the respondents opened their first bank accounts, and one-third obtained their first credit cards after becoming dacamented. As Gonzales and his colleagues conclude, "Although DACA does not address many of the problems these young people confront ... its beneficiaries experienced greater access to U.S. institutions, enabling them to better achieve their potential" (2014, 1866).

One of the most important points of access is higher education. As of August 2014, sixteen states have classified at least some unauthorized immigrants as residents for tuition purposes if they graduated from state high schools, have two to three years residence in the state, and apply to a state college or university. Another two states permit undocumented students to pay in-state tuition through board of regents decisions, for a total of eighteen states providing residency status (National Conference of State Legislatures 2014a).

New resources are making a college education and even graduate school a reality for some Dreamers. In October 2013, Janet Napolitano, former DHS Secretary and now president of the University of California, pledged $5 million in university funds to assist the approximately 900 Dreamers attending University of California campuses (Rainey 2013). These funds will supplement state and campus-based financial aid made available to California's undocumented students under Assembly Bills 130 (2012) and 131 (2013). Soon after, former *Washington Post* owner Donald Graham created "TheDream.US," a $25 million fund to award full-tuition college scholarships to 1,000 students in the next year "who want to study nursing, teaching, computers, and business." With support from the Bill & Melinda Gates Foundation, Bloomberg Philanthropies, and the Inter-American Development Bank, among others, Graham created this fund because "I'm not wise enough to know what is the right immigration policy for the United States of America. ... I know these students deserve a chance at higher education" (Layton 2014).

Washington Post journalist Pamela Constable has described DACA as "a legal ticket to self-respect." DACA recipients "are able to leave day-labor pools for steadier jobs in stores or trades and take part-time classes at community colleges. Their schedules are often grueling, but they are keenly aware that the clock is ticking. Every benefit DACA status confers—a Social Security card, a work permit, the right to drive—is valid for only two years." Again mirroring the complexities of mixed status families, however, she continues, "In the Washington region, immigration lawyers said that most of their DACA clients have parents who are in the country illegally. Some families have several children who received DACA; in other cases, one sibling was successful but another was too old or did not have enough documents to get approval" (Constable 2014).

What Is Next? Renewal of DACA

As DACA approached its second birthday, United We Dream and other advocacy groups called for substantial changes in "DACA 2.0," such as raising the maximum age of entry requirement from sixteen to eighteen, removing the age cap, including Dreamers in the labor force who do not meet DACA's education guidelines, making applying for DACA more affordable through a fee waiver for persons at or below 150 percent of the Federal Poverty Level, extending deferred action to five years rather than two, eliminating the "significant misdemeanor" bar and requiring that an individual must have served an aggregate of 365 days in order for their criminal record to bar them from the program, and granting DACA applicants parole-in-place if they are otherwise eligible for the program (Praeli 2014).

These requests were not met in the renewal of DACA, but Dreamers and other immigration advocates have continued to pressure the Obama administration to go beyond DACA, demanding that administrative relief be provided to all those who would have been eligible for legalization under S. 744, the comprehensive immigration reform bill passed by the Senate in 2013 (Praeli 2014; Preston 2014). As part of this strategy, Dreamers are actively engaging with key members of Congress whom they see as important allies in expanding administrative forms of relief.[10]

The Congressional Hispanic Caucus sent DHS Secretary Jeh Johnson a confidential draft memorandum, which was leaked to, and published by, the *Washington Post* on April 4, 2014. Reminiscent of the history of the leaked memorandum authored by Denise Vanison, Roxana Bacon, Debra Rogers, and Donald Neufeld suggesting the use of deferred action in 2010 (Vanison et al., n.d.), this memorandum begins by saying:

> The President shared with us in a recent meeting that he has asked you to do an inventory of the Department's current practices to see how it can conduct enforcement more humanely within the confines of the law. Below are several policy options that offer affirmative administrative relief within the purview of the law with the goal of family unity. In addition, we have also included recommendations on enforcement reforms that DHS can implement to better focus its resources on targeting those who pose a serious threat to our communities and reflect a more humane approach to immigration enforcement."
> (Congressional Hispanic Caucus, n.d., 1)

Among other recommendations, the Hispanic Caucus calls for DHS to protect parents and siblings of DACA recipients, as well as parents of US citizen or legal permanent resident children, against deportation, stating that this would help keep families intact and reduce the number of children in foster care. The caucus memo recommends that these family members be allowed to apply for a work permit, and for extension of humanitarian parole to immediate family members if they have been deported. The memo advocates for a review of ICE's civil enforcement priorities and of the use of prosecutorial discretion, termination of Secure Communities and the 287(g) programs, and limiting the use of detention to the highest-priority cases.

Yet consistent with the zigzag progress that has bedeviled immigration reform, in late May 2014, President Obama asked DHS Secretary Johnson not to make results of his review of administrative options public until Congress recessed in August, so as not to jeopardize last-ditch efforts to pass legislation in the House. Similarly, he asked the Department of Defense to delay a plan to allow persons granted relief under DACA, and who have specific language or medical skills, a path to citizenship by serving in the military (Kuhnhenn 2014). As the *Washington Post* reports, "The White House is concerned that Republicans would balk if the administration takes unilateral action to stem the deportation of undocumented immigrants, ending any slim remaining hopes of a legislative compromise" (Nakamura 2014). By late summer, House Republicans had made clear that a legislative compromise was not in the works. Rather, they promised impeachment proceedings if President Obama took unilateral action that they felt exceeded his authority.

Perhaps in an effort to strengthen President Obama's resolve, on September 3, 2014, more than 130 law professors sent a letter to the president reaffirming the constitutional basis for prosecutorial action, and for formalizing that policy decision through procedures such as deferred action and work authorization (Wadhia et al. 2014). Three days later, the president announced that he would delay taking executive action on immigration until after the midyear elections, as requested by fellow Democrats facing difficult contests. The delay did not achieve its objectives, as Democrats lost the Senate as well as the House. Finally, on November 20, 2014, President Obama announced his intent to pursue executive action to expand the deferred action program to shield five million unauthorized immigrants from deportation and provide them with work authorization, redefine priorities for ICE, and streamline the visa application process.

Complications and Contradictions

Focusing our lens on mixed status families, and especially the dreams and nightmares of the 1.5 generation, brings the complications and contradictions of contemporary immigration policy in the United States into sharp relief. We have seen multiple attempts to pass comprehensive immigration reform in the past decade. Whenever those attempts appeared at risk of failing, immigration advocates and their supporters in Congress and the White House tried for the more modest DREAM Act because there was more support for young people who came to the United States as young children than for their parents. Although some feared that the DREAM Act would peel off support from comprehensive legislation, others felt whatever might work should to be tried.

Early in the Obama administration, there was talk of what forms of administrative relief might be available to the executive branch. Deferred action was proposed, but instead the administration chose to demonstrate that it was taking a tough approach, hoping that so doing would make comprehensive reform more feasible. Instead, two million immigrants were deported under the Obama administration's watch, and the advocacy community began calling President Obama "deporter in chief." An organized coalition of Dreamers and their allies confronted the Obama administration with the necessity of offering administrative relief if they were to help get out the vote in the 2012 election. This strategy was successful, and half a million young people have been granted deferred action and permission to work in the United States. Yet close to eleven million undocumented immigrants still do not have such relief, and mixed status families are now further complicated, with some family members having US citizenship or legal permanent residency, others who are dacamented having a smaller set of privileges, and still others remaining undocumented. Within this shifting context, we next review the key structural mechanisms that have exacerbated harm for mixed status families and members of the Dreamer generation, and those that mitigate harm.

Structural Mechanisms That Exacerbate Harm

The educational and developmental ramifications for children of their parents' undocumented status are becoming increasingly clear. In part, this is due to families living in poverty and to the long hours that most undocumented immigrants work, often at multiple jobs. Compounding the problems faced by immigrants with legal status, who may also struggle with finding work that pays well, undocumented parents often have debts they must pay to smugglers, and they are vulnerable to exploitation by unscrupulous employers who may not pay them for a job completed. This translates into children not having access to good preschools, resources that might further their development, or even to their parents' time and energy. The multiple barriers to health care and to educational and social services further deprive citizen children of undocumented parents from services to which they are entitled. When children cannot access these services, their development is stymied, avenues for success are systematically closed off to them, and they are not able to contribute to society to the extent they might if they had received these benefits.

The exclusion of undocumented students from federal financial aid and from state-based aid in the majority of states is another structural barrier to full integration of the 1.5 generation in American society. When students who grew up in the United States, attending local schools for most of their life, suddenly realize that they are not considered residents of the state where they live, this has profound consequences for their sense of belonging. It also has serious financial implications. Having to pay nonresident tuition and lacking access to financial aid in most states means that higher education becomes an unattainable dream for youth who must watch from the sidelines as their friends, neighbors, and, in many cases, younger siblings go on to college.

Finally, exclusion of "dacamented" youth from the Affordable Care Act, while perhaps politically expedient, means that Dreamers must continue to struggle to pay for basic medical and dental care and reminds them of the liminality of their status—that they are not seen as fully American.

Structural Mechanisms That Mitigate Harm

In the absence of comprehensive immigration reform and even its more limited variant, the DREAM Act, Deferred Action for Childhood Arrivals has been the primary mechanism for reducing harm for members of the 1.5 generation. DACA represents a major victory for immigration advocates. Nevertheless, it has limitations. Chief among them is that DACA is a temporary status that must be renewed regularly. The program was probably limited in this fashion to make it harder for opponents to accuse the Obama administration of conducting an end run around congressional authority to legislate immigration law. As former INS Commissioner Doris Meissner told us, "That makes it uncertain and costly for beneficiaries because they must pay an application and fingerprint fee to obtain renewal of their status. Still, in the absence of immigration reform or any other avenue for legal status, DACA is life changing. It provides protection from deportation and the ability to work legally. Depending on state laws, it can also permit going to college and getting a driver's license. There are major pluses for young people."[11]

One of the key structural dilemmas when DACA was being developed in the summer of 2012 was how best to define its educational requirements. Advocacy organizations and immigration policy centers worked closely with government officials to define these requirements so as to include youth who may have dropped out of school, but who could now return and gain their diplomas or GEDs. The revised definition of being enrolled in school on the date when you apply for DACA—regardless of whether you had previously quit and now were returning to school—brings an estimated 350,000 more students out of the shadows and into the DACA eligibility pool (Batalova and Mittelstadt 2012). In addition, it gives families a reason to keep older children in school rather than allowing, or encouraging, them to drop out of school to take care of younger siblings while the parents work, or to go to work themselves to help support the family.

In his analysis of *Plyler v. Doe* and the education of undocumented children in the United States, Michael Olivas (2012b) describes the DREAM Act as "Doe goes to college." As federal law, the DREAM Act would have facilitated college education for eligible undocumented students nationwide by enabling them to obtain federal loan, grant, and work-study funding. DACA is not able to go this far. Yet as we discussed in this chapter, as of spring 2014, eighteen states have extended in-state tuition, and in some cases state-based financial aid, to undocumented immigrants who meet eligibility criteria, either through state legislation or through board of regents decisions (National Conference on State Legislatures 2014a). Thus, to borrow from Michael Olivas, Doe can more readily go to college, at least in some states.

DACA's most obvious benefit, of course, is to keep youth safe from deportation. But the increased numbers of undocumented youth who will now graduate from high school because of how the educational requirements were written, and who will continue on to college because of DACA and the state laws enacted in support of this program, are also tremendously important means of mitigating harm to youth and families.

In DACA's wake, there has been substantial state-level legislation permitting dacamented youth to obtain driver's licenses. In places where public transportation is limited, DACA's work authorization is seriously constrained without permission to drive. As of May 2014, eleven states and the District of Columbia allow undocumented immigrants to obtain driver's licenses, and another three states issued driving privileges to certain immigrants (National Conference of State Legislatures 2014b).

The coordinated engagement among government officials, nonprofit advocacy groups, Dreamer networks, local community organizations, and the media has been critical to informing relevant communities about DACA, including who is eligible, how to demonstrate residency and the other requirements, and how to apply. The degree of support across agencies and the speed with which those resources were engaged has been impressive and is in large part responsible for the early success of the program.

The expansion of deferred action in President Obama's November 2014 executive action will potentially affect five million people. As Dreamers had hoped, it removes the age cap for DACA, includes youth brought to the United States before January 1, 2010, and extends relief for three years at a time rather than two. It will go far to reduce family separations, offering deferred action and work authorization for parents of US-citizen or legal permanent resident children who have lived in the United States for at least five years and meet other eligibility requirements. Although Dreamers were disappointed that the administrative relief will not extend to their parents unless they have siblings who are citizens or legal residents, this carefully crafted expansion of deferred action illustrates that DACA was a viable vehicle for administrative reform and could serve as a blueprint for future forms of relief (Cavendish et al. 2014).

Conclusions

This reading focuses on the everyday experiences of undocumented youth and the children of undocumented parents. Millions of Americans live in mixed status families, with siblings encountering what may be vastly different opportunities depending upon where and when they were born. When parents are undocumented, the whole family lives in the shadows. The next generation suffers, because US-citizen children do not receive the educational, health, and other social benefits they are due. When teenagers realize they are undocumented, they see their options suddenly cut off. The implications for civic society are potentially huge, as large numbers of youth are made to feel that they do not really belong.

The Dreamer social movement has brought these teenagers and young adults out of the shadows and into the streets, where they are claiming the rights and privileges of membership in the society they have always called home. Fed up with congressional gridlock, they have pressured President Barack Obama to use the power of his pen and to enact administrative forms of relief so that their parents, siblings, and friends can live, work, and go to school without fear of deportation. On November 20, 2014, President Obama used his power and took such action.

[...]

References

Aber, Shaina and Mary Small. 2013. "Citizen or Subordinate: Permutations of Belonging in the United States and the Dominican Republic." Journal on Migration and Human Security 1(3):76–96.

Abrego, Leisy J. 2006. "'I Can't Go to College Because I Don't Have Papers': Incorporation Patterns of Latino Undocumented Youth." Latino Studies 4:212–31.

———. 2008. "Legitimacy, Social Identity, and the Mobilization of Law: The Effects of Assembly Bill 540 on Undocumented Students in California." Law & Social Inquiry 33(3):709–34.

———. 2011. "Legal Consciousness of Undocumented Latinos: Fear and Stigma as Barriers to Claims-Making for First- and 1.5-Generation Immigrants," Law and Society Review 45(2):337–69.

Abrego, Leisy J. and Roberto G. Gonzales. 2010. "Blocked Paths, Uncertain Futures: The Postsecondary Education and Labor Market Prospects of Undocumented Latino Youth." Journal of Education for Students Placed at Risk 15:144–57.

Batalova, Jeanne, Sarah Hooker, and Randy Capps with James D. Bachmeier and Erin Cox. 2013. Deferred Action for Childhood Arrivals at the One-Year Mark: A Profile of Currently Eligible Youth and Applicants. Washington, DC: Migration Policy Institute.

Batalova, Jeanne and Michelle Mittelstadt. 2012. Relief from Deportation: Demographic Profile of the DREAMers Potentially Eligible under the Deferred Action Policy. Washington, DC: Migration Policy Institute.

Boehm, Deborah A. 2012. Intimate Migrations: Gender, Family, and Illegality among Transnational Mexicans. New York: New York University Press.

Brabeck, Kalina and Quingwen Xu. 2010. "The Impact of Detention and Deportation on Latino Immigrant Children and Families: A Quantitative Explanation." Hispanic Journal of Behavioral Sciences 32(3):341–61.

Brotherton, David C. and Luis Barrios. 2011. Banished to the Homeland: Dominican Deportees and Their Stories of Exile. New York: Columbia University Press.

Capps, Randy, Rosa Maria Castañeda, Ajay Chaudry, and Robert Santos. 2007. Paying the Price: The Impact of Immigration Raids on America's Children. Washington, DC: National Council of La Raza and Urban Institute.

Capps, Randy and Michael Fix, eds. 2012. Young Children of Black Immigrants in America: Changing Flows, Changing Faces. Washington, DC: Migration Policy Institute.

Cavendish, Betsy, Steven Schulman, Amjad Mahmood Khan, and Erica Abshez. 2014. A DREAM Deferred: From DACA to Citizenship: Lessons from DACA for Advocates and Policymakers. Washington, DC: Appleseed.

Chaudry, Ajay, Randy Capps, Juan Manuel Pedroza, Rosa Maria Castañeda, Robert Santos, and Molly M. Scott. 2010. Facing Our Future: Children in the Aftermath of Immigration Enforcement. Washington, DC: Urban Institute. February. www.urban.org/uploadedpdf/412020_FacingOurFuture_final.pdf.

Congressional Hispanic Caucus. n.d. "Working Draft Memorandum to Secretary Johnson." www.washingtonpost.com/r/2010–2019/WashingtonPost/2014/04/04/Editorial-Opinion/Graphics/CHC_Request%20to%20Jeh%20Johnson.pdf.

Constable, Pamela. 2014. "Young Illegal Immigrants Get Two-Year Ticket to Earn, Learn, and Enjoy Self-Respect." Washington Post, April 6. www.washingtonpost.com/local/young-illegal-immigrants-get-two-year-ticket-to-earn-learn-and-gain-self-respect/2014/04/06/7693dbaa-bb5b-11e3-9c3c-311301e2167d_story.html.

Coutin, Susan Bibler. 2000. Legalizing Moves: Salvadoran Immigrants' Struggle for U.S. Residency. Ann Arbor: University of Michigan Press.

———. 2003. "Borderlands, Illegality and the Spaces of Non-existence." In Globalization under Construction: Governmentality, Law, and Identity, edited by Richard Perry and Bill Maurer, 171–202. Minneapolis: University of Minnesota Press.

———. 2007. Nations of Emigrants: Shifting Boundaries of Citizenship in El Salvador and the United States. Ithaca: Cornell University Press.

Flores, Stella M. 2010. "State Dream Acts: The Effect of In-State Resident Tuition Policies on the College Enrollment of Undocumented Latino Students in the United States." Review of Higher Education 33(2): 239–83.

Gleeson, Shannon and Roberto G. Gonzales. 2012. "When Do Papers Matter? An Institutional Analysis of Undocumented Life in the United States." International Migration 50(4):1–19.

Gonzales, Roberto G. 2010. "On the Wrong Side of the Tracks: The Consequences of School Stratification Systems for Unauthorized Mexican Students." Peabody Journal of Education 85(4):469–85.

———. 2011. "Learning to be Illegal: Undocumented Youth and Shifting Legal Contexts in the Transition to Adulthood." American Sociological Review 76(4):602–19.

Gonzales, Roberto G. and Leo Chavez. 2012. "'Awakening to a Nightmare': Abjectivity and Illegality in the Lives of Undocumented 1.5-Generation Latino Immigrants in the United States." Current Anthropology 53(3):255–268.

Gonzales, Roberto G., Veronica Terriquez, and Stephen Ruszczyk. 2014. "Becoming DACAmented: Assessing the Short-Term Benefits of Deferred Action for Childhood Arrivals (DACA)." American Behavioral Scientist 58(14):1852–72.

Hagan, Jacqueline, Karl Eschbach, and Nestor Rodríguez. 2008. "U.S. Deportation Policy, Family Separation, and Circular Migration." International Migration Review 42(1):64–88.

Hagan, Jacqueline, Nestor Rodríguez, and Brianna Castro. 2011. "Social Effects of Mass Deportations by the United States Government, 2000–2010." Ethnic and Racial Studies 34(8):1374–91.

Kuhnhenn, Jim. 2014. "White House Wants Delay in DOD Immigration Plan." Associated Press. June 2. http://hosted.ap.org/dynamic/stories/U/US_OBAMA_IMMIGRATION?SITE = AP.

Layton, Lyndsey. 2014. "Former Post Owner Hoping to Send Dreamers to College." Washington Post. February 3. www.washingtonpost.com/local/education/former-post-owner-launches-scholarship-fund-for-undocumented-students/2014/02/03/f41dea2a-8aaf-11e3–916e-e01534b1e132_story.html.

Menjívar, Cecilia. 2006. "Liminal Legality: Salvadoran and Guatemalan Immigrants' Lives in the United States." American Journal of Sociology 111:999–1037.

———. 2012. "Transnational Parenting and Immigration Law: Central Americans in the United States." Journal of Ethnic and Migration Studies 38(2):301–22.

Menjívar, Cecilia and Leisy Abrego. 2009. "Parents and Children across Borders: Legal Instability and Intergenerational Relations in Guatemalan and Salvadoran Families." In Across Generations: Immigrant Families in America, edited by Nancy Foner, 160–89. New York: New York University Press.

———. 2012. "Legal Violence: Immigration Law and the Lives of Central American Immigrants." American Journal of Sociology 117(5):1380–1421.

Menjívar, Cecilia and Dan Kanstroom, eds. 2013. Constructing Illegality in America: Immigrant Experiences, Critiques, and Resistance. New York: Cambridge University Press.

Nakamura, David. 2014. "Obama Orders Delay of Immigration Deportation Review." Washington Post. May 27. www.washingtonpost.com/blogs/post-politics/wp/2014/05/27/obama-orders-delay-of-immigration-deportation-review/

National Conference of State Legislatures. 2014a. "Undocumented Student Tuition: Overview." May. www.ncsl.org/research/education/undocumented-student-tuition-overview.aspx.

———. 2014b. "States Offering Driver's Licenses to Immigrants." April 3. www.ncsl.org/research/immigration/states-offering-driver-s-licenses-to-immigrants.aspx.

Olivas, Michael A. 2012a. "Dreams Deferred: Deferred Action, Prosecutorial Discretion and the Vexing Case(s) of Dream Act Students. "William and Mary Bill of Rights Journal 21:463–547.

———. 2012b. No Undocumented Child Left Behind: Plyler v. Doe and the Education of Undocumented Schoolchildren. New York: New York University Press.

Passel, Jeffrey and D'Vera Cohn. 2009. "A Portrait of Unauthorized Immigrants in the United States." Pew Hispanic Center. April 14. www.pewhispanic.org/2009/04/14/a-portrait-of-unauthorized-immigrants-in-the-united-states/.

Praeli, Lorella. 2014. "[Infographic] Five Things Obama Can Do Right Now to Provide Relief to the Undocumented Community. #WeCantWait." Last update May 1, 2014. http://unitedwedream.org/five-things-president-obama-can-do/.

Preston, Julia. 2011. "State Lawmakers Outline Plans to End Birthright Citizenship, Drawing Outcry." New York Times. January 5. www.nytimes.com/2011/01/06/us/06immig.html?_r = 0.

———. 2014. "Young Immigrants Turn Focus to President in Struggles over Deportations." New York Times. February 23. www.nytimes.com/2014/02/24/us/politics/young-immigrants-turn-focus-to-president-in-struggle-over-deportations.html.

Rainey, Libby. 2013. "Napolitano Announces New $5 Million Initiative to Aid Undocumented Students." Daily Californian. October 31. www.dailycal.org/2013/10/30/napolitano-announces-new-initiative-undocumented-students-uc/.

Shaina, Aber and Mary Small. 2013. "Citizen or Subordinate: Permutations of Belonging in the United States and the Dominican Republic." Journal on Migration and Human Security 1(3):76–96.

Sharry, Frank. 2013. "How Did We Build an Immigrant Movement? We Learned from Gay Rights Advocates." Washington Post. March 22. www.washingtonpost.com/opinions/how-did-we-build-an-immigrant-movement-we-learned-from-gay-rights-advocates/2013/03/22/8a0d2b9a-916e-11e2-bdea-e32ad90da239_story.html.

Singer, Audrey and Nicole P. Svejlenka. 2013. "Immigration Facts: Deferred Action for Childhood Arrivals (DACA)." Washington, DC: Brookings Institution. www.brookings.edu/research/reports/2013/08/14-daca-immigration-singer.

Suárez-Orozco, Carola, Marcelo Suárez-Orozco, and Irina Todorova. 2008. Learning a New Land: Immigrant Students in American Society. Cambridge, MA: Harvard University Press.

Suárez-Orozco, Carola, Hirokazu Yoshikawa, Robert T. Teranishi, and Marcelo M. Suárez-Orozco. 2011. "Growing Up in the Shadows: The Developmental Implications of Undocumented Status." Harvard Educational Review 81(3):438–72.

Taylor, Paul, Mark Hugo Lopez, Jeffrey Passel, and Seth Motel. 2011. "Unauthorized Immigrants: Length of Residency, Patterns of Parenthood." Pew Research Hispanic Trends Project. December 1. www.pewhispanic.org/2011/12/01/unauthorized-immigrants-length-of-residency-patterns-of-parenthood/.

Thronson, David B. 2010. "Thinking Small: The Need for Big Changes in Immigration Law's Treatment of Children." UC Davis Journal of Juvenile Law and Policy 14(2):239–62.

Van Hook, Jennifer, Nancy S. Landale, and Marianne M. Hillemeier. 2013. Is the United States Bad for Children's Health? Risk and Resilience among Young Children of Immigrants. Washington, DC: Migration Policy Institute.

Vanison, Denise A., Roxana Bacon, Debra A. Rogers, and Donald Neufeld. n.d. "Administrative Alternatives to Comprehensive Immigration Reform." http://abcnews.go.com/images/Politics/memo-on-alternatives-to-comprehensive-immigration-reform.pdf.

Wadhia, Shoba S. 2010. "The Role of Prosecutorial Discretion in Immigration Law." Connecticut Public Interest Law Journal 9:243–99.

Wadhia, Shoba S. et al. 2014. "Executive Authority to Protect Individuals or Groups from Deportation." Letter from 136 law professors to President Barack Obama. On file with the authors.

Willen, Sarah S. 2007. "Toward a Critical Phenomenology of 'Illegality': State Power, Criminality and Abjectivity among Undocumented Migrant Workers in Tel Aviv, Israel." International Migration 45(3):8–38.

Wong, Tom K., Angela S. García, Marisa Abrajano, David FitzGerald, Karthick Ramakrishnan, and Sally Le. 2013. "Undocumented No More: A Nationwide Analysis of Deferred Action for Childhood Arrivals, or DACA." September. Washington, DC: Center for American Progress. www.americanprogress.org/wp-content/uploads/2013/09/DACAReportCC-2-1.pdf.

Yoshikawa, Hirokazu. 2011. Immigrants Raising Citizens: Undocumented Parents and Their Young Children. New York: Russell Sage Foundation.

Yoshikawa, Hirokazu and Jenya Kholoptseva. 2012. Unauthorized Immigrant Parents and Their Children's Development: A Summary of the Evidence. Washington, DC: Migration Policy Institute. March.

Cases Cited

Plyler v. Doe 457 U.S. 2002 (1982).

Notes

1   Interview with Lorella Praeli, May 14, 2014.

2   Interview with Nina Rabin, February 23, 2012.

3   Between 2005 and 2011, more than 8,000 immigration-related laws and resolutions were introduced in state legislatures across the country, and 1,700 of these laws and resolutions were enacted (National Conference of State Legislatures 2012).

4   Interview with Victoria López, June 22, 2012.

5   Interview with Emily Butera, February 13, 2012.

6   Interview with Lorella Praeli, May 14, 2014.

7   Ibid.

8   Others will become eligible as they reach the age of fifteen or return to school, but they are not considered in the immediately eligible population.

9   Interview with Allison Posner, November 19, 2013.

10 Interview with Lorella Praeli, May 14, 2014.

11 Interview with Doris Meissner, December 6, 2012.

DISCUSSION QUESTIONS

1. Herbert Bolton is considered the "father" of borderlands history. How did he describe or conceptualize the borderlands?

2. Why did southern Texas become rife with violence following the Texas Declaration of Independence and the Mexican–American War?

3. How has the border region both changed and remained the same over time?

4. What was the purpose of the Border Industrialization Program (BIP)?

5. Despite the goal of curbing bracero unemployment, what was the reality of the BIP?

6. What reasons does Simon cite for Mexico's historic lack of enforcement of environmental law?

7. What is the leading cause of environmental destruction in the Lower Rio Grande Valley and what problems have developed as a result?

8. What is "garbage imperialism"? How is Mexico impacted versus the United States?

9. What is the "1.5 generation"? From where is this term derived?

10. How are mixed-status family dynamics impacted by family members' variances in citizenship status?

11. According to Lorella Praeli, directory of United We Dream, what five key lessons have Dreamers learned from earlier social movements?

Conclusion

*F*OREIGNERS IN THEIR OWN LAND WAS written to showcase an interdisciplinary range of information about the Mexican American experience in the United States, and introduces the breadth of Mexican American Studies. As I explained at the beginning of the book, its purpose is to raise awareness about an often-marginalized minority group and demonstrate how the Mexican American story can be interwoven with a traditional, American master narrative. The textbook sheds light on lesser-known facts about Mexican Americans while illustrating an American minority experience. I hope that it will serve as an example of how other minority groups can be studied.

Moreover, this work addresses the diversity of the Hispanic culture and reminds us that Mexicans are just one small part of the Hispanic story. This further emphasizes the complexity of American history and all the groups that have hyphenated identities in the United States. Students are introduced to the writings of several historians, a political scientist, a sociologist, an anthropologist, and a professor of criminology, law and society. Each scholar brings a unique perspective, which facilitates a well-rounded understanding of how Mexican Americans can be, and should be, interwoven with the American story.

Foreigners in Their Own Land takes readers on a thematic journey through Mexican American life, from United States Spanish heritage and exploration to twenty-first-century issues. It is far from all-encompassing, but allows readers to dip their toes into Mexican American Studies. The discussion questions at the end of each chapter encourage the reader to reflect on the readings and on their connection to contemporary representations and experiences of Mexican Americans in the United States.

The most important thing I want readers to understand is how Ethnic Studies enrich one's understanding of American history. The readings in this book showcase a range of topics in Mexican American history that are not often taught in K-12 education. And while this book emphasizes the Mexican American experience, my hope is that readers are inspired to pursue other Ethnic Studies courses and readings that will deepen their understanding of the diversity of the American experience. Master narratives generally skim over minorities and their accomplishments, but Ethnic Studies brings these minorities to the forefront to illustrate that they were, and are, changing the world in their own distinct ways as well.

Our personal experiences impact the way we learn and make decisions—this does not mean that one way is "right," and one way is "wrong." It is simply *different*. Accepting these differences and learning from them for personal and professional growth is a step toward creating a society that celebrates its diversity and uses it for advancement. The readings have demonstrated that, historically, this has not been the case for Mexican Americans and other minority groups in the United States. Minorities have been looked upon as inferior and treated as such. Learning about other cultures, and not pitting them against each other as "better" or "worse," is a move toward fostering positive change.

Minorities across the country have been calling for these changes for decades, and they are slowly starting to happen. More than 50 years ago, during the 1968 Civil Rights Movement, groups of African American, Latinx, Asian American, and Native American students "began a five-month strike at what is now San Francisco State University calling for, among other things, modifications to the traditional Eurocentric curriculum and creation of the first ethnic studies program."[1] These students were pushing back against the institutional racism they experienced in schools and demanded an education that reflected the ethnic diversity of the country. While it would be inaccurate to state that the demands they made 50 years ago have all been met, there continues to be an increasing call for K-12 education that "reflects and affirms students' racial and ethnic identities and, in doing so, helps improve student academic outcomes (Banks, 1991; Dee & Penner, 2016; Sleeter, 2011)."[2] Minorities in the United States continue to demand a curriculum that reflects the real-life diversity that exists in the country and in the classroom. However, there has been pushback against Critical Race Theory (CRT) being taught in K-12, and although Ethnic Studies and Critical Race Theory are not the same, they are often conflated in the media and seen as a threat to American patriotism, identity, and democracy.

The NAACP defines CRT as "an academic and legal framework that denotes that systemic racism is part of American society—from education and housing to employment and healthcare. Critical Race Theory recognizes that racism is more than the result of individual bias and prejudice. It is embedded in laws, policies and institutions that uphold and reproduce racial inequalities."[3] Ethnic Studies courses, on the other hand, aim to highlight traditionally marginalized or excluded groups and their history and perspectives. Unfortunately, opponents of CRT have used it to prevent discussions about systemic racism and the teaching of American history that addresses its racist past. They have used this term to unjustly "include all diversity and inclusion efforts, race-conscious policies, and education about racism, whether or not they draw from CRT."[4] The reality is that CRT is rarely taught in K-12 and is more often introduced at the college level. Regardless, it is being used as justification to censor K-12 education. This censorship makes Ethnic Studies courses even more critical. The goal of Ethnic Studies is not anti-American—in fact, one could argue the opposite is true. The United States likes to boast about being a melting pot of cultures, and Ethnic Studies is key to celebrating the country's diversity.

In 2021, Sylvia Kwon, from the Region 15 Comprehensive Center, published a state scan that summarized recent and on-going states' Ethnic Studies legislation.[5] The report found that in the years since the 1968 Civil Rights Movement, "more than a dozen states have introduced legislation in support of ethnic studies, multicultural education, or a similar form of coursework that incorporates the narratives, histories, and lived experiences of historically marginalized communities in the United States (Au, 2020; CSAI, 2019; Depenbrock, 2017)."[6] The implementation of legislation has varied, with some states passing laws requiring African American or local Indigenous history to be taught in public schools, while other states have created broader policies to include the LGTBQ+ community.[7] Gains in several states have resulted in Ethnic Studies being offered as an elective course. In Texas, for example, Mexican American Studies was approved as an elective high school course in 2018, and in 2020, the State Board of Education approved an elective high school course in African American Studies.[8] While this is certainly a step forward, the goal is to make Ethnic Studies a requirement for graduation to ensure that all students are exposed to the varied cultural history of the United States.

Change is on the horizon, and textbooks like this lead us forward by showcasing the history and stories of Mexican Americans. I urge students to seek out texts that explore other minority groups as well. The more one learns about other marginalized peoples, the better understanding one will have of United States history. Moreover, the history of American marginalized peoples informs current events, such as the Black Lives Matter movement. This history provides centuries of context for present-day events and movements. My hope is that readers walk away from this textbook with an interest in, and an understanding of, Mexican American heritage and a desire to learn about marginalized groups in our country and around the world.

Notes

1. Sylvia Kwon, *Ethnic Studies Legislation: State Scan*, Center For Standards, Assessment, & Accountability (Comprehensive Center Network: Region 15, February 2021), https://csaa.wested. org/wp-content/uploads/2021/03/ES-State-Scan-FINAL-v1.pdf, 1.
2. Kwon, *Ethnic Studies Legislation*, 1.

3   *Critical Race Theory*, NAACP Legal Defense and Educational Fund, December 22, 2021, https://www.naacpldf.org/critical-race-theory-faq/?gclid=CjwKCAiA6Y2QBhAtEiwAGHybPecCnkJtQ1SYvoh8W5sqNgn0ac1Vx_Pk19tXvSenPcpm0b1we3ZHVhoCj5kQAvD_BwE.

4   *Critical Race Theory*, NAACP Legal Defense and Educational Fund.

5   Kwon, *Ethnic Studies Legislation*, 1. The report includes 19 states that currently have ethnic or multicultural studies legislation in place (California, Connecticut, Illinois, Indiana, Kansas, Kentucky, Louisiana, Massachusetts, Michigan, Mississippi, Nevada, New Mexico, Oklahoma, Oregon, Texas, Vermont, Virginia, Washington, and Wisconsin) and the District of Columbia.

6   Kwon, *Ethnic Studies Legislation*, 1.

7   The following states have passed laws requiring the teaching of African American history in public schools: Arkansas, Florida, Illinois, Mississippi, New Jersey, New York, and Rhode Island. The following states have passed laws requiring the teaching of local Indigenous history in public schools: Hawaii, Maine, Minnesota, Montana, and Wisconsin.

8   Kwon, *Ethnic Studies Legislation*, 7–8.

CPSIA information can be obtained
at www.ICGtesting.com
Printed in the USA
LVHW060236110622
721014LV00003B/10